The Scar of Montaigne

An Essay in Personal Philosophy

The Scar of Montaigne

An Essay in Personal Philosophy

BY

PHILIP P. HALLIE

Wesleyan University Press

MIDDLETOWN, CONNECTICUT

Copyright © 1966 by Wesleyan University

Quotations herein from *The Complete Works of Montaigne,* translated by Donald M. Frame, are reprinted with the permission of the publishers, Stanford University Press; copyright © 1948, 1957, 1958 by the Board of Trustees of the Leland Stanford Junior University

Library of Congress Catalog Card Number: 66-23925
Manufactured in the United States of America
First edition

FOR DORIS ANN

One day at Bar-le-Duc I saw King Francis II presented, in remembrance of René, king of Sicily, with a portrait that this king had made of himself. Why is it not permissible in the same way for each man to portray himself with the pen, as he portrayed himself with a pencil?

So I do not want to forget this further scar, very much unfit to produce in public: irresolution, a most harmful failing in negotiating worldly affairs. I do not know which side to take in doubtful enterprises.

"Nor yes nor no my inmost heart will say" (Petrarch).

— Michel de Montaigne
"Of Presumption," *Essays,* Book II

Contents

Preface	ix
Acknowledgements	xiii
Introduction: Plain Talk and Life	xv

PART I: THE SOIL OF A PERSONAL PHILOSOPHY

Chapter 1: Montaigne's Century	3
A. The wars of religion	3
B. The humanists	9
1. Language	12
2. Living	13
C. The healthy cannibals	17
Conclusion	20
Chapter 2: Doubt and Man	22
A. Affirmation	24
B. The general function of doubt	26
C. The techniques of doubt	27
1. Antithesis	27
2. The tropoi	30
D. The sceptic's doctrine of man	31

PART II: THE ROOT AND BRANCHES OF A PERSONAL PHILOSOPHY

Chapter 3: Men and Mixtures	37
A. General	37
B. The mild objection	40
C. The pestilence	44
D. The beginning of the therapy	45
E. The fount of knowledge	48
F. The end of the *a fortiori* argument	49
G. Epilogue on public docility	50
Chapter 4: Common Sense and Habit	53
A. Our common sense	53

	B. Custom and common sense	61
	C. Action and individualism	64

PART III: LANGUAGE THE INTEGUMENT

Chapter 5:	Language and the Troubles of the World	71
	A. Humanism and language	71
	B. Imagination and its vagaries	72
	C. Lies, prayers, and our troubles	86
	D. The modern diagnosis: Wittgenstein	89
Chapter 6:	The Powers of Language	94
	A. Expression and communication	94
	B. Essaying a mind	97
	C. Two kinds of order	101
	D. The style of Montaigne	105

PART IV: THE FRUIT OF A PERSONAL PHILOSOPHY

Chapter 7:	The Scar of Montaigne	117
	A. Freedom, ease, and stability	118
	B. The two laws of man	120
	C. *Mens sana in corpore sano*	125
	D. The scar	130
Chapter 8:	Personal Philosophy and Privacy	134
	A. Absolute privacy	134
	B. Introspection	136
	C. Aloneness	139
	D. Privacy and publication	140
	E. Conclusion	152

APPENDIX: MONTAIGNE AND DESCARTES

Introduction	157
Appendix A: Montaigne's and Descartes' Doctrines of Language	159
Appendix B: Montaignian and Cartesian Doubt	168
Notes	177
Critical Bibliography	185
Index	197

Preface

Several years ago I resolved to spend a year working in the Bibliothèque Nationale reading everything I could find that was directly relevant to Montaigne himself, his essays, and his century. With the help of the Guggenheim Foundation I was enabled to get away for that year. But about three-fourths of the way through it, I began to feel that even the most useful, illuminating scholarly research on Montaigne was leading me *away* from what had always interested me in his *Essays*. And so, having read much of the scholarship, I went back to the muscular French of Montaigne himself. I wanted to recover and articulate the excitement Montaigne had for decades been arousing in *me*. It was then I discovered that Montaigne had excited me not only because he used language as if he had invented it himself, but also because his essays embodied a way of doing philosophy that spoke to my condition as a person and as a philosopher. They combined for me some of the best traits of twentieth-century philosophy: the lucidity of some Analytic philosophers, the urgency of some Existentialist philosophers, and the vision of some Metaphysical philosophers. And they combined these traits while avoiding many of the excesses that these movements had fallen into in our century. In short, they avoided jargon, arbitrariness, and dogmatism.

And they avoided these excesses by what John Dewey in *Experience and Nature* called "intellectual disrobing": Montaigne admitted "*dès l'entrée,*" in the Preface to his *Essays,* that all he was trying to do was to show (to himself and any other persons who might be interested in him) what *he* thought and felt. The *Essays* are a self-portrait, he said; for him, to "essay" essentially meant to show oneself in the act of thinking, to put into words the impact of a certain topic on a particular man's mind. He intended his essays to be neither objective, eternal truth about the topics they treated nor subjective babbling, but a faithful picture in understandable language of the way his mind encountered these topics. Throughout the three books of the *Essays* he makes it plain that for him an essay is not a treatise, makes no claims to finality or universality — it does not presume to speak for all men in all times and places. The purpose of the Montaignian essay is *"une fin domestique et privée,"* a local and private goal: after all it seeks to reveal the essayist as he is, with his common sense, his idiosyncrasies, his passion, and his way of using language.

In what is usually called "the history of philosophy," most philosophers end up telling us that the writer is as a matter of fact privy to the ultimate truth and to the best way of putting that truth into words. Modern Analytic, Existentialist, and Metaphysical philosophers, for example, usually make it clear in their work that they are not merely "showing" or "essaying" themselves: they are really telling the Truth, or at least using the only Method worth using to get at the Truth. Most philosophers are not candid enough to engage in Dewey's or Montaigne's intellectual disrobing.

Having found, and for a long time having admired, this candor in Montaigne, and having found it so rarely in others, I finally decided to write a candid book on him — a book that essayed, that showed and plainly *said* that it showed what his writings mean to me. I am a teacher of philosophy who has been deeply influenced by the so-called "ordinary language" school of thought which Ludwig Wittgenstein and Gilbert Ryle have led; and I have been influenced also by some phases of Existentialism, as well as by the Greek Sceptics. But no more need be said about this here; these influences will be shown in what follows.

Even as Montaigne warned you in his Preface, I warn you here that this is no treatise purporting to give *the* truth about that infinitely complex thinker, Montaigne. This is a book — as the Introduction will indicate in somewhat more detail — written by a person who thinks philosophy has grave weaknesses now, and who finds in Montaigne an example of a way of philosophizing that could mitigate some of these weaknesses. Because I have avoided much of the scholarly apparatus on Montaigne and his century, some of my interpretations of the *Essays* are somewhat more problematic for technical Montaignian scholars than I make them out to be here; but none of my interpretations, I firmly believe, is arbitrary or palpably wrong or wrongheaded. After long study and thought, I believe that what I have said is faithful to, and at worst merely consistent with, the most persistent insights and the governing intent of Montaigne's work.

In fact this whole book will scandalize specialists: sometimes it deals with history, sometimes with literary style, sometimes with traditionally "philosophic" problems, and it never leans very heavily on all the scholarly apparatus and distinctions that specialists in these areas would employ. As I have said, it is a second-order essay, my essay of Montaigne's way of essaying his mind, and I am a person who is rather impatient with apparatus that attenuates feeling and with distinctions that depart too far from a colloquial way of writing. And I am convinced that Montaigne was such a person. Anyway, the uninformed reader may begin to assess the claims I make in this book if he will use the rather extensive Critical Bibliography at the end of it. As for the specialist, all I can do is write a preface like this, reminding him of the over-all goals of my book.

In this book I want to make it clear how Montaigne's *Essays* show his mind, and how and why they do not try to inflict that mind on others with proofs or recipe-methods. I believe that philosophy is more personal than the exact sciences and less arbitrary than man's inarticulate passions. I think Montaigne would not object strenuously to my using his *Essays* in the twentieth century to give substance and credibility to this belief. But if he would, or if the reader does, then I am sorry; but here I am in the time and place that I am, and this is the best I can do with the most candid philosopher I have ever encountered.

PHILIP P. HALLIE
Middletown, Connecticut
March 1966

Acknowledgments

I am grateful to:
- The John Simon Guggenheim Memorial Foundation for the Fellowship in 1958–1959 which made this book possible;
- The Wesleyan Center for Advanced Studies for the Fellowship in 1962–1963 which gave me the leisure to deepen my thought on Montaigne;
- The Stanford University Press for permission to use Donald Frame's edition of the *Essays* as the main English translation referred to in this book;
- René Dubos for all his stimulation and encouragement;
- Donald M. Frame for his translation and for his reading of this manuscript;
- Marian N. Haagen for bringing typographical order out of chaos;
- Hiram Haydn for his criticism and encouragement;
- Henri Peyre for all his help from 1957 on;
- Michael Polanyi for developing the basic categories of personal philosophy in *Personal Knowledge;*
- Gilbert Ryle for his stimulating interest in Montaigne as a philosopher;
- Hao Wang for helping me one day with his logician's mind to simplify my task;
- The owners of Montaigne's castle in 1959 for letting me stay there on such short notice;
- Above all, Doris Ann Gabriele Hallie for enduring me and helping me through these difficult years, but mainly for setting me an example with her lucid, vivacious spirit.

None of these institutions or persons should be held responsible for the inaccuracies that may occur in this book.

Introduction

Plain Talk and Life

I

LANGUAGE always comes from a particular tongue moving in a particular mouth or from a particular hand moving under a particular pair of eyes. This means that a particular person's mind is directly involved in every instance of language — a mind with its own characteristics and its own environment, whatever traits and environment it may share with other minds. These particularities are heavy with significance, but many philosophers have chosen to ignore or minimize this significance, at least for their own language. The fact that it is always *a* man who is talking or writing has certainly been acknowledged in the great tradition of confessional writing that runs through Augustine, Pascal, and Rousseau; but no thinker in the history of the West has kept this fact perpetually and centrally in mind in the way Michel de Montaigne has done. No philosopher has explicitly acknowledged the particularity of *his own* language (never forgetting its plain, strong ties with the language of other men) as fully as Montaigne. His *Essays* lie before us as essays of himself: "Reader, I am myself the matter of my book," he tells us in his very important preface "To the Reader." He is trying out, experimenting with "my powers," not the Representative Right-Thinking Mind in possession of a final public Truth. Essays are for him a set of actions which reveal a particular mind in the process of staggering ignorantly, inquisitively, but above all personally through time and space. Kierkegaard once imagined a philosopher suddenly sneezing while writing a sentence of his Science of Being, and the Dane wondered how this metaphysician could possibly continue to take his metaphysics seriously after this sudden eruption of his feeble particularity. It is very easy to imagine Montaigne sneezing while writing an essay (he himself tells us that he liked to scratch the inside of his ear) and then continuing without a qualm to essay "without straining or artifice ... my defects ..., and also my natural form." His essays are soaked with the explicit particularity of a sceptical man watching himself acting in various situations.

One of the reasons philosophers have battled with each other across the centuries is that, seeking universal truth, they choose to ignore the particularities that all human claims are heirs to, their own as well as others'. They lay down criteria as if God himself were creating a universe anew, and they are appalled when these criteria are not accepted or correctly applied by all men; they are appalled when they read massive objections to their contentions. And so, for instance, Descartes will argue with objectors sometimes with patience, sometimes with disdain, always with genius, but seldom with decisiveness. He will confront the recalcitrant judgment of Hobbes (in the Third Set of Objections and Replies) on the criterion of clarity and distinctness, and say, "No one can be unaware that by mental illumination is meant clearness of cognition, which perhaps is not possessed by everyone who thinks he possesses it." So clearness is not itself a workable criterion: if you think you have something clearly in mind, you may be wrong, and perhaps only Descartes will be able to tell you whether in fact you are thinking "clearly." The frustration, the barely hidden impatience and anger of a philosopher trying to shore up a Universal Science — these are what Montaigne avoided by speaking explicitly *in propria persona,* according to his own lights. Sometimes Montaigne is carried away by the force of his own beliefs, and he seems to feel that he is speaking for all men, but the title of the essays (the way Montaigne himself uses the term *essais*) reminds him and us that it is always he, Michel, who is speaking this way. His signature, his own responsibility for what he is saying, is essential to the form and content of the *Essays*. Every published edition of the *Essays* opens with that little preface "To the Reader":

> This book was written in good faith, reader. It warns you from the outset that in it I have set myself no goal but a domestic and private one. I have had no thought of serving either you or my own glory. My powers are inadequate for such a purpose. I have dedicated it to the private convenience of my relatives and friends, so that when they have lost me (as soon they must), they may recover here some features of my habits and temperament.

And the complete editions end with this generalization about signature-philosophizing:

It is an absolute perfection and virtually divine to know how to enjoy our being rightfully. We seek other conditions because we do not understand the use of our own, and go outside of ourselves because we do not know what it is like inside. Yet there is no use our mounting on stilts, for on stilts we must still walk on our own legs. And on the loftiest throne in the world we are still sitting only on our own rump.

There is no such thing as life apart from lives, man apart from men, species apart from individuals; each person (like each animal) has a rump upon which he alone sits, legs upon which he alone stands, a mind upon which he alone relies; and in whatever other jobs he has to perform, he must make do with whatever he is.

One of the purposes of this book is to examine the meaning of the last two passages quoted from the *Essays* — to examine them in philosophic depth. These words have behind them a theory of the scope and function of human knowledge. Great scholars like Pierre Villey have traced the evolution of some aspects of these ideas through the various editions of the *Essays* published in Montaigne's lifetime. But after all, Montaigne signed his name to the *totality* of the *Essays*. He did not progress beyond any of them in the sense of repudiating them. I am convinced that arching across the three books is this constellation of ideas I have just mentioned (about the limits and utility of human knowledge). It is not the only constellation to be found there, but it is a very important one. When one has studied it with some care there still remains much to be studied in the *Essays* of Montaigne; but what one has learned is, I think, important not only toward understanding Montaigne's thought but also toward understanding human understanding itself.

2

SOMEHOW in the twentieth century, at least in the English-speaking world, philosophy has come unstuck from living. It has moved toward the sort of disinterested rigor and detachment that a highly developed theoretical science exhibits, and young philosophers have found themselves philosophizing in a way reminiscent of Axel in Villiers de l'Isle-Adam's *Axel:*

> Live? Our servants will do that for us. . . . Oh, the external world! Let us not be made dupes by the old slave, chained to our feet in broad daylight, who promises us the keys to a palace of enchantments when it clutches only a handful of ashes in its clenched black fist!

Descartes' split between a rigorous method of achieving and guaranteeing certitude and the mental relaxation (he uses this metaphor) of everyday life has helped subsequent philosophy make "wisdom" in living a matter quite *à part* from the business of doing philosophy. Of course everybody agrees with Descartes that someday philosophy and everyday living will meet, in a universal science, an Encyclopedia perhaps.

On the other hand, Montaigne has been neglected by philosophers because he is not subtle enough for our "philosophy," for our way of "loving wisdom." First of all, he treats matters in "bigger morsels" (as Montaigne himself puts it), without the precision demanded of a man when he is "doing philosophy." And this is supposed to be bad, even though philosophers from Aristotle to Wittgenstein have warned us to seek only that degree of precision that the subject matter can bear without crumbling into dust in our hands. Moreover, it is simply tender-minded, to be dismissed by a sweep of the hand, to suggest that giving "guides for living" (a phrase some philosophers of my acquaintance dismiss with an open sneer) has anything to do with philosophy as it is now being done. Especially in current Anglo-American philosophizing, we leave the bigger morsels, the vague, broad problems, to our wives or to that philosophically peripheral self who crosses the street carefully in order to get to his library without having his head knocked off.

Of course it is absurd to blame Descartes for this Axel-like split. What one must do is see the split and decide whether it should endure. The fact seems to be that a "technical" philosopher is often one of the few intellectuals who have not thought long and hard about a philosophy of life. Many of us have, like Descartes, preempted the word "philosophy" (and the careful and sustained activity of thinking) for problems that are comfortably distant and distinct from the "bigger morsels" of everyday life.

What we learn when we compare these two ways of philosophizing is that even though you push practical common sense outside the realm of philosophy, you, an active, socially dependent human being, still have to use it. And when that practical sense is treated as diametrically opposite to philosophic sense, as opposite as body is to mind, it becomes not only irrelevant for philosophers to reflect about the problems of living carefully and sustainedly; it becomes downright blasphemous, "relaxed," to do what Socrates wanted us to do: examine life.

I believe that we understand both Montaigne and philosophy better when we see that he presents us with the proposition that we are *not* being derelict of our duty as careful thinkers when we think long and hard about the whole business of living. We understand both better when we comprehend in depth what he meant by refusing to be a man "who turns his mind from a good meal and laments the time he spends on feeding himself." The ambition, the jealousy, the anxiety, the fear, the sudden spasm of loneliness, that one sees and feels so often at conventions of lovers of wisdom and that one experiences when one comes down from his "supercelestial thoughts" and deigns to live — these feelings are exacerbated by this invidious contrast and separation of thought from life. It is my living, says Montaigne, that suffers from such a division, and also it is my philosophy itself that suffers, because it cuts itself loose (despite all its assurances for the future) from the immediate demands of the only life and the only everyday language we have. When living and philosophy *stay* separate from each other, both become vagabond and quarrelsome, like a pair of divorced people who still need each other.

Montaigne communicates the ridiculousness of unexamined living in the pursuit of great goals in the last pages of the great essay "Of Experience." In reading this passage I think of Descartes as the "master," Montaigne as Aesop, and the goals of much modern philosophy as the goals toward which both of them are moving. Here is the passage: "Aesop, the great man, saw his master pissing as he walked. 'What next?' he said. 'Shall we have to shit as we run?'"

Despite the profound differences between their two ways of philosophizing, Montaigne and Descartes have been spoken of by various commentators, notably Brunschvicq in his *Descartes et Pascal, lecteurs de Montaigne,* as similarly concerned with the solitary, thinking individual. But because of those differences, comparisons can be misleading. Comparisons can minimize the fact that Descartes was creating the foundations of a universal science, whereas Montaigne was drawing a portrait of himself in the act of living his own life. They can also minimize the fact that Descartes proposed an impersonal, objectively rigorous, and fruitful method for achieving such a science, while Montaigne presented mainly what he called *"mon stile,"* his way of thinking and living. That is to say, as we have been noticing, for Descartes philosophizing is (at least for the time being) radically different from and unrelated to the way he or anyone else acts in his everyday life, while for Montaigne such a separation is the cause of man's making lovely systems in the air and living in slime here on the earth.

For instance, compare the Second Part of the *Discourse on Method* with the famous Third Part, which presents the Method itself. In doing so you will see that his "code of morals for the time being" is in flat opposition to the Method. According to that Method he would "accept nothing as true which I did not clearly recognize to be so." And this meant accepting only those beliefs which "are presented to my mind so clearly and distinctly that I could have no occasion to doubt [them]." But in the *"morale provisoire"* he tells us that he would "follow faithfully opinions the most dubious." Descartes assures us and himself that someday he will adjust his everyday life to his theoretical life, his practice to his theory. But you read his works in vain if you seek that adjustment. There are some efforts at such an adjustment, but they are minor and inconclusive. The fact writ large in Descartes' writing, personal letters and all, is that theory and practice are distinct, like mind and body, and different in kind, like mind and body, capable of being thought of together only when we relax, when we are *not* being philosophic.

But no such separation occurs in Montaigne, either in his letters or in his more formal writings. Throughout his career as a philosopher he was essaying himself, Michel, presenting a way of thinking as intimately involved with his life as his hands and eyes were. In fact, he called his essays a *"membre de ma vie"*: an instrument, an organ, of his life. We fail to see the specific powers and the specific weaknesses of both philosophies if we think of them simply as partaking in a common concern for the solitary, thinking individual. The epistemological and metaphysical isolation of Descartes' thinking thing, the mind (its solitude makes it problematic whether there are other thinking things or minds), is radically different from Montaigne's doctrine of privacy, which involved no such isolation. Here are two quite different notions of what philosophizing is and two different sets of conclusions about the "solitariness" of a thinking man.

But our subject is Montaigne, and I have mentioned Descartes (and will do so again) only in order to illuminate or set off that subject more strikingly. We are concerned with a philosopher who distrusts impersonal languages, whether scientific (in the modern sense of this word) or metaphysical. This distrust and the way he has expressed it have earned him a place *outside* most histories of philosophy, because most historians of philosophy assume that philosophizing and personal style have little to do with each other, that personal speech or writing belongs to belletristic enterprises alone. Within these assumptions Montaigne's *Essays* are "literature, not philosophy." And indeed, there is no disputing the fact that Montaigne influenced Locke, Berkeley, Hume, and the rest of modern philosophy far less than did, say, Descartes. As far as his influence on such "technical" philosophers is concerned, he is out of the mainstream. This book suggests that the mainstream be widened so that it flows through a man who loved wisdom as sustainedly, as lucidly, and as freshly as did any of these men.

3

BEFORE going on it is important to avoid a certain misunderstanding. From what has been said, the reader might surmise that the present writer and Montaigne himself would unreservedly oppose modern Anglo-American philosophy. It will be one of the purposes of this book to show that this is not the case. One of the compelling reasons for my writing this book has been the important affinities I have found between the thought of Montaigne and the thought of the boldest modern "linguistic analysts" in England and America. All these thinkers are aware of the deep pitfalls and the great powers of language, and they all implement this awareness with great skill and deep insight into the human mind. People like Montaigne, Ludwig Wittgenstein, and Gilbert Ryle see human language as intimately involved in human action and in the common sense that is (hopefully) man's guide. It is the failure on the part of so many contemporary Anglo-American philosophers to *use* these insights in the service of the particular problems of particular men that has led to the criticisms expressed in this Introduction. But after we have noticed these failures it becomes easy to see that Montaigne's way of thinking is in some respects very close indeed to our modern ways. And after we see this closeness, we can envisage more easily the widening of the mainstream of philosophy to include Montaigne's kind of personal philosophizing.

Montaigne loved and respected the language spoken in the streets of France, especially in and around Bordeaux. Like him, many modern thinkers see our everyday language as the home from which philosophy should not stray very far. Surely it is in such "ordinary" language, skillfully and lucidly employed, that we must each think our best thoughts about our various lives. This book is dedicated to explaining and defending this proposition. In a later book I hope to elaborate on this proposition using first-order essays, in the language I have learned to speak and the life I have learned to live in America and England.

PART I

The Soil of a Personal Philosophy

Chapter 1

Montaigne's Century

A. *The wars of religion*

IN 1528, five years before Michel de Montaigne was born, two intense young men went opposite ways through the halls of the Collège de Montaigu in Paris. One was leaving, the other entering. One was soon to become the most articulate leader that the Protestant Reformation of the sixteenth century was to produce; the other was to become the most militant — even military — leader that the Catholic Counter-Reformation of the sixteenth century was to produce. One was John Calvin, from French Picardy, and the other was Ignatius Loyola, from the Spanish Basque country. In 1533, the year of Montaigne's birth, Calvin wrote the sermon that was to drive him from France and start him on his path to Geneva; one year later Loyola organized the Jesuits.

In 1590, two years before Montaigne died, Paris, always *"très Catholique,"* was being besieged by a Protestant claimant to the throne of France, Henry of Navarre, the future Henry IV. Henry was trying to starve the Catholic Parisians into submission. Pierre de l'Estoile, in his journals, gives us an eyewitness account of the last days of the siege:

> During this time, which was six days before the lifting of the siege of Paris, and up to the end of it, you could see the poor, dying, eating dead dogs on the street; others ate garbage that had been thrown in the river, or rats, or meal made of bones....
>
> Toward the end ... the most barbarous ... began to chase children on the streets as well as dogs ... and three were actually eaten....
>
> I personally heard the proposition made and defended by a well-known Catholic ... that there was less danger [in the hereafter] by eating a child, in such circumstances, than by recognizing ... a heretic ... and that all the best theologians of the University were of this opinion.[1]

This was what France had come to by the end of Montaigne's life. He died in 1592, two years before Henry entered Paris and began to pacify France. He started writing the *Essays* in 1572, the year of the St. Bartholomew's Day Massacre, and never breathed a breath at a time when his country was not beset or threatened by the religio-civil conflict between Catholic and Protestant. To read the *Essays* without looking at the physically and morally suicidal century in which he lived is to read them ill. To try to understand his notion of a personal philosophy — a philosophy involved with his way of life — without knowing what he means by such phrases as "the strife that is tearing France to pieces" is to fail at the important task of seeing the way of life to which he was reacting. We need not speculate on what phases of this strife "caused" him to write what he wrote; all we need do is glance at the religious wars and his role in them so as to understand these phrases. Montaigne's philosophy was to a great extent a response to a concrete, particular situation, rather than being only the result of philosophical analysis. And an important part of that situation was the religio-civil strife that lasted the whole fifty-nine years of his life.

It would be impossible to analyze here in any detail all the causes[2] of the "higher anarchy" in which Montaigne wrote his essays. One of those causes was economic: inflation had impoverished many of the nobility, with their fixed incomes, and had helped strengthen the hands of the bourgeoisie and peasantry, whose incomes were more fluid. Consequently, many of the nobility roamed the countryside and found themselves in a similar economic condition to that of the poor German artisans who were immigrating into France and bringing Protestantism with them. Thus, many nobles found Protestantism a handy form of social protest against the rich, very Catholic bourgeoisie. Montaigne, incidentally, got his inheritance from a bourgeois family in Bordeaux and kept his Catholicism as part of his inheritance, though his mother was of Jewish ancestry. Another cause was local politics: many cities became states within the state of France, fortresses against the others. Power was in the hands of local groups more than in the hands of the King. Montaigne, as a Catholic Mayor of Bordeaux, had to keep the Protestants and Catholics in his city from killing each other off, and he had to do this without much help from the throne. Still another cause was international politics: France was surrounded by powers trying to win the country over to their respective sides; for instance, one of the de Guise (the extremist

Catholics) was quite probably in league with Catholic Spain, actually in their employ. And the Protestants were pulling from other points on the map.

Some of the causes were, of course, theological. But the number of sacraments, the metaphysical interpretation of Communion (transubstantiation and so on), justification by faith or by works, the particular translation of the Bible to be used, the existence of Purgatory, and such matters were all unimportant to people like Montaigne. In his "Apology for Raymond Sebond" he makes it plain that as a Catholic he was interested mainly in the immediately practical conflict between the Protestant doctrine of the priesthood of all believers and the Catholic reliance on tradition and authority. The Church gave great weight to these public forces and denied that there was a direct flow of meaning from the page of the Bible to the private, individual mind of each believer. And so did Montaigne. He gladly made profession of his Catholicism before the Parliament of Paris, and he makes it clear whenever necessary that he is in favor of the Church's tradition and authority. In a later chapter we shall explore his grounds for holding this doctrine.

The effect of these economic, political, and theological forces was a power struggle, in which Montaigne was directly involved. We should consider this in somewhat more detail. To the left, among the advocates of change as against tradition, there were the radical Huguenots (called "Lutherans" before 1560). These were the extremist "Huguenots of Religion" who frequently destroyed churches, refused compromise, and one day in 1534 (one year after Montaigne's birth) tacked on the very chamber door of King Francis I foot-high posters (*placards*) bitterly and insultingly attacking the Roman Catholic Mass. By this last "Incident of the Posters" the friendship between the court and the Reform was once and for all destroyed (it was one of the causes of Calvin's eventually leaving France). Finding these posters on his own chamber door, Francis felt himself and his France threatened, insulted, and challenged by the Reform. He vigorously accepted the challenge.

One of the leaders of these Huguenots of Religion was the talented Agrippa d'Aubigné, whose "Prayer to God that He May Avenge the Protestants" was one of his many writings that called for vengeance against their persecutors. His and his colleagues' religious zeal added fire to their human resentment and made them on the whole more ferocious and impatient than were the "Huguenots of State," the disenfranchised, sometimes poverty-stricken, nobles who resented the "foreign" extremist-Catholic de Guise (they were from Lorraine) who were wielding great power over Paris and the King.

To the far right, in defense of tradition and the Church, was the Catholic League, formed officially by the de Guise in 1576, but long a-borning. At its most extreme — and it was often extreme — it wanted to exterminate or chase out of France the whole Huguenot sect. Warriors like Blaise de Monluc (a friend of Montaigne) were the lieutenants of the de Guise in this group. Here is a poem by one of its poet-members, Jean Antoine de Baïf, called "Epitaphe," whose subtitle is "For the Protestants killed on the day of Saint Bartholomew." I shall give a literal translation:

> Poor bodies where once those stormy spirits lodged,
> Once the terror of the princes of the land,
> Daring even against heaven to wage war,
> Disloyal, obstinate, perverse, and violent;
>
> Today the meal of flying creatures
> And creeping scavengers, and of those worms contained in
> The sinking sewers, of the tribe that wanders
> Under the deep rivers flowing into the sea:
>
> Poor bodies, sleep; if your miserable bones,
> Nerves, and veins and flesh are worthy of sleep,
> Who could not allow France to be at peace.

Such unforgiving, bitter hatred, thinly masked by an unfelt sympathy for the *bodies* of the Protestants massacred on that dreadful day, expresses, even better than an account of the many atrocities committed by both sides, the depths of the conflict dominating France while Montaigne wrote his *Essays*. The *Ligue* argued, when it argued at all, somewhat as follows: There must be religious unity in France at all costs; the only appropriate religion for France is the True Religion, Catholicism; if any group contests the True Religion, it is one's double duty as a Frenchman and as a Catholic to eliminate them. There were differences within the League,[3] but there was general agreement that the primary desideratum for the souls of Frenchmen and the whole French nation was unity of religion.

Between the extremist Huguenots and the League there was a wide range of moderates. There was the great-minded La Noue, the Protestant leader who could fight brilliantly and bravely, yet who sought always to reconcile Frenchman with Frenchman. But the most influential moderates were those Catholics often designated by the broad name "Politiques," but including people like Montaigne who refused to call themselves by this or any other political name. One of those Catholic moderates who refused to take on the name of Politique was the widow of Henry II, Catherine de' Medicis, the Queen-mother of France during most of the religious wars. She was the daughter of Lorenzo de' Medici, who had been associated at least for a while with that philosopher of naked political expediency, Niccoló Machiavelli. Her position, the position of the Politiques, and Montaigne's position are well epitomized by a little story. One day she turned to her son, then the Duke of Anjou, after he had told her how firmly he held his Catholic faith, and she told him (he had been fasting, and hearing three masses a day) that she "had rather he were an Huguenot than be so foolishly precise to hurt his health."[4] This little anecdote — true or false — is the best brief summary of Montaigne's (and the Politiques') position I have been able to find, if you put the French nation in the place of her "lean and evil-colored" son. *Health,* the pleasurable well-being of the nation, was more important to them all than was "foolishly precise" theological or devotional zeal. The fact that she participated in the "King's secret"[5] (which was that the Catholic throne was secretly sympathetic to and cooperating with the Protestant leader Henry of Navarre, behind the back of the Catholic de Guise) and her many acts alternately weakening and strengthening each of the two extremist parties so as to keep her sons on the throne — these show how alien her thinking was to the extremist insistence on a purely Catholic France. Because it was apparently best for the health of France (and because the health of France meant the continuance of her sons on the throne), she was reconciled to a France with two religions; and this was one of the key points that marked the moderates off from the League.

There were finer minds and firmer leaders than Catherine among the moderates. There was Jean Bodin, whose *Six Livres de la République* appeared the same year the League was officially formed (1576) and while Montaigne was writing his "Apology." Bodin, like the other thinkers in the right-center of the power struggle, defended religious moderation, not for reasons of morality, but primarily for expediency, for the order, the peace, the "health," of the country. There was also Michel de l'Hôpital, Chancellor of France during the early Civil Wars (1560–1568), humanist, poet, and champion of religious toleration.

It was l'Hôpital and Bodin who became the spokesmen for the group called the Politiques, which firmly supported Henry of Navarre's claims to the kingship toward the end of the century, after the King's secret was out. Their arguments, following the general pattern of Catherine's remarks to her "evil-colored" son, went, broadly, as follows: No one party is powerful enough to destroy the other; therefore, continuance of the religious wars would involve interminable bloodshed and a sickness unto death for France; and so we must allow both parties to exist by keeping the demands of both as moderate as possible. Again, expediency, the health of the country, not moral or religious righteousness, was at the heart of the argument. One enemy of the moderates put their position this way:[6] the Politiques, he said, "preferred the repose of the kingdom, and of their own homes, to the salvation of their souls; they ... would rather that the kingdom remained at peace without God than at war with Him." The second remark is an overstatement. The Politiques were Catholics; they did not think of a kingdom "without God." They thought in terms of a kingdom with *more than one way* of worshiping God.

Not the least of these Catholic moderates was Montaigne himself, who spoke through the *Essays* in favor of the "health" of France. Not only a Mayor under Henry of Navarre but his personal friend, he felt himself personally and politically close to both Henry and l'Hôpital. Like the Politiques, he was still a Catholic and thought that it would have been best if France had followed the time-tested traditions of the Church (this is the gist of the "Apology") instead of arousing the "private judgments" of men to arguments on issues those judgments could never understand and settle. But things being where they were, he stood for moderation for the sake of the health, the peace, of France. Some commentators have taken this moderation as equivalent to atheism, but in my opinion this is to misunderstand his personal and political position in the sixteenth-century wars as well as his Scepticism.

Our scanty evidence[7] indicates that he was a liaison between a counsellor to both bitter parties in his own province of Guyenne and was privy to the fact that through the King's secret leaders of both parties, to use his own words, "even up to the best, defended their cause with disguises and lies."[8] Whatever his exact role or importance, he was an active force in the unification of Bordeaux, of Guyenne, and of France itself and was always a moderate.

All these considerations give some meaning to phrases that are for our purposes crucial to the *Essays,* like "this notable spectacle of our public death, its symptoms and its form."[9] They prepare us for his reaction to those "unhealthy" times. That reaction understandably involves disgust with the times and a desire to withdraw from them; but it also involves an aspiration to help remedy them through moderation. This is where he stood in his century: a Catholic moderate, inhabiting the "golden mean," the *"juste milieu"* that the Romans and Greeks had taught him to respect, but an active moderate, acting to help cure a diseased France. In the context of this stand, this active moderation, and in the midst of these wars, he wrote his *Essays* and developed his personal philosophy.

B. *The humanists*

SOMETIMES Montaigne is classified as one of the French "Humanists" of the sixteenth century. Since, because we are human, it is always human beings we are dealing with, no matter what the particular point of our dealings, the word "Humanism" has been pretty much emptied of meaning over the centuries by being applied to all sorts of convictions. But if we are careful to specify the original meaning of the term *humanista,* we find that this classification of Montaigne is helpful and right. *Humanista* in the high Renaissance referred to someone involved in the teaching or learning of the "humanities." And the humanities in turn (the *studia humanitatis* of Cicero and Gellius) was a specific group of studies revolving around ancient writings and concerning itself with only such subjects as grammar, rhetoric, poetry, history, and moral philosophy. The latter was the only "philosophy" this curriculum emphasized, and it specifically excluded such fields as logic, the natural sciences, metaphysics, mathematics, and such special areas as astronomy, medicine, law, and theology. A *humanista,* then, was someone who through reading the classics learned and/or taught grammar, rhetoric, and so on, and did not, as a *humanista,* deal with what we might describe as "science" or "pure knowledge" regarding either nature or God. He was someone preoccupied with the art of writing and the art of living, the way (Montaigne's word is "façon") in which men use language and act. Knowledge that was only indirectly or not at all relevant to linguistic or to life-style was only indirectly or not at all relevant to the Humanist's concerns. This emphasis has been described as part of "the rhetorical tradition in Western culture."[10] But this is misleading, since writing and speaking well are quite plainly not our only purpose in reading or writing history and morals;[11] these latter subjects involve *doing* well (or ill). The Humanist was someone far more interested in language than is the metaphysician or scientist, but he was also more immediately, even pressingly, interested in human actions and interactions as historical and moral phenomena than are logicians, natural scientists, theologians, and the like. Here is a workable definition of a *humanista* which fits Montaigne like a glove and covers the area of Humanism that the "rhetorical tradition" phrase leaves out: a Humanist is somebody more interested (via his interest in antiquity) in ways of using language and of living than he is in knowledge of the conclusions of such fields as physics, mathematics, or theology. It is a fact plainly evident after even a cursory reading of the *Essays* that Montaigne was far more interested in the *studia humanitatis* — the classics — as they bear on linguistic and life-style than he was in physics, metaphysics, mathematics, or theology. In this sense of the word *humanista,* he was a Humanist, and so was his personal philosophy, as we shall see. For his personal philosophy had a great deal to do with both antiquity and the way in which man writes and lives.

Like the religious wars, Humanism in France had origins too complex for any adequate brief summary. Certainly the otherwise futile Italian wars waged by the Valois kings Charles VIII and Louis XII brought the whole Humanistic Italian Renaissance down hard on France, and so did the many Italians who were migrating to France. The Turks had invaded Constantinople in 1453 and had chased the great scholars (especially on Greek antiquity) into Italy; when the Valois kings entered Italy they found, to their surprise, not a decadent culture, but the art and learning of the Italian Renaissance. They found a rebirth stimulated not only by those scholars but by such events as the invention of the printing press in the fifteenth century and the consequent widespread availability of the Bible, Homer, Virgil, Plato, and Aristotle — texts unobscured by commentary, moralizing, or authoritarian tradition.

It would be misleading to say that Italian Humanists like Petrarch civilized the French as far as antiquity was concerned; after all, the study of Latin literature had flourished in France's brilliant Middle Ages (especially in the twelfth century), when Italy was making no great contribution to classical studies. But the verve, the concentration, and the originality that the Italian *humanista* brought to these studies, coupled with the authoritativeness of Italy's Byzantine scholars in the area of Greek studies, reawoke the French to an intense interest in antiquity and to an emphasis on linguistic and moral style.

By the time Montaigne's father was fighting under Francis I in another futile Valois Italian war, it was a commonplace that Italy was the exemplar of art and classical learning. And Montaigne's whole upbringing by that same father was one of the many tributes French soldiers paid to the Italian Renaissance. His father Pierre saw to it that the only language Michel heard, read, or spoke during his early years was Latin; he was awakened by the sound of music, heard no threats, felt no punishment, shed no tears, but quite naturally spoke, read, and wrote Latin. In 1539, at the age of six, Michel went to the great "college" of Guyenne; his Latin was so far beyond that of his contemporaries that his instructors (including the great Latinist George Buchanan) let him browse around in Ovid while the other students labored their way through the fundamentals. Such was his childhood, full of ease and pleasure, freedom, art, and especially the Latin classics. And his childhood left its mark on him: all the rest of his life these were the things he would love above all others.

You will still be able to read in Montaigne's tower his famous inscription dated February 28, 1571, his first birthday following the sale of his post as magistrate. It tells of a man "long since displeased with slavery to Parliament and to his public duties" who wished above all now to take his rest upon the calm bosoms of the Muses in freedom, peace, and leisure. These are the words of a man yearning for the early years of his Humanistic upbringing, and now at last able to satisfy that yearning. As we have already noticed in some detail, this retirement was not to an ivory tower absolutely separate from the "public duties" the inscription speaks about, for they were by no means forgotten by him; what he was doing was putting himself in a position to pursue the studies and way of life of his childhood, to develop along Humanistic lines more than those sixteen years of "slavery" had permitted him to do. Privacy for him would be no clean break with public life; his retreat was not a final separation, but a means of escaping *slavery* to public duties. This famous retirement into his father's peaceful estate outside of Bordeaux was a means for developing what his childhood had given him, a love of leisure and freedom, a love of antiquity, and a love of the *studia humanitatis* we have been talking about. Whatever other motives he may have had, he was escaping slavery to public duties in order to continue his development as a Humanist.

1. LANGUAGE

The most important French Humanists, including, of course, the great translator of Plutarch into vigorous, idiomatic French, Jacques Amyot, were profoundly interested in what Amyot himself had called the "renovation of language." The Humanists of France (and all the poets of France in the sixteenth century were Humanists) had one great ideal: the revivification of the French language, and thereby of French thought and art, by grafting French onto the still living stalk of ancient literature. Henri Etienne and Estienne Pasquier (a friend of Montaigne) did their best to bring the sap, the inner vitality, rather than the external forms, of antique literature into the French language.

Of course, this is not the place to examine in detail all the facets of the Humanists' massive concern for revivifying language by drawing from antiquity *and* speaking spontaneously, directly, simply. Du Bellay, of the famous "Pléiade," in his prose works and in his poems strove to "illustrate," amplify, invigorate, humanize, language, though early in his career he came close indeed to antiquarian, superficial pedantry. In the closing years of his life, especially in his last collection of poems, *Les Regrets,* he emerged from the temptations of that new pedantry, as deadly as the medieval sort; in these allusive but at the same time simple and direct poems, side by side with lines about Ulysses and about his barber (who wants Du Bellay to leave his books and go out and make love), there occur these lines:

> Je me contenteray de simplement escrire
> Ce que la passion seulement me fait dire,
> Sans rechercher ailleurs plus graves arguments.

He will content himself to write simply and only what passion makes him say, without borrowing themes or arguments from "elsewhere." What he wanted in these last poems of his short life was a minimum of artifice, a maximum of direct, passionate humanity. Even Ronsard, the greatest of the Humanist poets of the French Renaissance, struggled to revivify his native language against the temptation to make a new inhuman pedanticism. He once wrote an epic called *La Franciade,* which is as cold as a key, leaning on a dead religion, using borrowed, tattered comparisons and a bloodless decasyllabic meter that kills even Ronsard's efforts to keep it alive. But happily this was an aberration, and we have those blood-fed lyrical poems of *Les Discours* and *Les Amours de Marie,* among others. This same struggle between a beloved past and a precious present appears in Rabelais' *Gargantua* and *Pantagruel,* where the heroes make asses of the pedants, when the pedants are not making asses of themselves.

And Montaigne's *Essays,* as Humanistic documents, exhibit that struggle, though in a special way. He too had a great concern for language; but he was less concerned with "illustrating" or amplifying and revivifying the French language than he was with speaking revealingly in *any* language. He too had an awareness of the problem of assimilating an alien, dead language and culture (in various places he tells of his struggle to find "my style" after having written some early essays that, as he put it, "smell a bit foreign"). But throughout the *Essays* he was not as much worried about having imitated Latin or Greek classics as he was about the dead, artificial, inhuman, impersonal languages of metaphysics, theology, medicine, and jurisprudence. He too found a solution to the problem of speaking powerfully and directly, and here he comes close indeed to the solutions such Humanists as Du Bellay, Ronsard, and Rabelais found. He was to use the gifts of antiquity in order to express *himself,* not primarily what Du Bellay had called *"plus graves"* matters like the nature of things or of God. The main force of his writing would ultimately not come from "elsewhere," but from his own freshly and directly experienced thoughts and passions, with a minimum of borrowed, alien artifice. His style of writing was to be formed by *his* way of dealing with anything that came to hand: the words of the ancients, the incidents and demands of the religious wars around him, and so on. His way of writing was to be the permanent image of his personal, transitory life, a permanent record of himself in dynamic interaction with various matters. Primarily he would essay, experiment with, discover, himself, not *"plus graves"* matters, and not by using conventions alien to his own way of thinking and feeling.

2. LIVING

Another use the Humanists made of antiquity, as we have noticed, had to do with a way or style of living. Not only did they find in antiquity models for writing; they found models for living. In general, they admired Greeks like Socrates, Romans like Cato the younger and Caesar, and Epaminondas, who accomplished deeds that the scholarly *humanista* would in all likelihood be unable to imitate. Nonetheless, he could admire them, give reasons for admiring them, and be guided by them in his active life.

To say that they were concerned with a "style of living" as well as a way of writing is not to say that they were primarily interested in the superficial manners or mannerisms of men, nor is it to say that they were primarily interested in men's public stations or occupations. The *façon* of living they were concerned with had to do with the basic ways a man thought, felt, and acted, whatever his superficial eccentricities or public station. Consider one of the greatest of the Humanists, Erasmus, who died in 1536, three years after Montaigne was born, and who was greatly admired by Montaigne. According to Erasmus, the occupation of a man did not in itself reveal that man's way of living, nor did his personal or social mannerisms. Erasmus, like the ancients, saw a distinction between what a man appears to be from the point of view of the public and how a man feels and thinks and acts in the intimacy of his day-to-day personal life. The task of a student of human beings is, according to Erasmus, to deemphasize casual appearances or classifications and to make men look long at "their naked selves," as he put it in his *Praise of Folly*. A king or a prince can be wealthy and powerful as far as his occupation and public privileges are concerned and at the same time be a beggar and a galley-slave as far as controlling his own lusts and passions is concerned. According to Folly and Erasmus, you must lay a man open, look *through* what he is to the public, and see how he lives in the intimacy of his own soul and his own household. In doing this you see the reality of the man, not simply "the part he is to act ... on the stage." When you are laying a man bare you are not asking whether he is a king or soldier or even what his scientific and religious convictions are in detail; you are asking, "What woman would be content with such a husband? Who would invite such a guest ...?" The test of his real worth involves his way of feeling, thinking, and acting in his constant, intimate relationships with himself, his family, and his friends.

And so, insofar as the style is the man, insofar as life-style involves the most intimate, basic patterns of a man's thought, feeling, and action, Humanists like Erasmus and Montaigne were interested in what we have called the "style of living." This is the sort of "style" that interested Montaigne when he wrote, in his little preface to the reader, that he was presenting *"ma façon simple, naturelle et ordinaire."* And this is the sort of "style" or "way" he was thinking of when he wrote in the essay "Of the Art of Discussion":

> And every day I amuse myself reading authors without any care for their learning, looking for their style, not their subject. Just as I seek the company of some famous mind, not to have him teach me, but to come to know him.

He, like Erasmus and so many of the other Humanists, did not seek knowledge of the universe, "the dimensions of the sun, moon, and stars," as Folly puts it, "knowledge" in the form of puny conjectures, "castles in the air, and infinite worlds in a vacuum." They were not interested in what was external to man, nor were they interested in the externals of men. What they sought to become acquainted with (not to have a categorized, conclusive knowledge of, but simply to become familiar with) was the ways men encounter various subjects, the ways they engage in their various occupations, the ways they live in their various stations.

In general, the way of life that the Humanists admired and appropriated for themselves was a way that "followed nature," apart from divine or human threats and promises. But living according to nature meant different things to different Humanists, just as it had meant different things to different ancients who had adopted this rule of life. To some it meant primarily knowing oneself, as Socrates and the Oracle had advised, and pursuing in all one's thoughts and actions the *ariston metron*, the moderate path between extremes, the healthy middle way between cold, dead indifference and hot, feverish involvement (notice how this metaphor of health resembles the "health" the Politiques were seeking for a France sick with extremism). According to this way of thinking, if you know yourself, your own powers and limitations, if you know your "nature" (the more or less permanent needs, habits, capacities, of your body and mind), and if you follow the somewhat permissive but firm laws of nature, you will in that very process be avoiding sick extremes, and you will be living well. Such notions occur again and again in crucial places in the *Essays*. The Humanists found them described in the works of philosophers like Plato, Aristotle, the Stoics, and the Epicureans, as well as exemplified in the lives of men Plutarch wrote about (and Montaigne, like other comparatively Greekless fellow Humanists, read about these men in Jacques Amyot's vivacious translations of Plutarch).

But withdrawal into the bounds of one's "nature" and living in moderation according to its reasonable demands was not the only meaning the Humanists — and Montaigne among them — found in the injunction to "follow nature." A second meaning is most strikingly illustrated by the earlier writings of Rabelais. In those earlier writings, following nature meant living without circumspection or moderation. To follow nature was to follow one's physical appetites, one's mental caprices, and one's protean, sometimes rather brutal, conscience. Ask a philosopher of antiquity how much a man should drink, and what will he say, no matter what his school? The most likely answer is "Not too little of course; but not too much. After all, excess brings in its train misery, ill-health, remorse, and so on." But what does Rabelais answer, though he is a physician? "Drink until the cork on the soles of your shoes swells up to half a foot in thickness." Look at his ideal monastery, Thélème. Its only rule is "Do what you wish." True, he is talking to and about people who were *"bien nés, bien instruicts,"* gentlefolk: for *them* spontaneous pleasure-seeking is what he recommends, since they have the "instinct and spur that always pushes well brought-up people toward virtue and away from vice." But in general, freedom from authoritarian rules, freedom to satisfy one's needs as they arise, simply for the *joy* of that satisfaction — this is *his* blueprint of the *ars vivendi* that Cicero had identified with wisdom. Pleasure, spontaneity, the joys of health in mind and body, with one's only discipline coming from occasional discrete whispers from one's conscience — all this is what Rabelais celebrated, at least before that Prologue to the Fourth Book wherein he praises "golden mediocrity," which was now "pleasing in all places." And all this is what we find more quietly expressed in the *Essays* of Montaigne. It is a great moment when Gargantua, after reaching for this and that, finally wipes his bottom with a live goose's neck, just for the warm joy of it; you will not find such moments in Montaigne, but you will find praise of spontaneity and immoderation in many of his *Essays*.

Some commentators have called Montaigne, especially in his later years, an "Epicurean." But no Epicurean celebrated bodily pleasures (the itch inside his ear that he loved to scratch, and the other little pleasures) as gleefully as did Montaigne. As far as such pleasures are concerned, Epicureans were kill-joys, not very different from the Stoics or the other philosophers of antiquity. Perhaps Horace, Martial, or Petronius might be blamed for these moments of license in Montaigne (and Rabelais); but whatever the origin in antiquity or in the hearts of these men, sixteenth-century French Humanist thinkers sometimes asserted that carping moderation and public regulations were not as valuable as what we now call "doing what comes naturally." And from time to time, when Montaigne was not being the restrained, rational philosopher, he was a likely candidate for Rabelais's Thélème.

C. *The healthy cannibals*

ONE of the most massive contributions that the fifteenth-century Europeans had made to human knowledge was their exploration of the rest of the world. In the sixteenth century these explorations were not only pushed further as scientific enterprises but were utilized abundantly in commerce. The Near East, India, and China were consequently fairly well known to the informed late sixteenth-century European, whether he was a practical man or a theoretical one. These were highly civilized countries, and the bulk of their explorations had been done by the Spanish and the Portuguese, not the French.

But there were explorations of other countries in which the French (and the English) played a vital and continuing role, and these countries were by no means as verbally sophisticated as the others. It was in the explorations of the Americas that men like Villegaignon and Jacques Cartier made their discoveries. And the reports of such men, as well as the popularizations of their explorations by so-called "cosmographers," helped create in the minds of Frenchmen a very strong image. It was an image of a man naked, firm of will, innocent of verbal refinements, and, above all, vigorously healthy. This was an image different from the one that most Humanists transmitted by their uses of ancient Greek and Roman letters. And Montaigne was one of the many Frenchmen who became intensely interested in these "savages," whose actions spoke louder than their words. The Old World had helped teach him subtleties; the New World helped teach him plainness and innocence. Once he spoke with a savage chieftain who with two others of his tribe were at Rouen in 1562. At other times he spoke with sailors and merchants who had visited the primitive lands, usually Brazil, on business. But, as he tells us in his essay "Of Cannibals," he got most of his information from a "simple, crude fellow" who had lived more than a decade in Brazil. He kept this man at his castle for a long time, where he also kept native beds, ropes, swords, and shield-bracelets fresh from "that other world which has been discovered in our century." I am convinced that this guest was a *truchement,* or "interpreter," quite possibly a Norman, like many of the *truchements,* and certainly one of the rough, curious, and often greedy, often even criminal men who went to Brazil and stayed for a while, usually as minor leaders of the natives. Here was no man wedded to verbal constructions or possessed by an arrogant desire to attract his hearer to his own judgment. From him Montaigne learned much concerning the cannibals of Brazil.

Like a good Humanist, he made notes on their language (which he found to be "like Greek in its endings") and studied their poetry, a "warlike song" and a "love song," to prove that their naturalness, their simplicity, was not the result of a deficiency or of sheer stupidity. Still, it was their actions that most interested him, not their art or inventions. And in their actions he found a lifelong and overwhelming concern for what is directly useful to living. For the cannibals the useful was the natural, and only those actions were thought useful that preserved life or preserved honor. For instance, when a man set himself up as a prophet and his prophecies did not come true, he was cut into a thousand pieces. And Montaigne approved this pragmatic approach to divination:

"Men who come to trick us with assurances of an extraordinary faculty that is beyond our ken, should they not be punished for not making good their promise, and for the temerity of their imposture?"

The test of their prophecies was action, experience, not subtle verbiage. As for the cannibals, their "whole ethical science contains only these two articles: resoluteness in war and affection for their wives." Honor, love, and life — these were what they lived for; and the vices of civilized countries with more subtle ethical codes, with evils like treachery, disloyalty, and cruelty, were unknown to them.

Yes, they ate their enemies, and Montaigne plainly acknowledges "the barbarous horror of such acts." But he insists that there are worse acts committed by verbally subtle and arrogant civilized persons, such as torturing on a rack a live body full of feeling (the cannibals killed their enemies swiftly before dismembering and eating them). And even worse than inflicting this pain is "the pretext of piety and religion" that people were now using in civilized France to *condone* roasting a man bit by bit or having him mangled alive by dogs and swine. The cannibals killed and ate out of a plain desire for extreme revenge, Montaigne tells us, not under the cover of subtle pretexts. They always acted out of a straightforward love of valor and of life and out of the powerful emotions that these two loves generated in them. No theory was allowed to "smother" what Montaigne calls "our great and powerful mother Nature" in their actions; and this plain allegiance to conscience and to life was what Montaigne meant when he said that they were "still very close to their original naturalness."

But not only does the "naturalness" of the cannibals teach us that the simple pursuit of life and of self-respect is admirable; it also teaches us that nature herself is full of variety. We must, Montaigne insists, accept this variety without calling "barbaric" everything that is not our own practice. We must become aware of our own provinciality (and, of course, in so doing mitigate it). We must see that "we have no other test of truth and reason than the example and pattern of the opinions and customs of the country we live in. There is always the perfect religion, the perfect government, the perfect and accomplished manners in all things." And this is the second major point Montaigne makes concerning the cannibals and nature: variety is part of nature too. Of course, Montaigne is not asking us to change this, but simply to recognize it without rancor, or with as little rancor as we can manage. We shall continue to be provincial, because this is "natural"; but if we recognize this, our manner, the way we judge others by our own standards, will be affected: we shall be milder in living with those different from us.

There is a third element in Montaigne's notion of the naturalness of cannibals. It gives an honorific tone to words like "nature" and "natural" as they occur in his writings. This third element is that of healthfulness. The cannibals are healthy, and Montaigne's eyewitnesses "never saw one palsied, bleary-eyed, toothless, or bent with age." It is important to notice that in the essay on cannibals he attributes this health to their climate and to the food they eat, not to any special knowledge on their part. And throughout his *Essays* this will be exactly the point he will be making when he uses the term "healthy" with respect to individuals or nations: health will be the result of fitting into the established "ordinary" course of things with a minimum of artifice or special knowledge. It will be the result of simply allowing yourself to be ruled by the laws of your environment, be they the "laws of nature" that Montaigne talks vaguely about in the essay on cannibals or the man-made laws and customs of the land one lives in. Fitting into the established, abiding way of doing things, this is important to health for Montaigne. He will talk this way when he talks about his own personal health, and he will talk this way when he criticizes France for destroying her health by breaking with the old religious and civil traditions.

This last notion, health as adjustment to the established order, is directly related to our second point: we recognize the variety in the world, but not in order to change it; we recognize the variety in order to see "more sanely" where we stand in it, and we continue to take our stand where our feet are. In fact, for him, health and the recognition of variety in the world are much the same thing. As he puts it in the essay "Of the Education of Children":

"So many humors, sects, judgments, opinions, laws, and customs teach us to judge sanely of our own, and teach our judgment to recognize its own imperfection and natural weakness, which is no small lesson."

Once we become aware that our way is one among many, we have come far toward avoiding the feverish, deadly fanaticism of, say, the extremists in the religious wars. Once we see that our judgment is not the sole arbiter of the truth, we begin to moderate our passions and can both live and let live, judge and let judge. This point can be generalized: the religious wars, Humanism, and the explorations helped teach Montaigne that a feverish attachment to one's own cause and an equally feverish desire to extinguish other causes were inappropriate to the way things are. They were inappropriate to the inextinguishable variety of men's ways.

Conclusion

POLITICALLY and religiously, Montaigne was a moderate in an age when political and religious fanaticisms were infecting and destroying the vigor and order of French society as well as the health of individual Frenchmen. A dynamic commitment to moderation on public matters (for, as we have seen, Montaigne was a Catholic and a political leader) worked side by side in him with *both* moderation and occasional unbuckled spontaneity as far as personal matters were concerned. He lived in the sixteenth century in France, and he believed like Catherine de' Medicis and the Politiques that the health, the orderly, balanced operation, of the state was a very important matter, all the more important because France was sinking fast. And so he had to be a pathologist for the body politic, circumspect, and so forth. But in the *Essays,* which were in the end about him — which were, indeed, the image of him — a public sickness was not usually being cured; an individual private person was usually being discovered and presented in all his richness. And this richness was the richness not of a public man, a Mayor of Bordeaux, counsellor to the Protestant Henry of Navarre and to a Catholic king. These activities are hardly mentioned. They play a tiny part in the *Essays.* The richness he presented here was the richness of a person who had withdrawn in his heart from a sick public situation so that he could *be* more fully, more vigorously, than that situation could permit. His style of writing, his style of living, would therefore be personal not public, would not be the limited, circumspect style of a public man in those times; and his way of writing, his way of living, these two *façons,* images of each other, would be his own. That this should be so was, as we have seen, consistent not only with the public problems of the time but with the tensions and fruitions that the Humanists of his era were experiencing. Moreover, his yearning for healthy simplicity had much to do with what he learned from the cannibals. To step back somehow from the public sickness and to write and to be himself were complementary projects that appealed to Michel de Montaigne as Politique, as Humanist, and as an admirer of simple men.

Chapter 2

Doubt and Man

Here is a paragraph from the classic study by Pierre Villey called *Les Sources et l'évolution des Essais de Montaigne* (Villey is speculating on the effect that the Scepticism of Sextus Empiricus had on Montaigne):

> His head is swimming; he loses his footing, and the forces that have been accumulating for so long in his brain come together, and carry him toward the fatal conclusion. He will go wherever Sextus will wish to lead him.... Montaigne proclaims that [no belief] ... will stand up under criticism.... He does not see clearly into himself, but do not be afraid: this dimness will pass. Let Montaigne put a little distance between him and Sextus, and his ideas will get calm again; he will restore his doubts to their proper proportions.... He will contradict Pyrrho, he will handily formulate his judgments, and hold on to them.[1]

Villey saw Pyrrhonism as an "ocean" of doubt,[2] a totally negative philosophy from which one must escape in order to stand or walk like a man. The Sceptic, Villey thought, was somebody afflicted with "infinite uncertainty,"[3] unable to find "a solid point where he could stand." And thinking of Scepticism in this way, while seeing the obvious firmness in so much of Montaigne's thought, Villey concluded that Scepticism "did not last" in the mind and in the essays of Montaigne.

In this chapter we shall not try to refute the charge that Scepticism was only *"un moment,"* and a very brief one, in Montaigne's life. This whole book, and especially the first two Parts of it, will try to show that Scepticism is a large and integral part of Montaigne's concept of a personal philosophy. In this chapter, all we shall do is try to see what the Scepticism of Sextus Empiricus actually is. To do this is important, not only because it will help counteract Villey's description and evaluation of it but also because only if we know what it is can we see its actual role in Montaigne's thought.

Doubt and Man

But as an introduction to this explanation, and by way of contrast with Villey's somewhat melodramatic description of Montaigne's Sceptical dizziness, consider the following paragraph from an essay in the First Book (not usually thought of as the "Sceptical" Book of the *Essays*) — the essay entitled "That the Taste of Good and Evil Depends in Large Part on the Opinion We Have of Them":

> Pyrrho the philosopher being one day in a great tempest, showed the most frightened among his companions a pig that was there, not at all concerned at this storm, and encouraged them by its example. Shall we then dare to say that this advantage, reason, that we make such a fuss about, and on account of which we think ourselves masters and emperors of the rest of creation, has been put in us for our torment? What good is the knowledge of things if by it we lose the repose and tranquillity we should enjoy without it, and if it puts us into a worse condition than Pyrrho's pig? The intelligence that has been given us for our greatest good, shall we use it for our ruin, combating the plan of nature and the universal order of things, which says that each man shall use his tools and means for his comfort?[4]

Now *this* is a just summary of the Scepticism to be found in Sextus Empiricus' *Outlines of Pyrrhonism*. Notice that this *agoge,* or way of life, is flatly contrary to the way of life Villey had in mind when he thought of Pyrrhonism: Pyrrho, far from having lost his mental footing, is apparently the only one on the ship (other than the pig) who is stable, calm, and comfortable. Far from subverting intelligence or belief and throwing man into *"une incertitude infinie,"* Pyrrho is using his mind to achieve those beliefs or attitudes conducive to "his comfort." Actually the only point these two accounts of Scepticism share is a reference to the sea, and even here the difference is profound: Villey says that Pyrrhonism throws one's mind into the tempestuous sea; Montaigne says that Pyrrhonism rescues that mind.

The Scepticism Montaigne actually found in Sextus' *Outlines of Pyrrhonism* uses incertitude as a negative means to a very important positive end: healthy-mindedness, unperturbedness. Pyrrhonism is a therapeutic philosophy, and the Sceptic is a doctor (indeed, Sextus and many others of the Sceptics were practising physicians) who uses doubt to cure man of a swollen imagination and to restore him to his natural common sense. We shall be examining the key terms in this last sentence throughout the rest of this book.

Scepticism (like Stoicism and Epicureanism) is part of the Hellenistic-Roman wisdom-tradition of philosophy, which extended from the traumatic breakdown of the empire of Alexander the Great in the fourth century B.C. to the third century A.D., when Sextus wrote his *Outlines*. It is one of various *Lebensphilosophien,* whose philosophic tools (like logic, metaphysics, and such) were used in the service of a practical ideal — the ideal of happiness, *eudaimonia*. They all sought mental poise, tranquil self-control, spiritual health, though they advocated fundamentally different ways of achieving it. In logic, in epistemology, in metaphysics, in ethics, they differed profoundly from each other, but they all sought in those centuries after the fall of Alexander's great empire the one thing Villey denied Scepticism: stability.

A. Affirmation

THE originating cause or *arche* of Scepticism is the hope of living peacefully, without the offensive or defensive passions displayed by those who think they have found the "substantial truth" behind the "seeming" of everyday life. In accordance with this *arche,* the Sceptics drew up what they called a "Practical Criterion." That Criterion states that the Sceptic must live his life in a manner "in accordance with the customs, the laws, and the institutions of our country, and with our own natural feelings [hunger, thirst, and the like.]"[5]

And actions, perceptions, and talk involved in everyday life are not accepted on moral or metaphysical "foundations." I do not follow that rule because it is morally right or metaphysically realistic; I follow it because doing the sorts of things it loosely describes is living. Our "natural feelings," our *oikeia pathe,* lead us to want food, drink, and continuing life. The Sceptic is not claiming by way of metaphysics that there is something — or nothing — beyond these feelings. He is saying that they are a part of life, and either we continue to live or we don't.

The "tradition of laws and customs" of our country is on the same footing as the constraint of our bodily needs. We need justify none of them; they are part of the basic, normal rules of life, and to play the game of life is to live according to them. Obviously, then, the Sceptics would doubt any doctrine of Natural Law "underlying" the positive laws and customs of a country. To deviate from the local tradition is to invite trouble, just as to deviate from the urge to satisfy hunger and thirst is to invite trouble. We follow the traditions of our country for ultimately expediential, not moral or metaphysical, motives. But we should not think of motives as precisely defined ideals of any sort; rather we should think of them as "natural feelings" for peaceful existence, not requiring any precise definition at all.

Now, this motivation (or lack of moral and metaphysical motivation) does not make the Sceptic's adherence to the laws and customs of his country any more irregular for being expediential or "part of the game." The Sceptic follows those laws and customs as regularly as he follows the guidance of his appetites for food and drink. The only palpable difference between the Sceptic and the dogmatic good citizen is that the Sceptic quietly goes about the business of living, while the dogmatist

> is continually disturbed. When he lacks those things which seem to him to be good, he believes he is being pursued, as if by the Furies, by those things which are by nature bad, and pursues what he believes to be the good things. But when he has acquired them, he encounters further perturbations. This is because his elation at the acquisition is unreasonable and immoderate, and also because in his fear of a reversal all his exertions go to prevent the loss of the things which to him seem good. On the other side there is the man who leaves undetermined the question what things are good and bad by nature. He does not exert himself to avoid anything or to seek after anything, and hence he is in a tranquil state.[6]

There is, in short, an adverbial difference between these two good citizens' allegiance to the laws and customs of their country; they both follow traditions, but one does so disquietedly and the other does so quietly. Scepticism is a way of living, thinking, and using language, a way consistent with various types of laws and customs.

Another consequence of not holding the Practical Criterion dogmatically (on the basis of metaphysical proofs) is that we follow our own traditions and laws without having to attack bitterly opposing or different traditions and laws. It becomes inappropriate, even foolish, to be either offensive toward differing traditions or defensive in the face of them. The fact remains that the broad, vague Practical Criterion is not accessible to doubt; it is up to our common sense to administer it precisely, but is an indefeasible rule of conduct for *me*. And so Sceptics follow their traditions and laws, but always with the right adverbs attached, and always with a permissive attitude toward the fact of other traditions and laws.

Thus Scepticism is an appropriate way of living and thinking for a man who finds other, strange customs and laws attractive, but is still a Frenchman and a Catholic by birth and upbringing. To him, pagan antiquity itself, even Protestantism (when it did not violate the laws and customs of its host country), could be neither an object of destructive hatred nor a source of defensive counterclaims. The moral and metaphysical rectitude of all these laws and customs would be dubious; all one could judge them on would be their capacity to promote a peaceful, continuing life in accordance with one's natural feelings; and even this judgment would have to be cautiously made after a long, hard look at the facts of everyday living, which are the only meaningful matrix for those laws and customs.

B. *The general function of doubt*

THE way doubt operates in Scepticism is well expressed in the metaphor of the laxative (a metaphor Montaigne delightedly re-used). As Sextus the physician puts it, "Just as aperient drugs do not merely eliminate the humours from the body, but also expel themselves along with the humours,"[7] so doubt cancels itself out with the dogmatic claims it works upon. The last word belongs to everyday life, to the Practical Criterion, to experience or "appearances."[8] After doubt has brought about a suspension of judgment on dogma, both doubt and dogma lose their importance, and the functions and objects involved in an orderly, undogmatic life take over. Food, drink, the customs and laws of our country; the "instruction of the arts," that is, the pleasures involved in creating and appreciating the arts; simple piety without dogmatic claims about invisible reality; the things that a civilized man needs in order to have a peaceful, vigorous life — all these are there when the doubting is done.

Implicit in all we have been noticing in this chapter is the belief that we do not doubt certain matters of fact called "evident." The reason we do not doubt them is not that we have *proved* them to be the case; on the contrary, anything that needs to be proved is non-evident and therefore subject to doubt. The term "doubt" is applicable only to so-called "proofs" concerning what is beyond phenomena, beyond our consciousness and its immediate objects. What we suspend judgment on, or doubt, is Indicative Signs — signs that are supposed to point *beyond all possible experience* to hidden "substances" or "laws" or "essences"; but we do not suspend judgment on Recollective Signs — signs that refer, *within experience,* to other parts of our experience: the way smoke signifies fire or reminds us of fire. The function of doubt in classical Scepticism is severely limited by what the Sceptics wanted most: contented living amongst Recollective Signs. The purpose of doubt, like the purpose of Scepticism in general, is not to produce infinite uncertainty; it is to find tranquillity by removing a main source of our discontent — dogmatism. Common sense is not the source of misery; plain talk about plainly observable attitudes and objects does not produce fanaticism, defensiveness, and so forth, and so doubt is irrelevant to them, since it is a practical instrument which functions only in places where peace is threatened by that "trickster," reason. A healthy man does not need a laxative.

C. *The techniques of doubt*

THERE are two main constituents of doubt. In the writings of Sextus each of these elements has a technical name and a carefully specified set of characteristics. The two are "antithesis" and "mental suspense."

1. ANTITHESIS

Given two conflicting judgments, the awareness of the fact that neither of these conflicting judgments takes final precedence over the other, as far as being true is concerned, is the awareness of antithesis. Consider an example that Sextus used and Montaigne re-used in the "Apology." You have a plump, fragrant apple before you, fresh from the orchard. It is smooth, sweet-smelling, and yellow. To the ordinary man, everything is plain: there is an apple on the table, and it looks and smells a certain way. But the dogmatist enters with a queer terminology that resembles ordinary talk, and he refuses to be satisfied with Recollective Signs, with "announcing his impression" of the apple. He says: "The apple does not *really* possess all these qualities." And he goes on: "It really has only *one* underlying quality that only *looks* like the various qualities of smoothness, yellowness, and the like, because our various sense organs distort it." Then another dogmatist enters and says: "The apple really has *other* qualities as *well* as these — and if we had different kinds of sense organs we would see these other qualities."

Consider the first dogmatist's suggestion: that there "really" might be only one basic quality differentiated by our different sense organs into smoothness (by our sense of touch), yellowness (by our sense of sight), and so on. Now, this is plausible. After all, a tree sucks up water, and the water is transformed in one place into leaf, in another into twig. A flute receives one stream of air, but because of the various stops the stream comes out at one time one note, at another time another note, and all from the same stream of air.

Now consider the second dogmatist's statement: that the apple may possess more basic qualities than are apparent to us. This too is plausible. It is easy to imagine a man born with only the senses of touch, taste, and smell, but unable to hear or see. To such a man visible or audible existence "makes no sense" in any definite, clear way. Now we perceive only the number of qualities in the apple that our sense organs are equipped to perceive; if we had other sense organs we might perceive more and different ones.

These are possibilities, and the more you think about each, the more plausible it becomes. You may in fact spin out of any one of these answers a whole dogmatic philosophy of perception and reality, as have many philosophers. But the Sceptic's question is: is there any *criterion* for resolving the controversy to the satisfaction of all dogmatists? And the answer thus far in the history of human thought is No. Since all of them are talking about what is not available in perception, that trickster, reason, is perfectly free to fabricate defenses of one's own interpretations and to attack other interpretations. The dogmatists are not all bound by any decisive factual criterion. And if one of them says, "Now, gentlemen, let me settle the controversy: the apple is really such-and-such," then the others can say quite rightly that he is a party to the controversy himself and therefore cannot be a judge in it, given that there is no criterion he can use to arbitrate the dispute "objectively" and conclusively. They are all on the same footing, and so are all their claims: equally plausible, equally implausible, depending upon what point of view you happen to have. And this equality is symbolized by a scale whose plates are in perfect balance. It is this condition that Montaigne is talking about when he says that reason is made of wax and can be molded into any shape a man desires. The Sceptic has the impression that no one claim about facts beyond experience is in the end more certain (or uncertain) than any other.

The awareness of antithesis brings about a suspension of judgment concerning the "real" qualities of the apple; I withhold assent from any set of such claims without denying any one, since I also, as a Sceptic, have no criterion for attributing truth or falsity to such a belief. Sometimes Sextus comes close to dogmatism when he looks at a set of Indicative claims, as in his book *Against the Physicists,* when he says: "The variety of the modes of conception ... stamps them with the ignorance of the truth." But he usually recovers his mental poise quickly and says that one of them may be true, for all we know, but we do not know which. We are still in the midst of a battle between various claims.

Now, our example of the two dogmatists is perhaps misleading. There need not be only two members to an Indicative set. Speaking in the language of logic, the relationship of antithesis is not necessarily one of Contradiction. Ultimately there is only one Contradictory of a given statement ("All horses are black" has as its only Contradictory "Some horses are not black" or some phrase meaning the same thing). But an Indicative set can be, and usually is, vast, containing many conflicting claims. You can have a dozen dogmatists in the room. Here is a sample set of Indicative antithetical claims:

1. There is only one quality underlying your sense impressions (the Materialist or the Idealist).

2. There are no qualities underlying your sense impressions (Phenomenalism or Solipsism).

3. Only those qualities which are measurable really underlie the phenomena (Galileo, Descartes, Locke, *et al.*).

4. There are no qualities, but there is a Spirit or a God causing these sense impressions in me (Berkeley).

And so on. The whole history of dogmatic philosophy is the history of the growth of such sets. In fact an "original" dogmatic philosopher is one who increases one or more such sets by one. This is his immortal contribution to the chaos of the human mind.

Of course, the relationship between members of such a set has something to do with contradiction or nay-saying; members of it are "in opposition" to each other. No two can be true at the same time. There is a conflict between them. But since the conflict is not necessarily between only two claims, it can be as broad and manifold as the whole history of philosophy with respect to a given problem. The sum-total of all the various laws and customs of all the various countries of the world, each claiming to be "right" or "true," can be as vast as the wide world itself. The dogmatic claims of Italian, Brazilian (see Montaigne's essay "Of Cannibals"), French, and all the other cultures — all these claims could make up an antithetical Indicative set, and an awareness of this set could bring about a suspension of judgment. For instance, antithesis in the "Apology" often involves putting down a dazzling variety of conflicting claims. In fact, sometimes Montaigne tries to get you to suspend judgment by sheer weight of numbers.

Scepticism, in short, is an injunction to recognize a brute fact when it grabs you by the throat and to distinguish it from a phantom that assails you by the imagination or by that trickster, reason. The art of being a Sceptic is the art of seeing these brute facts (whether they be food, drink, hunger, thirst, or habitual actions) as Recollective Signs and as Recollective Signs only.

2. THE TROPOI

These general remarks about doubt and *ataraxia* are inadequate even for so brief a discussion of Scepticism as this. They do not show how the Sceptic goes about setting up his antithetical sets, and therefore they are about Scepticism's end-product, not about its all-important instruments or means. The means the Sceptics use in seeking out antitheses are called by them *tropoi* — modes of argument. The early Sceptics had ten tropes or guides for setting up an Indicative group; later Sceptics (that is, those who lived after the birth of Christ) added five tropes, not to refute the first ten but to elaborate and add to them. And there are other modes, but the first ten are the backbone of classical Scepticism and the main ones Montaigne uses.

Here the conciseness of Sextus' *Outlines* makes further condensation unnecessary. The *tropoi* are, he says,

> First ... that in which suspension is caused by the variation in animals. In the second it is caused by the differences in human beings. Third, by the difference in the construction of the organs of sense. [This is the one that the Indicative set about the apple used.] Fourth, by the circumstances. Fifth, by the positions, distances, and places involved. Sixth, by the admixtures present. Seventh, by the quantities and compoundings of the underlying objects. Eighth, by the relativity of things. Ninth, by the frequency or rarity of occurrence. Tenth, by the institutions, customs, laws, mythical beliefs, and dogmatic notions.[9]

But the mode of arguing that overarches and contains these ten tropes is the mode of *relativity*. For instance, using the first trope, we learn that other animals can see better or hear better than we can; looking at other animals, we see that they can judge on matters concerning life and pleasure as well as we can. Looking at other animals, we see that we creatures get diverse sense experiences from the same objects (Sextus tells us that quail are fattened by hemlock and deer eat poisonous plants). When we see all this, we find ourselves suspending judgment concerning *whose* sense experiences indicate *the* non-evident structure and stuff of the universe. And this suspense becomes even more plausible if we try to judge amongst all these ways of experiencing things and find that we are being judges at our own trial, begging the whole question in favor of our own kind of perceptions: we cannot pull ourselves up by our bootstraps, much less the other animals. We are down with them. In short, the truth of our impressions is relative to ourselves; there may be as many different kinds of truths as there are different kinds of animals. As for the independent, essential nature of objects "behind" those impressions, these conflicting impressions and effects lead us to suspend judgment.

And having found no acceptable criterion for adjudicating such conflicts or differences, each must use relative, practical criteria appropriate to his condition and appropriate to the *changes* in this condition. From an awareness of this condition and its changes springs Montaigne's concept of personal philosophy.

D. *The sceptic's doctrine of man*

IF you slice off and throw away the old contemplative *theoria* of the dogmatists — the old confidence that human reason has some special, unique insight into the underlying stuff of the universe — you deemphasize the ascendancy of man himself in the universe, as the incident with the pig suggested toward the beginning of this chapter. Seneca, in his letters to Lucilius, follows the Stoical doctrine that reason alone sets man off from animals, and for him the greatest good for man is to be found in the use of reason, since man's greatest good lies in what is unique to him. But to a Sceptic this is all groundless reasoning, dogmatic cant; and when the Sceptic claims *this,* and uses his various modes of argument to back up his claims, it becomes clear that he thinks about men as "on the same footing" with animals, not as "masters and emperors of the rest of creation." If a Stoic like Seneca tends to think in terms of man's superiority over other animals, a Sceptic like Sextus tends to think in terms of man's equality with the other animals. Certainly the use of the very important First Mode furthers this way of thinking, and so do the others. And thinking this way, he emphasizes human actions as they are related to other animals' actions. As a Sceptic, when you use the word "nature" you do not mean the laws of nature rationally discoverable by man alone; you mean "the passions ... whereby hunger drives us to food and thirst to drink." You mean the forces that drive both men and animals — forces just as evident to the animals as to us.

Pure reason and the hidden laws discoverable only by reason fall away when doubt gets through corroding them. And what is left is a life of action that is "on the same footing" with the actions of other animals. You simply act for "reasons" of hunger, thirst, and the like. Instead of sovereign, even divine, reason (as Seneca and the other Stoics would have it), you have common sense, something similar to the sense that keeps other animals alive and thriving. Ours is a basic sort of reasonableness, according to the Sceptic; and, contrary to the Stoic, it is a kind of canniness whose perfection lies solely in keeping its possessor alive and healthy. The antique doctrine of following nature is not for the Sceptic an exordium to rise above the other animals by using reason to penetrate all the laws of the universe; it becomes an invitation to resemble the other animals in a search for health and long life — a pedestrian, empirical search that moves humbly amidst the Recollective Signs that constitute our living experience. The mind of man, instead of being a beacon that searches out and illumines the depths of the universe around it, becomes a tool for the survival of the individual creature who possesses it.

Of course the "Guidance of Nature" and the "constraint of the passions" are not all there is to the Practical Criterion. The rest of it has to do with more or less peculiarly human institutions, like enacted laws. But, as we have noticed, the Sceptic does not follow these laws because he believes he has any special insight into their moral or metaphysical validity. He follows them for "reasons" similar to the "reasons" a wolf follows his pack and participates in their running and hunting habits. He follows them for the sake of living, and living healthfully. They are modes of healthy action, ways of attaining a healthy unperturbedness. For the Sceptic, life needs no other goal but healthy living itself. And knowledge of anything or any ethical standard beyond everyday life is not only *not* the goal of living for him; its pursuit is plainly a grievously distracting force in life.

Insofar as Montaigne is a Sceptic, in the classic meaning of that term, he will have no detailed conclusions to offer either about what is Right for all men or about what is Real for all men. He will neither deny nor affirm any absolute or universally valid Indicative statement. As a Sceptic he will be committed to living a life amongst Recollective Signs, or within "living experience," as Sextus put it, and he will not be living that life as if his were the only valid way of living or his beliefs the only tenable beliefs: he will, as a Sceptic, be aware of the intimate relationship between his particular condition and his own ways of thinking. This awareness, as we have been seeing, will by no means throw him into a paralytic trance or make his actions and beliefs less regular or less effective. It will make those actions and beliefs more self-conscious: it will temper them with permissiveness toward others' ways of acting and believing; but it will not destroy his own capacity to act and to believe effectively, happily. On the contrary, because he is not passionately denying or affirming anything about the absolute truth of morality or metaphysics, he will live out his life and think his thoughts calmly, at least with respect to morality and metaphysics, without the negatively offensive or the positively defensive passions of the dogmatist. Sextus summarized the relativism of Scepticism by saying that the Sceptic does not speak for all men; he "announces his own impression" at the moment of speaking. As a Sceptic, this is what Montaigne will do, but in a far more personal way than did Sextus. Sextus usually spoke as an anonymous member of a school; Montaigne usually spoke not in terms of "us," but in terms of *me,* this particular man, with this particular name — a particular man whose particular yearnings and insights and impulses overflowed the categories or methods of any school.

But, whatever the differences between Sextus and Montaigne, they both cherished a way of life and thinking that left room for other ways of living and thinking, and they cherished that way far more than they cherished pure, objective knowledge *or* the denial of it. In this emphasis upon what we have called the "adverbial," or the *façon* of one's own life, Montaigne was a Humanist with a Sceptical turn of mind. And in his desire to do things, not for metaphysical or theological reasons, but for reasons of expedience — peace and health — he was a Politique with a Sceptical turn of mind.

It is time now to turn to the *Essays* themselves and see how he produced his personal philosophy. To begin to do so, we shall consider the one essay in which Montaigne most fully and profoundly expressed both his Scepticism and his position vis-à-vis the public disputes of his day: the "Apology for Raymond Sebond."

PART II

The Root and Branches of a Personal Philosophy

Chapter 3

Men and Mixtures

A. General

Doubt is the heightened awareness of insistent variety. In the dubitative stage of his philosophizing, the Sceptic is more aware of the differences amongst creatures, conditions, and beliefs than he is of any detailed similarities. When the doubting is washed away, he sees broad similarities (the Practical Criterion is a statement of these similarities), but *epoche* itself is nothing but the suspension of judgment that a man feels when faced with many different points of view, each of which is insisting on its rights.

In our introductory chapter we considered some of the sources of Montaigne's awareness of variety: Protestantism and the religious conflicts it created, and the Renaissance with the cultures of Rome and Athens that it brought to France. We have also discussed the exploration of the New World[1] and mentioned the explorations of Middle Eastern and Eastern countries. Montaigne was deeply interested in all these movements, and this interest widened and deepened his awareness of the variety in the universe.

A glance at his longest and most ambitious essay, the "Apology for Raymond Sebond," shows how much he respected a democracy of points of view: quotations, anecdotes, pithy observations, desultory inferences, all spread out on the page, iconically represent his image of a multifarious world. A dogmatist usually moves in a straight line from lucid axioms through cautious, small steps up to an irrefragable conclusion. But a Sceptic like Montaigne wants "change indiscriminately and tumultuously. My style and my mind alike go roaming. 'A man must be a little mad if he does not want to be even more stupid,' say the precepts of our masters, and even more so their examples."[2]

But the "Apology" is not simply an embodiment of *epoche,* just as Classical Scepticism is not simply the process of doubting. The essay has a specific, explicitly stated goal, and Montaigne's writing of it was triggered by certain events — events that determined both the nature of his doubts and the goal those doubts were intended to serve.

In 1569, at his father's request, Montaigne translated into French a book entitled *Theologia naturalis, sive liber creaturarum, specialiter de homine et de natura ejus.*[3] The writer of this book was a certain doctor and theologian named Raymond Sebond, who had died in Toulouse in 1432. Montaigne's translation had a large sale and was reprinted in 1581. As its original Latin title indicates, one of its main points was a doctrine of man. The Spanish-born theologian saw man as the most perfect of God's creatures; in fact, he believed that all other creatures were created to serve him. He also believed that man's perfection lay primarily in his rational powers, and Sebond himself used these powers to work out a natural theology, a demonstration of the nature and existence of God, as well as proofs of the specifically Catholic doctrines of the Trinity, Original Sin, and the Incarnation. In many respects he was an imitator of St. Thomas Aquinas, but he was rather more sanguine about the powers of human reason than was the Angelic Doctor.

By the time Montaigne sat down to write this essay in anything like its present form, Sebond's book had been attacked as well as praised. And we are almost certain[4] that the daughter of Catherine de' Medicis, Margaret of Valois, then wife of the future Henry IV, asked the translator of the book to defend it against the attacks of Protestants and atheists.

The "Apology," then, is a Sceptical essay written to defend an unsceptical Catholic theologian whose beliefs were pleasing to at least one member of the Catholic court of France. But before we can read the essay as it was intended to be read, at its face value, we must remind ourselves of one more element in the situation. The essay was thought through and composed between 1575 and 1580, after the St. Bartholomew's Day Massacre, at the height of the French religio-civil wars; at this time theological controversy was at high heat and was helping to destroy the very life of France. Theological refutation and counterrefutation constituted a spiritual disease that was issuing in physical violence, and Montaigne wrote his essay as a "preservative" against this disease. Men were arrogantly tearing up the highroad of French religious custom, and a public personage of great power had assigned a moderate Catholic to defend a

Catholic theologian against such arrogance. The "Apology" is a spiritually therapeutic document written to help preserve the health of France against the disease of disputatious pride.

Much has been written by Sainte-Beuve and others[5] about the irony and even the atheism that Montaigne is supposed to be exhibiting in this massive essay. And indeed in the essay Montaigne implies that he has his doubts about the Trinity and the Incarnation. But most of these writers do not see that Sceptical doubt is in the service of peace and of what Sextus calls "the tradition of laws and customs." When we see this, we realize that Montaigne had little time and less reason to desire to kick under the table the dead body of this imitative natural theologian (whose writings he had translated at the behest of his beloved father). The plain fact is that he had a preventive to a personally and nationally dangerous disease to concoct right on top of the table, in full view. His doubt was in the service of a particular "assignment,"[6] and in the fulfillment of that assignment his personal philosophy will begin to emerge as part of a broad vision of man, nature, and God.

But before studying this emergence more closely, let us briefly summarize the argument of the essay. The essay is a "final fencer's trick" whereby a man wraps his sword around his opponent's and lets both their weapons fly out of their hands and land on the ground. It is an effort to show the weakness of human reason itself, Montaigne's included, and it is a desperate measure, suitable for desperate times. The arrogant critics of custom have made this measure necessary.

Still, when the swords of theological disputation are fallen, when radical doubt has done its work, where can a man turn for stability, for the very peace the essay seeks? One thing is clear: he cannot turn to any one set of metaphysical claims that purport to tell the pure, unsubjective truth. Now, there are three sources of stability: two of them natural, and the third supernatural. The first is the beliefs dictated by the traditions and laws of one's country. If you cannot find the absolute truth about the pure essence of things, you must stand on relative truths, mixtures of objects with a nation's customary ways of seeing them. The second source of stability, deeply involved with the first, is my own common sense, the way I deal with the world in my efforts to survive and be happy. My common sense is soaked with the history of my country, of my region, but its specific function is to maintain my own health. It is like the *sens* other creatures have, an instrument for maintaining an individual's health.

And the third source is a Fideist's simple, non-metaphysical faith in God (in most of his writings and in most of the "Apology" he does not emphasize his Fideism).

Here in outline are the roots of Montaigne's thought. The world is full of a number of things, and when we appropriate this fact we are individually and as a nation well through the gateway to wisdom. It is obvious that such a pluralistic way of thinking is a rich ground in which to grow a personal philosophy similar to that mentioned in our Preface and Introduction.

At the outset of the essay he says:

"Because many people are busy reading it, and especially the ladies, to whom we owe additional help, I have often found myself in a position to help them by clearing their book of two principal objections that are made against it."

And with all its variety, the structure of the essay is simple: Introduction (how Montaigne got involved in this project of defending Sebond); Part One (the first objection, and Montaigne's response to it); finally, the longest part, Part Two (the second objection, and Montaigne's response to it. It is this part that contains the "Warning to the Princess" which talks specifically about *"ce preservatif"* against arrogant dogmatism of any sort). Montaigne is trying to "clear" (*"descharger"*) Sebond of these two objections. This is what he wanted to do for the sake of the public weal and at the behest of a royal personage. The essay is as simple as this. For all his great gifts, Montaigne was at bottom a tough, plain-spoken Gascon; he was doing a job; and the essay is the way he did it.

B. *The mild objection*

"La première repréhension" against the book is this: matters of faith are separate from matters of reason; indeed, such proofs as Sebond's can only do Christians harm, mixing as they do human reason with divine matters. Now, Montaigne will support something like this kind of Fideism (faith and Grace, not human reasons, are relevant to religious belief). But the notion that *"les Chrétiens se font tort"* whenever they try to support their belief by human reasons — *this* notion has two flaws. The first flaw is that it simply is not the case that Christians always do themselves harm when they try to support their faith with reasons. They may do themselves harm when they try to attack or judge this faith with reason:

this is the very sort of thing that leads to Protestantism and rationalistic Atheism as well as Catholic fanaticism. But when they use reason to embellish and enrich the faith of their own childhood and of their fathers, they are doing something quite worthy of a Christian. And its worth lies in its effect on our erring minds; it prepares us for Grace and keeps us always receptive to God, even in the face of temptations. If "reasons" have no ontological justification, they certainly have a psychological, homiletical one, insofar as they help us *"concevoir et loger en nous"* the faith God grants us. Montaigne himself knew a man of some power and learning who "confessed to me that he had been brought back from the errors of unbelief through the medium of Sebond's arguments." This was plain evidence that reasoning in support of one's religion can be useful to Christians. The objection had been confusedly saying that Christians can do themselves only harm by thinking about their religion. This objection was belied by Montaigne's friend, if by nothing else.

Of course, without faith, without Grace, all Sebond's arguments are only "purely human fancies." But with faith, or in preparation for it, they are quite useful and even solid. At this point Montaigne makes an orthodox Sceptical move: if we strip Sebond's arguments of this faith, "they will still be found as solid and firm as any others of the same type that may be opposed to them. . . . [Protestants for example] must admit the force of our proofs, or show us elsewhere . . . proofs better woven and of better stuff." The reader will recognize this for what it is: a statement of antithesis. Montaigne is simply suspending judgment on whether such proofs are true or false, apart from faith. And he is implying that Catholicism is preferable to these other proofs solely because of everyday, experiential reasons — reasons to be found in the realm of Recollective Signs. Violating the old way has created the religious wars which are destroying Frenchmen and France; let us therefore not violate the old way of worshiping God, and let us use whatever means we can to keep ourselves receptive, attentive to the old ways and the old faith.

But there is a second mistake in the criticism of Sebond which claims that Christianity is "conceived only by faith" and not by human reasons: it assumes that we can separate faith from human reasons, or even distinguish them when they occur together. And this assumption is plainly belied by history, especially by the history of the religious wars in France. If we could distinguish divine Grace from "human accidents," then that Grace and our faith would be everywhere the same and would be independent of human or wordly changes. If there were a ray of divinity that appeared in all believers, and if that ray could be distinguished from purely human, changing passions and imaginations, then we could all follow that ray, no matter what selfish or brutal human passions tried to make us swerve. Our faith would be like that pure ray, eternal, unchanging, independent of circumstance. "And yet I am afraid," says Montaigne, that in the religious wars that "are oppressing our state" we see "events fluctuating and varying in a common ordinary manner." This must be because men cannot distinguish divinity from humanity — cannot separate faith in God from private, ordinary human accidents. On the contrary, their religion is as variable and selfish as their own passions and circumstances. And all this is so not only because religion is a mixture of human accidents with whatever "ray of divinity" may be there, but also because we make use of religion to flatter and satisfy our own passions. Religion involves human accidents, but not only as recessive, pettily disturbing elements. These human accidents dominate whatever "ray of divinity" may be involved; they so thoroughly obfuscate that ray as to make it predominantly human. This ray does not lead us; we "lead it, drawing, as if from wax . . . many contrasting figures" from it and calling them all "religion." No, the ray of divinity is not distinguishable here; there is only the plain fact that men in the name of religion "are driven . . . by private and accidental considerations according to whose diversity they are stirred."

It is always man we are dealing with when we talk about religion, man whose nature is *"merveilleusement corporelle,"* subject to change and diversity. Try to distinguish yourself from rays of divinity, and you are always a man trying to distinguish between these things, a man changing with circumstances, differing from other men. We are creatures who

> receive our religion only in our own way and with our own hands, and not otherwise than as other religions are received. We happen to have been born in a country where it was in practice; or we regard its antiquity or the authority of the men who have maintained it; or we fear the threats that fasten upon unbelievers, or pursue its promises . . . human ties. Another region . . . might imprint upon us in the same way a contrary belief.
>
> We are Christians by the same title that we are Perigordians or Germans.[7]

In religious as in secular knowledge Montaigne, the good Sceptic, is reconciled to living with mixtures of human with (perhaps) trans-human elements. He will not try to distinguish the ray from the human being who "lodges" it in his mind; he will simply look at the whole man. If you cannot untangle the mixture because you have hands *"merveilleusement corporelles,"* then you simply live with the mixture and do the best you can. To live with mixtures is to withdraw from making truth-claims about pure, trans-human rays. It involves learning to cope with individual men and individual countries made up of men.

Montaigne was Sceptical about human reasons and receptive to faith and Grace; but he never denied what he was saying in response to this first objection: he never denied that thinking on religious matters can have a useful psychological function. On the contrary, his whole apology for Sebond was an example of such thinking and was written to be useful as a psychological "preservative" in religious matters. There is not a single bitter drop of destructive irony in Montaigne's defense of Sebond *against this first objection.* Of course, Sebond himself would have taken grave exception to Montaigne's Scepticism about "knowledge . . . supernatural and divine." He was a rationalistic theologian claiming to have such knowledge. But all this is irrelevant to the fact that Montaigne set out to clear Sebond's book of this first objection and of its implications. This he did as best he could, and he never once withdrew any claims he made in Sebond's defense. Again I must say that those who accuse Montaigne of an elaborate, subtle, ultimately destructive irony directed against Sebond's book do not see exactly what Montaigne thought he was doing in "clearing" this book "of two principal objections that are made against it." We should not forget that Scepticism does not assert the falsity of any Indicative truth-claim; nor should we forget that it has a Practical Criterion which adjures Sceptics to follow the customs, laws, and institutions they were raised in. We should remember that Montaigne was a Catholic writing in defense of a Catholic theologian at a time when Protestants were by *their* theologizing creating "this dangerous pestilence that spreads day by day in your courts." This book is preventive medicine against that pestilence. Whatever his disagreement with Sebond, Montaigne's only task as he saw it was to clear this book of these objections and in the process to offer this *"préservatif."*

In short, as far as the first objection is concerned, he was saying that Grace and human considerations are sometimes fortunately (as in Sebond's book with its psychologically effective defense of staying on the "highroad"), sometimes unfortunately (as in the religious wars), but always as a matter of fact indistinguishable from each other. In saying this he was preparing the reader for the second objection against Sebond's book.

C. The pestilence

THE second objection claims that Sebond's arguments themselves are "weak" and that one can "shatter them with ease." In meeting the first objection, Montaigne had shown mildness and even admiration toward his pious objectors; they were not trying to rock the boat of "ancient usage"; they were not claiming great things for human reason. On the contrary, as we have noticed, Fideism with regard to faith and Scepticism with respect to human knowledge were very close to Montaigne's own heart, and the first objection expressed both. But this second objection is neither so useful for the tranquillity of society nor so modest in its claims. This one is full of foolhardiness and arrogance, rather than caution and humility. The first objection underestimated the power of reasons by ignoring their important psychological effects; but the second was more dangerous because it overestimated the power of reasoning. It alone presumed to make certain claims about God apodictically and in detail. Now, human arrogance and pride had led men to claim that their own reasons can "shatter with ease" tradition and the claims of other men on religious matters. And this attitude "must be shaken up a little more roughly" than the pious attitude embodied in the first objection. For it alone bears chaos in its womb, is full of danger, since ultimately it encourages us to leave *"la route commune"*[8] of tradition and custom, only to wander in the unregulated byways of conflicting imaginations, each way as likely or as unlikely as the next.

Because of the social and personal dangers that the second objection alone creates, Montaigne devotes the rest of this, his longest essay, to meeting it. He had spent only a few pages on the first objection. However, instead of taking the critics' arguments one by one and showing that they all failed to do what they claimed to do, as was traditional in theological disputation, Montaigne during most of the rest of this essay turns his back upon Sebond's book itself and upon the particular criticisms leveled at it by his enemies. He tries to "crush and trample underfoot" the arrogant *attitude* toward religion and reason that produced this objection. And this he does by way of a gigantic a fortiori argument having the following form: if the finest minds from antiquity onward have not been able to find The Truth about *anything,* then a fortiori these critics of Sebond cannot shatter with ease the best argument Montaigne has ever read on so vast a subject as *God.*

It is the second objection — that Sebond's arguments are *not* part of an antithetical set, that they can be crushed or refuted with ease — that Montaigne sets out to demolish with his a fortiori argument. Of course, what emerges is the antithesis of the best opposing positions with Sebond's as far as finding The Truth is concerned; but again, this by no means refutes Sebond, antithesis being what it is. Moreover, the Practical Criterion — which in Montaigne's case is to follow the highroad of Catholicism, using whatever psychological aids you can muster along the way — this rule is part of the preventive medicine Montaigne was offering to the court of France.

D. *The beginning of the therapy*

ABOUT subjects like the existence and nature of God, the basic stuff and structure of the universe, the nature of man, and the essence and the location of the soul, the human mind has insistently produced antithetical beliefs. Whenever it has sought clarity and universal approbation on such matters it has failed. Sometimes it has been willing to acknowledge that it could not find "the bean in the cake," the precise truth amongst the various possible truths, and *then,* no longer claiming to have found The Truth, it offered the "most excusable" doctrines. For instance, concerning religion, of all the opinions, "that one, it seems to me, was most probable and most excusable which recognized God as an incomprehensible power, origin and preserver of all things ... accepting and taking in good part the honor and reverence that human beings rendered him, under whatever aspect, under whatever name, in whatever manner." In an earlier edition[9] he had added to this last permissive phrase the notion we have spoken of so often, his form of the Practical Criterion: "He who asked the Delphic Oracle how it was proper to serve God got only this response: according to the custom and law of your country." Here we find not a precise, contentious, universal truth, but a broad, vaguely stated claim that breaks down into home truths.

In the field of astronomy Copernicus is offering us "legitimate fictions," plausible remarks (the *De Revolutionibus* had appeared in 1543, about thirty years before Montaigne wrote his "Apology"), and has very logically used his remarks on nature in astronomical deductions.[10] But Montaigne wonders: first Ptolemy; then our clever Copernicus; *then* who? He gives Copernicus a thousand years of ascendancy, just to show his admiration for the Pole, but he asks, "Who knows whether a third opinion ... will not overthrow the preceding two?" He uses an interesting term to describe victorious theories about the nature of the universe; he speaks of them as "in vogue." Lacking an eternal guaranty of their truth, they will suffer a deposition, the fashions of the ages being fleeting. In time, all these precise legitimate fictions about the nature of the universe have become illegitimate, have no longer been *"en vogue."* Let us hesitate long before we assert that they will obtain approbation from all men in all times.

Now, Montaigne does not deny that men have practical acquaintance, know-how, with respect to the stars and the sea and other parts of the world around us. We may not be able to present conclusive proofs about the exact nature of the stuff and structure of the universe, but we can still act in this world with more or less success. We can still survive in our environment by living cannily amongst Recollective Signs. We can adjust our actions to our sense experiences, even though our "proofs" about Indicative Signs may be as shaky as our moods.

Montaigne was once talking to a physicist[11] who claimed that the innovations of his science had refuted our previous working knowledge of the winds and tides. He asked the man: "What? ... Then did those who navigated under the laws of Theophrastus go west when they headed east? Did they go sideways, or backward?" The practical know-how of the ancient sailors who navigated successfully could not be refuted by new knowledge about the nature of the universe. The fact that, barring accidents, they got where they wanted to go and back in their maritime environment was of tremendous importance to Montaigne and quite a different matter from the "novelties and reforms" in physics and astronomy, quite another matter from systematic deductions based on presuppositions of convenient fictions. Despite the fact that with this trickster, reason, the physicist could make the new theory "so palpable that I could touch it," very "full of likelihood," still to Montaigne the know-how of the sailors was more durable, plainer, and more reliable than these precise claims to The Truth. Men who could deal successfully, without proofs or precision, with the complexities of life on the sea were to him possessors of a kind of knowledge that no wielder of deductions "full of likelihood" could match. And all of this is what Montaigne meant when he concluded his account of the conversation with the physicist with these words: "I then replied to him that I would rather follow facts than reason."

This respect for successful action, for successful adjustment to the broad necessities of living, is one of the main positive doctrines of the "Apology." He never tried to cast doubt on the practical know-how that made no claims to having found and proved The Truth. It permitted no arrogance like that of the objectors to Sebond: if you do not know how to navigate your ship, you drown yourself and your crew sooner or later; and if you do know how, with some luck, you do your job and stay alive. If arrogance is failure to know the limitations of one's own powers, that arrogance was soon corrected, Montaigne felt, in the rough-and-tumble of trying to act successfully in nature. In verbal claims to The Truth, there was no such corrective. Arguments could go on for centuries with nobody admitting defeat because of this trickster, reason. The trickster can pull plausible and almost palpable proofs out of any hat, and interminably.

But not only has reason failed to yield us The Truth about the world; reason has led to chaos about man himself when it has tried to get precise knowledge of the nature of man. People have patched him together like a puppet made out of a thousand "fantastic bits." They have invented an "imaginary republic," whose parts they rearrange, "each according to his fancy," in their search for detailed, universal knowledge of him. We feel our own impulses, sensations, and the like quite plainly, but still we must imagine parts of ourselves: a soul, faculties, functions, orders, stages, and so on. We are racked with an insatiable yearning for precision; but with the increase of precision the disagreements multiply, universal approbation is lost, and our sets of imaginary republics grow fatter and more numerous. Elsewhere Montaigne had shown that students of medicine have invented many contradictory hypotheses and unsuccessful cures (if he could have found one that would help him with the stone in his bowels, he would have acknowledged medicine to be a True Science out of sheer gratitude). In medicine, as in psychology and metaphysics, all one can do is throw up one's hands and say: "How many contradictory opinions they form!"

It is beginning to look as if a Socratic awareness of our ignorance is the way to wisdom. It certainly is the case that Montaigne's relationship with the arrogant critics of Sebond is similar to Socrates' relationship with a certain arrogant politician of Athens. In that other great *apologia* Socrates said of this politician:

"Well, although I do not suppose that either of us knows anything really beautiful and good, I am better off than he is, — for he knows nothing, and thinks that he knows; I neither know nor think that I know. In this latter particular, then, I seem to have slightly the advantage of him."[12]

There is no need to review in detail this great array of often amusing claims and counterclaims: the God men worship, the goodness men seek, the laws they erect to help them in the fulfillment of this goodness, the conscience of man which supposedly intimately reminds him of Goodness and of its laws — all these vary from country to country, from time to time, from circumstance to circumstance, and from man to man. The Truth concerning them all — the precise, universally cogent truth on these matters — is in doubt. Given this doubt, we must turn to a local life — a life using mixtures and abjuring dogmatic claims to public or universal validity. This is the substance of the great middle part of the "Apology," and there is no better way to see its richness and style than to read it.

E. *The fount of knowledge*

BUT the last and gravest move Montaigne makes in this middle part should be looked at by us here. It has to do with the cognitive powers of man: the fount, the origin, of all these claims about the world, God, goodness, and so forth. This is the crucial part of the essay where Montaigne's great a fortiori argument is drawing toward its climactic close. He holds up to scrutiny our judgment and our senses, our instruments of knowledge themselves, and he finds them to be "of lead and wax, stretchable, pliable," mixtures like the conclusions that emerge from them.

If we do not know what the fount of all knowledge — our senses — gives us in the way of sound, objective knowledge, then how can we presume to know enough about an infinite God to "shatter" Sebond's arguments "with ease"? Ignorant of finite things, how can we presume to know enough about infinity to disrupt the health of our country with dogmatic theological strife? In asking this rhetorical question, Mon-

Men and Mixtures 49

taigne draws most directly and frequently from the *Outlines* of Sextus Empiricus. Here, in attacking the "sovereign masters," the origin and ultimate criterion, the "greatest foundation and proof" of our knowledge, he leans most heavily on Sextus and reveals himself unambiguously as an orthodox Sceptic after the manner of Sextus.

In order to cast doubt upon the senses as Indicative Signs of Reality he uses most of the tropes Sextus mentioned in the First Book of his *Outlines*. In fact, he uses Sextus in what might now be thought of as a plagiaristic way. For instance, a passage that shows how the organs of animals can affect what they see appears as follows in the "Apology":

"The moisture that the root of a tree sucks up becomes trunk, leaf, and fruit; and the air, being but one, by being applied to a trumpet is diversified into a thousand kinds of sounds. It is our senses ... which likewise fashion these objects out of various qualities."[13]

In Sextus this is put as follows:

"Water also, which is one and uniform when it is absorbed by trees, becomes in different places bark, branch, or fruit. ... The breath of the musician, also one and the same when it enters the flute, becomes in turn a high-pitched tone or a low one."[14]

There are various places where this sort of thing happens in this attack upon the "sovereign masters," the origin and ultimate criterion of knowledge. At one point he mixes one trope with another in exactly the same way Sextus confuses them.

F. *The end of the* a fortiori *argument*

WHETHER you look for The Truth in the senses or in the thought of man you find that "we, and our judgment, and all mortal things go on flowing and rolling unceasingly. Thus nothing certain can be established about one thing by another, both the judging and the judged being in continual change and motion." Whatever we know is intermixed with whatever we are and with other things; and all is changing: our moods, the light on things, everything.

Moreover, if we would elevate some Stoic Sage to the status of absolute judge concerning the true essence of things, he would be a mixture himself, changing with the elments that make *him* what he is. Our Sage would have to be someone who is neither healthy nor sick, has no moods, no structures to his organs, needs no media in which to sense things:

"We would need someone exempt from all these qualities, so that with an unprejudiced judgment he might judge of these propositions as of things indifferent to him; and by that score we would need a judge that never was."[15]

We are all, in short, biased, and our bias is always changing with a thousand unconsidered accidents of environment, body, and mind. In a liquid world, how can a liquid hand grasp anything? Or to put it logically: in a world of conflicting, mutually antithetical criteria, how can we discern the precise, universally cogent Truth about anything?

Toward the beginning of the "Apology"[16] Montaigne told us that in defending Sebond against the arrogant second objection he would "consider for the moment man alone, without outside assistance, armed solely with his own weapons, and deprived of divine grace and knowledge." It is such a man who claims that by reasoning he can "with ease" shatter Sebond's arguments about God. And so Montaigne has stood up to him with the only weapons he respects — human weapons — without any recourse to grace or faith.

Now the moment of combat is over; now it is permissible to drop to one's knees after both swords have been flipped from the hands of the contestants. We can receive "outside assistance" through faith and Grace, and we can see how incommensurate both combatants have been with the God they have been arguing about. Faith reveals, says Montaigne, that God is eternal, that He abides; our battle, using the best of human and natural weapons, has revealed that men and nature are changing together and are deeply involved in each other's changes. Unable to understand little changing things, how can we understand an infinite unchanging God?

G. Epilogue on public docility

BUT with the a fortiori argument now complete, the essay is not finished, though the arrogance that motivated the second objection may be purged. To conclude the essay Montaigne makes two zigzag moves that are of summary importance to his whole philosophy. First, he quotes Seneca, who recommends that since the difference between man and

God is so great, man must "raise himself above humanity!"[17] Next, at the moment when the unaware reader is saying to himself that this is the moral of the whole "Apology," he turns on the reader and on Seneca with the final summary of his essay: Seneca's exhortation expresses a "useful desire" and is absurd:

"For to make the handful bigger than the hand, the armful bigger than the arm, and to hope to straddle more than the reach of our legs, is impossible and unnatural. Nor can man raise himself above himself and humanity; for he can see only with his own eyes and seize only with his own grasp."

And *this* is what he has been saying all along. It is always man with all his limitations, all his changes, all his dependencies, that we are dealing with, and it is ignorance of these limitations, it is vanity, to talk as if man with his own powers transcends these limitations. Our powers are commensurate only with satisfying human needs, natural needs. Only by giving them up, not by trying to use them to go beyond ourselves, can we rise above humanity:

"He will rise, if God by exception lends him a hand; he will rise by abandoning and renouncing his own means, and letting himself be raised and uplifted by purely celestial means."

Not by human aggressive activity, but by passivity before God's will; not by pretexts of reasons, but by a docile faith-full will, can we rise above humanity, if God lends us His hand. Of course, the "If" is gigantic in the light of a whole essay which illustrates how anything from without, including God's will, gets mixed in with human passions and circumstances.

But the "If" is not important. What is important is the docility that it is the basic purpose of the essay to encourage. Docility before God's will, docility under the traditions and laws of our country — these are what our shifting private judgments must learn. The Protestants lacked docility under customs, but so did the Catholics who militantly argued with them, for example, at the Colloquy of Poissy.[18] As for Sebond, he was following the traditions of Catholicism. But those who raised the second objection were not docile. Like the Protestants and the extremist Catholics, they used the pretext of reason contentiously on matters concerning God. They were the activists in the religious wars. They were the ones who lacked the docility that Montaigne and all Sceptics find appropriate to man's condition as a poor, mixed, and changing creature.

But if this is the main theme — against activism and for docility in matters relating to God and to public institutions — there is another which is almost as important to the "Apology" and by far the most important theme of most of Montaigne's other essays. This second theme is as follows: if you want to *act,* if you want to do something with these human tools of yours — your senses, your judgment — do not use them in verbal battles about the divine; use them to obtain mixed but "tangible, and palpable goods: peace, repose, security, innocence, and health — health, I say, the finest and richest present that nature can give us."[19]

Montaigne has written his apology in the same spirit that moved a certain Miletian maid[20] to throw a stumbling block before the feet of Thales the philosopher as he walked along looking heavenward: she wanted to remind people to look to themselves rather than to heaven. She, like the Socrates of Plato's *Apology,* had something of the Sceptic in her. And so did that servant of Democritus[21] who laughed at her master for seeking out secret and devious causes for plain events. Laughter, stumbling blocks, laxatives, fencer's tricks — all amount to the same thing: the humiliation of an arrogant man and the turning of his attention to the particular circumstances in which he lives. The only time Montaigne attacked Scepticism was when, briefly, he suspected the Pyrrhonians[22] of using their arguments to shake our faith in Recollective Signs, *"pour ruiner l'apparence de l'expérience."* Scepticism is a useful tool, to be dispensed with when it is no longer necessary. It is something artificial, a "device," an *"invention"*[23] concocted by men to make way for the natural. It is a spiritual purgative.

Once Montaigne praises Pyrrhonism directly: "There is nothing of man's invention that has so much verisimilitude and usefulness." And our study of the "Apology" has shown that every word of that eulogy was carefully considered: Scepticism is itself an artifact, created by man, not found by him in nature; it is useful for curing sick souls; and it does all this by showing the world to us in all of its actual, common-sensically evident variety.

Chapter 4

Common Sense and Habit

A. Our common sense

Pyrrho's pig can serve as the emblem of the "Apology" as well as can the Sceptic's balance-scales. The pig was eating quietly instead of troubling itself with painful imaginings. It was *using* its common sense, and so was Pyrrho, who was admiring it in that tempest; the other passengers were *abusing* their good sense. As a therapeutic public document the "Apology" is a plea for common sense — a plea for using our heads to save our hides. And so, from this massive document there begins to emerge a notion, typically broad and imprecise, of what common sense is. And it turns out in this essay (as well as in the others) that *"sens," "jugement,"* or *"sens commun"* is the power (in pigs as well as in men) to keep its possessors in physical and mental health. It is a mixture of inheritance, upbringing, and circumstance which Montaigne never tries to analyze down to its pure, objective elements. But because it is so important to him, because his *Essays* are indeed a hymn to common sense, he makes some rather revealing efforts to understand the shape of it. The purpose of this chapter is to study some of these efforts. In doing so we shall be concentrating not on the variety but on the uniformity of nature, not on Montaignian doubt but on Montaignian affirmation.

The shortest essay Montaigne ever wrote was also one of the few he never revised after the first edition. It is the twenty-second in the First Book and is entitled "One Man's Profit is Another Man's Harm." A certain Athenian, Demades, once condemned those who sold funeral supplies because they were profiting from other men's miseries. That unrealistic man! How blind he was to life around him and within him! If you condemn these funeral-suppliers, then you must condemn all gain, because profit comes at the expense of others. The architect profits from the ruin of houses; doctors profit from disease; soldiers profit from war;

and "the very honor and function of ministers of religion is derived from our death and our vices."

Having said this, Montaigne makes two typical moves to conclude one of his most revelatory essays. First he says, "let each man sound himself within, and he will find that our private wishes are for the most part born and nourished at the expense of others."

He is talking about himself, but also about the people he has known. If one wants a victory, one wants somebody's defeat. Many of our satisfactions come from somebody else's deprivation, and in wishing for satisfactions we are often wishing for the failure of others. Now, Montaigne is not reducing all our desires to egocentric proclivities; in this brief essay the phrase *"pour la plus part"* plays an important role. It tells us that he is not presenting a "nothing but" simplification like that of Thrasymachus or Hobbes; he is simply pointing out something plainly visible if we will only look. What he is saying is not that *all* of us are *always* and *only* bloodthirsty or indifferent to others. He is saying that often we are. We are so fond of preserving our own comfort and life that we often do so at the expense of others. And for a confirmation of this, he asks us to look at our own lives.

But his second and last move in the essay is not a request that we look into our "private wishes." It is a request that after having done so we look around us at the *générale police* of nature. There we shall find that "the birth, nourishment, and growth of each thing is the alteration and corruption of another." The child hurts, ages, and depletes its mother. We eat the meat of animals; we cut short the lives of vegetation to sustain our own lives; living, we are in the midst of death, preferably the death of others.

Struggling in a world of private interests, we are called upon by nature to look out for our own comfort and life. In this struggle we see, if we will only look, that each living thing is a distinct organism trying to fulfill its natural duty to preserve its health. Again, it is important to notice that in all the rest of Montaigne's writings "the expense of others" is not what he emphasizes when he talks about the *générale police* of nature: it is the preserving of one's own life and tranquillity that he emphasizes. He is interested in our "tools and means" primarily as positive instruments for living healthfully, not as negative weapons for hurting or destroying others. Montaigne himself was acutely sensitive to the infliction of pain upon other creatures. He could not bear to see a chicken killed, and he was upset even when he saw trees tremble under the blows that are given them. His aversion to the infliction of pain amounted almost to a mania, and was for him a fact far more important than any generalizations one could draw about the viciousness of man in nature.

Now, the *"jugement naturel"* of man is his main tool for attaining health of mind and body. But to understand what Montaigne means by "judgment" it is necessary to turn again to the "Apology," specifically to the large section which occurs toward the beginning of the essay. This whole section is quite similar to what Sextus called the First Mode, which brings about the suspension of judgment by pointing out the variety in animals. But Montaigne, unlike Sextus, emphasizes the similarities between animals, not the variety; and he does this because, as we have noticed, the larger part of the "Apology" is an attempt to humiliate us by crushing the dangerous second objection to Sebond's book. What Montaigne is trying to do in this (perhaps the only readable) section of the "Apology" is to cure us of this "natural and original malady," vanity, which makes us imagine that we are the only animals capable of understanding God. He wants to show how we are, like the other animals, provided with certain instruments for the preservation of our lives, and that it is only by the vanity of our imagination that we plant ourselves above them and in the confidence of God. We are all creatures with just enough power and just enough knowledge to keep ourselves alive, with luck, and none of us has more power or more knowledge than is necessary for the preservation of its being.

This "parity ... between us"[1] and the other animals Montaigne tries to show by pointing out the uniformities of nature. For instance, as far as communication is concerned, he finds that our bodily movements *"discourent et traictent"* with great eloquence, no matter what the species. Animals use their eyes, their paws, and many other parts of their bodies to communicate love, hatred, fear, obeisance. They act out, and in that action communicate what they mean, what they are. To show that the language of motion or gesture is not so limited as not to deserve the name "language," he gives a Rabelaisian list of silent mutual services that we perform for each other. Our hands, our head, our eyebrows, our shoulders — all these and more "vie with the tongue" for flexibility and power to bring about direct, swift communication. Moreover, though many of these gestures may not be readily intelligible to members of another species, they are more or less uniform and more or less readily intelligible to all members of our species. Far more than our various, deeply differing verbal languages, the language of gesture is the "one proper to human nature," the language that is natural to our species, common and readily intelligible. For Montaigne, not only in communication but in all the other phases of life, guided bodily action is the basis for equality and similarity among the living creatures that make up nature. After leaving the topic of communication he asks a very daring question: "What sort of faculty of ours do we not recognize in the actions of animals?"

Finally he will answer it by saying: an unruly imagination.

Look at the honeybees: orderliness, division of labor, calculation and foresight (*discours et providence*), are all plainly visible in the lives of these tiny creatures, even more consistently than in human activities. And what about the swallows? When spring comes, they find the most suitable dwelling place. They use squares, circles, and obtuse angles instead of collapsible right angles; they mix water and clay to the right consistency, put soft floors in their dwelling because of the tender feet of the yet unhatched birds, and face the opening of their dwelling away from the rainy wind. They know what is in fact harmful or helpful to themselves and their fledglings. They are part of nature: equipped to save their hides.

All of this orderliness and planning, reflected directly in action, Montaigne describes with various words, but the key word is *"jugement."* The power to order the world and ourselves for the preservation of our being, a power given to *all* creatures by a benevolent Mother Nature, is "judgment." And by "preservation" Montaigne means not only the bare maintenance of life but the maintenance of a vigorous, healthy life. Judgment brings the "comforts" of life, the "repose and preservation," the "security and contentment,"[2] that he had talked about in the first version of his First Book. For each creature, what is his, what is inborn in him without any benefit of elaborate education, is the drive and the fundamental capacity to protect itself and find contentment using its *"sens naturel."*[3]

In this power to act for our repose and preservation, we find the same sort of similarity to ourselves that we find when we compare the way we are "born, beget, feed, act, move, live, and die" to the way animals do these things.[4] "There is some difference, there are orders and degrees" distinguishing animals from each other, but all creatures try to combine "skill and judgment" (*d'adresse et de jugement*) for their own best advantage.

These two terms, "skill" and "judgment," are inextricably tied together in Montaigne's thoughts. Natural knowledge for him is basically knowing how to do something, how to act successfully. It is very close indeed to skill, since the proof of both is in successful action. You check up on a man's skill and his judgment by the same means: you see how successfully he acts. Judgment and skill centrally involve observable, ordered, successful action in one's environment.

But though we have a judgment capable of contributing to our own long and tranquil living, it is muddled, disturbed, and in some cases ruined by the vanity and unruliness of our imaginations.

> if it is true that he [man] alone of all the animals has this freedom of imagination and this unruliness in thought that represents to him what is, what is not, what he wants, the false and the true, it is an advantage that is sold him very dear . . . for from it springs the principal source of the ills that oppress him: sin, disease, irresolution, confusion, despair.

Montaigne thinks that animals have some vestige of this imagination as well; but in men alone does he find imagination working dramatically against man's own needs for self-preservation and tranquillity. We yearn for everything but what we are equipped by the gifts of nature to achieve. In the rest of nature animals yearn for what they can, with only a little good fortune, achieve; they are aware of their own powers and limitations: a zebra will not (unless it is insane) attack a hungry lion; a deer will not attack a tiger. But man will try to know God, will try to be "master and emperor" of the world, because his unruly imagination has outstripped his awareness of his own powers and limitations.

And so, following Pyrrho, Montaigne often says: look to the animals for the healthy state of your natural judgment. Look to the animals, and notice what we are all here for, what we are equipped by nature to achieve: tranquillity and preservation. An animal usually shows by his actions that he knows the business of life to be living in health, within the limits of his powers. He knows what it is to live without artificial desires, without *"cupiditez estrangers,"* desires that he has not been given the powers to gratify.

A passage in the First Book, the essay "Of Solitude," goes as follows:

> Among our customary actions there is not one in a thousand that concerns ourselves. The man you see climbing atop the ruins of that wall,

> frenzied and beside himself, a mark for so many harquebus shots; and that other, all scarred, pale and faint with hunger, determined to die rather than open the gates to him — do you think they are there for their own sake? They are there for the sake of a man whom perhaps they never saw, who is not in the least concerned about their doings, and who at that very moment is plunged in idleness and pleasures.[6]

Only those who in their madness, in their unruly imaginations, have forgotten that they are alive on this planet to find health and peaceful life — only they are beset by artificial, "extraneous desires." I must add the vignette that follows the one just quoted, because it is a little masterpiece like the other and also because it will be useful to have in mind when we talk later in this chapter about educating our judgments:

> This fellow, all dirty, with running nose and eyes, whom you see coming out of his study after midnight, do you think he is seeking among his books how to make himself a better, happier, and wiser man? No such news. He is going to teach posterity the meter of Plautus' verses and the true spelling of a Latin word, or die in the attempt. Who does not willingly exchange health, rest, and life for reputation and glory, the most useless, worthless, and false coin that is current among us?[7]

We have ignored the desires we are equipped to satisfy, the ones that enhance vitality. When Montaigne says in that same great essay, "Let us bring back our thoughts and plans to ourselves and our well-being," he is simply saying: let us go back to that way of life which takes our own health and tranquillity as the solidest goods and which uses each individual's equipment to try to get them.

Later in the Second Book (in a passage strikingly similar to the opening sentence of Descartes' *Discourse on Method*), Montaigne uses a different approach to point up the presence in us of our *"sens naturel."* He looks at himself and at other men and asks,

"Who ever thought he lacked sense (*sens*)? That would be a proposition implying its own contradiction [saying 'I lack sense']. . . . To accuse oneself would be to excuse oneself in that subject, and to condemn oneself would be to absolve oneself."[8]

That is, if I say "I lack sense," and I mean it, then I am also saying that I do not lack sense! I am showing that I have enough sense to see my faults. We have here a contradiction.

But there is not only a logical situation here. There is also a psychological one:

"There never was a porter or a silly woman who did not think they had enough sense to take care of themselves.... And the arguments that come from simple natural reasoning in others, we think we would have found *if we had merely glanced in that direction.*"[9] [My italics.]

Here the word *"sens"* means just what he took it and the word *"jugement"* to mean in the "Apology": the capacity to take care of oneself. But now he is emphasizing the peculiarly human aspects of natural judgment, the psychological situation that makes us all quite confident that we have it.

What emerges from this is a richer meaning for the word *"sens"* and its cognates. Now it means not only the power to take care of oneself, to seek and find one's own advantage, but also the power to understand what is broadly obvious, to grasp principles that are *"grossiers et apparens."* Common sense is now a power to know what is plainly the case. When we say, "It's just a matter of common sense," we usually mean, "Just look at it and you'll see!" This is what Montaigne always meant by his notion of a "good nose": simply sniff and you'll smell what there is to smell.

This notion of seeing things *"évidemment,"* by only turning to them, without proofs or precision, is important to what Montaigne means when he calls his writings "essays" of his judgment. What he means is that, at least for himself, simply turning one's attention to a certain subject reveals certain things about that subject. For instance, in the last paragraphs of the *Essays* he informs us that kings sit on their own bottoms, though kings may have tremendous power, and he also informs us that "gay and sociable wisdom" and health are what we want. These remarks would be banal to us if we always thought of man as one of nature's creatures; but they are revealing because we do not always think of man this way, and Montaigne is asking us to do so. When Mme. de Sévigné commented on the immense common sense in this book of Montaigne's she was saying: "My God, how obvious he is after all! This would be common knowledge if only everybody looked at the facts he points to."

But there is another sense of the "obvious," besides that of being plainly true once you look at or think of it. The obvious is that which nobody ever thought of contradicting or putting into antithesis. Who would ever think of saying kings *do not* sit on their own bottoms, no matter how lofty their thrones? The obviousness, even the banality, that Sainte-Beuve found in the *Essays* is a direct consequence of Montaigne's desire to point to matters that are irrelevant to doubt, once you state them. Who could contradict or doubt the claim that we eat, sleep, are born, or that we often do things at the expense of others? Only somebody who is not using his common sense.

It would be absurd to say that all the essays are essays of Montaigne's "natural judgment" in this sense of pointing out gross, incontrovertible facts. For instance, the "Apology" itself, as we have seen, is an elaborate proof of a conclusion that is by no means obvious to just any untutored person with a "good nose," and it is by no means incontrovertible. The same holds true of various other essays.

But firmly accepting this, one must see two points. Though "simple natural reasoning" is sometimes not important as far as the overarching structure of a given essay is concerned, Montaigne always emphasizes it in the individual, often epigrammatic sentences that make up each essay. His most ambitious essays, the "Apology," "On Vanity," and "Of Experience," emphasize the individual sentence, the epigram, the self-enclosed, unproved, unexceptionable remark. One of the reasons for the tendency to dispersion that is an important trait of his essays[10] is that *in a given sentence* he is frequently following his "good nose." Montaigne is not by accident famous for his epigrams. After all, the epigram appeals not to proofs, but to a simple willingness to look. Montaigne had a grasp of his subject that held his longest and most complex essays together; but such unity in complexity is not the salient feature of the essays. The salient feature is the individual, self-contained, incontrovertible maxim or epigram; and it is this feature that expresses Montaigne's "simple, natural reasoning."

The second point to see is this: Montaigne's appeal to the obvious, or to what is obvious to him, is not the only use he makes of his *"sens"* in writing the *Essays*. Natural judgment is primarily for Montaigne the use of one's powers to take care of oneself. Sense is *"sens pour sa provision,"* and he is sometimes willing to sacrifice obviousness, willing to disregard his *"bon nez,"* in order to take care of himself or his nation. The main thing he is after is to reveal himself in the process of finding and keeping health. This is what he started writing the essays in order to find, and what he never loses sight of. Judgment that affirms the obvious and incontrovertible is an ancillary tool and can be, should be, dispensed with when it is useful to do so. As our analysis of the "Apology" indicates, Montaigne's concern to take care of himself and his nation can take him far beyond his *"simple discours naturel."* In the end *"sens"* is a purely practical instrument for obtaining the "essential tangible, and palpable goods: peace, repose, security, innocence and health — health, I say, the finest and richest present that nature can give us." If he can obtain these by simply looking, good; if it is necessary to marshal epigrammatic insights in a complex essay, then this is good, too. Living well is mainly what we are here for.

B. *Custom and common sense*

COMMON sense is what we are using when we avoid a precipice or move into shelter away from the cold winds of evening. It is what makes us shun pain and seek comfort, what makes us act to preserve and satisfy ourselves. In our awareness of pain and our yearning for comfort, "all does not consist in imagination. We have opinions about the rest; here it is certain knowledge that plays its part."[11] The yearnings, the "foreign desires," that make us forget our concern for self-preservation and tranquillity for the sake of metaphysical truth are stuffed with imaginings. Trying to satisfy them, we leave behind the healthful orderliness of nature and enter the deadly, vagabond fields of contentious assertion.

But we have been treating judgment as if it were innate, as if it had nothing to do with learning. Montaigne sometimes says that his natural judgment is what was "born with me."[12] But even then he never fails to point out the importance of what we acquire, "the authority of others and the sound arguments of the ancients, with whom I found my judgment in agreement. These men have given me a firmer grip on my ideas and a more complete enjoyment and possession of them." In most other passages on this subject he says that what one learns is Circe's drink: it transforms one profoundly instead of giving only a "firmer grip" on what one already knows. In these passages what we learn is "second nature." It is no less powerful than what we are born with, and it "steeps and dyes" what we are born with.

In general, habituation or learning can have two effects upon man's senses, desires, bodily movements, and opinions; it can stupefy or root out, or it can intensify or develop. In either case, men do not actually need the pure Truth in order to believe or act as they do; all they need is appropriate habits. Habituation exerts so great a force upon us that it requires no foundation deeper than itself.

In fact, as far as one form of habituation, *"la coustume,"* or public patterns of action, is concerned, looking for a foundation can be disappointing. In "Of Custom" he tells us that once he tried to justify a certain firm custom; he set about tracking it to its rational basis. But instead of finding in its early history a solid foundation, he discovered the earliest reasons for following it to be so weak that he almost became disgusted with it. And so he came to the conclusion that to tear off the mask of custom, to tear off its appearance of universal truth, is to do something difficult and painful. But he also found out that once you have been disappointed, your judgment[13] can be restored to a much firmer base than reason: habituation itself. When we realize that we are Christians for much the same "reasons" as we are Germans or Frenchmen, when we see that chastity is believed in not simply because it is the Truth but because it is the custom, we learn to attach ourselves only in moderation to our local customs. Besides, we then realize that a custom cannot be "refuted," since it usually has little to do with reasons, and we are very reluctant to replace what is indeed the bone-structure of our country, its public patterns of action and belief. And so we are satisfied with a peaceful community; we do not try, like the Reformers, to shatter the law-abiding pace of our country's existence.

As we noticed at the end of the last chapter, there is a kind of basic passivity involved in this position as far as political action is concerned. Montaigne had enough of the Greek *metriopatheia,* or resignation to the inevitable, to leave alone matters beyond our private jurisdiction. And if a certain custom did not hurt our health and tranquillity, he was inclined not to meddle with it. There was enough of the Stoic in him to say, as he did in "Of Children and Fathers":

"Let us let things take their course: the scheme of things that takes care of fleas and moles also takes care of men who have the same patience to let themselves be governed as fleas and moles. There is no use in our shouting 'Giddap'; that will indeed make us hoarse, but not get us ahead. It is a proud and pitiless scheme."[14]

Here he is talking about doctors and their contradictory and useless counsels and about the physical health of an individual human body; but the attitude is the same when it comes to customs and laws: "It is the rule of rules, and the universal law of laws, that each man should observe those of the place he is in."[15] Stuck with antitheses and the vagaries of our own fancies, we should be willing to submit to local laws, realizing that our private "reason" has no jurisdiction either over "public" nature or over public laws and customs. It can understand neither of these basically, and it can alter neither without danger. But does this mean that Montaigne's is a passive attitude toward living?

Far from it. As we have been noticing, human judgment is an instrument of action, of doing and changing. It seeks tranquillity and self-preservation for the individual, but it involves the individual in doing things in order to insure these. In the first place, there are many actions we perform that do not involve changing the laws or customs. They are simply private actions, like the timing of our vital functions. Moreover, Montaigne makes a distinction between "our thoughts" and the actions "of the crowd." Let me quote a very important passage relating to this distinction:

> It seems to me that all peculiar and out-of-the-way fashions come rather from folly and ambitious affectation than from true reason, and that the wise man should withdraw his soul within, out of the crowd, and keep it in freedom and power to judge things freely; but as for externals, he should wholly follow the accepted fashions and forms. Society in general can do without our thoughts; but the rest — our actions, our work, our fortunes, and our very life — we must lend and abandon to its service and to the common opinions, just as the great and good Socrates refused to save his life by disobedience to the magistrate.[16]

He is saying that we should not interfere with the laws and customs of our country by our actions, though we have a right to be mentally active, to think our own thoughts about them and other things. In a later chapter we shall see what he means by the passage that begins, "Society in general can do without our thoughts." But Montaigne is far from advocating mindless passivity. We have a judgment equipped with all the powers necessary for the maintenance of our own tranquillity and health, and it can do many things, both physical and mental.

Still, with all its limitations, custom is important; as Montaigne put it in the essay "Of Husbanding Your Will," "What my habit lacks, I hold that I lack. And I would almost as soon be deprived of life as have it reduced and cut down very far from the state in which I have lived it for so long."[17] Prevent him from mixing his wine with water, as was the custom in France, or from praying the way he does, or from using the French language he speaks, or from following his other customary patterns of behavior, and you are taking away an important part of Michel de Montaigne. The preservation of our customary patterns is involved in the preservation of life itself.

The upshot of his thoughts on common sense and custom is this: we are deeply involved in public habitudes, yet we can live our own lives. We dare not destroy these habitudes; and yet it is nonsense to say that they are all there is to life. We are Frenchmen or Americans, but we are still ourselves, different and distinct from our countrymen. We are mixtures of public and private elements.

The fact is that these differences and distinctnesses are far more important to Montaigne than the public habitudes. Montaigne is not a political theorist or a sociologist as much as he is an individual trying to keep mentally and physically alive. Whatever political theory or social psychology he presents is a propaedeutic to a certain remark in "Of Glory": "As for me, I hold that I exist only in myself." The *Essays* are not predominantly public documents; they are mainly private ones. They are primarily an expression of Montaigne's own common-sensical desire to take care of himself. When he says, *"Je ne suis que chez moy,"* he is talking about the heart of his essays, his own concern for his own life. He is not only saying that his skin is ultimately (and obviously) the boundary of his being; he is saying also that he is concerned with the public only insofar as it can "get under his skin." Like every other animal not corrupted by vain dreams, Montaigne is mainly concerned with taking care of himself. True, that self is involved with public habitudes and with public order and disorder; but that self must be a place unto itself, as Pyrrho's pig knew. This metaphorical way of talking summarizes Montaigne's notion of a personal philosophy. We shall be making that notion more specific throughout the rest of this book.

C. Action and individualism

THE independent individual is usually a somewhat shadowy notion in the essays on custom; but in the essays on education (especially in the two famous ones "Of The Education of Children" and "Of Pedantry," in the First Book) the individual steps forth as the exemplar of all that Montaigne believes to be "natural" for man. These essays are dramatic in that there is in them a hero and a villain, and in them we see most pointedly how this "second nature," habit, is of a piece with man's basic drive for self-preservation and a secure existence.

Foreshadowing Rousseau's *Emile,* his message is this: if you train a child to be passive and dependent, to be protected by his parents or his money, to do nothing but carry the words of other men around in his head, to hold nothing but borrowed ideals, follow nothing but standardized rules, know nothing but dates, places, names, and words — if you train a child to "know" only such things as these, he will be a poor, passive, dependent thing, an ass loaded with books. Your training will stifle his inborn power to mature into independence, will twist the rules of nature,[18] will put to sleep the eye of his independent judgment.[19] You will transform a creature born to act on his own hind legs into an anonymous beast of burden staggering under a pile of other men's words. These essays on education show how habituation can transform a dependent baby into a free, healthy man.

The villain of Montaigne's two essays on education — anonymous passivity — is a very complex one in detail; Montaigne finds many faults with the educational methods of his day. Children have been educated not as individual human beings with various sorts and degrees of powers; they have been educated by people who are not interested in those various powers or limitations. Educators are interested in a wordy, standardized, theoretical body of "knowledge."[20] They are teaching not people but words.

And there are two consequences of pouring words through a funnel into a child's passive memory. The first is the loss of what Montaigne calls "freedom."[21] The second, closely related to the first, is the loss of cheerful, tranquil good health. A man who knows nothing but what he has learned by rote is the slave of words and authorities, not their master. Montaigne knew a man who, when asked what he knew, could answer only if he had a book nearby and could point to the passage he had learned. He could not even tell Montaigne whether he had an itchy backside unless he went to his dictionary to find out what "itchy" and "backside" meant. A man who depends on verbal formulas or external authorities is in the same condition as a certain rich Roman;[22] he kept around him authorities in various fields, so that when an occasion arose to talk about a certain field he could let the one who knew it hold forth. He was completely dependent upon these men, and yet "he thought that this knowledge was his own."[23] A man who has memorized words and dates all his life is leaning so heavily on the arms of others that his own powers have atrophied. He has "no free motion left"; his "vigor and liberty are extinct." What he has acquired by his education is nothing but a "dependent and mendicant ability" — the ability to beg for a handout and to depend on the fancies of other men. When he is alone he is a feeble slave without a master.

The thing that is not intimately our own, that is not a *"naturelle possession,"*[24] is outside of us, is not part of ourselves; and when we are dependent upon it we are like slaves or prisoners waiting for food or death to be doled out. The key distinction for Montaigne is between an "acquisition"[25] and a *"naturelle possession."* One is an object outside of ourselves, like our clothing, upon which we depend; another is a part of ourselves, and there is no subjection; there is simply the use of it. One is mere hearsay; the other is the very *"complexion et habitude"*[26] of the person who has it.

If we disgorge food unchanged, it has not become a part of us. To make something a natural possession is to change that thing under the pressure of one's needs.[27] "The bees plunder the flowers here and there, but afterward they make of them honey, which is all theirs; it is no longer thyme or marjoram."

Anything a student has changed is "all his own,"[28] like the bee's honey that was once sharp-tasting thyme or marjoram. The honey that each man is creating, the natural possession he is developing, is primarily his judgment. In the two essays that summarize Montaigne's views on education, he is concerned mostly with educating a person to put the stamp of his own personality on what he touches. Memory does not do this, except in its failures. This is all judgment does. It asks: how is this relevant to my health and tranquillity? How is this relevant to my actions, my conscience,[29] my living? To question is to transform; to memorize is to reproduce. Only by personal questions do we make what is proposed to us part of ourselves; only by such questions do we stop disgorging undigested food and start transforming it; only by such questions do we act, instead of simply suffering or enduring. The *Essays* themselves with their many quotations are efforts Montaigne himself made in the process of using his judgment. Especially in his later essays he used these quotations as bees use flowers, to form his own honey, to educate and observe his own mind.

There is a second set of consequences that follow upon the mnemonic type of education: the loss of cheerful, tranquil good health. Montaigne despises the pedants, the fine fruits of so much Humanistic learning. All they can do is make a show of their learning by spouting words in profusion — words they carry around "floating on the surface of their brain." They are so busy with others' words that they do not have the time or interest to take care of their own lives. Having been confronted with theories, they are like doctors who "know Galen well, but the patient not at all."[30] That bleary-eyed Humanist dealing with words miles away from the actions and passions of his everyday life: we have met him in the essay "Of Solitude" with his eyes watering, his skin pale, stumbling down the street half alive, muttering his words. He is one of those who have suffered one long hammer blow from words and theories, and he wanders through life confused mentally and impotent practically.

Here Montaigne makes a typical remark: "In truth, most of the time they seem to have sunk even beneath common sense."[31] And he means what he says: a peasant and a shoemaker go about their ways "simply and naturally, talking about what they know,"[32] not getting involved in verbal battles and confusion, not using words with one part of their brains and living with another part. The common man applies what he hears to his life or he is bored with anything you tell him; he is practical, interested in turning what he knows to his own advantage, not interested only in repeating it. The lackey and the fish-wife at the Petit Pont can talk common-sensically even though they do not have all your theories and precise divisions of language committed to memory. Their language is of a piece with their lives, a part of the action and passion of living. It is not encapsulated in some little area on the surface of their brains. Compared to that of the pedant, their lives have integrity, constancy, the moderateness of opinion that comes with trying out opinions in the open air, in everyday life. Compared to the wise man, they are far from perfect: for one thing, they follow the herd too slavishly. But in contrast to the pedant, their lives are regulated, moderate, of a piece. Whatever they learn they directly interpret in terms of their "behavior and ... sense."[33] For the common man with all his weaknesses, the ultimate test any new "knowledge" must pass is the *"essay de l'action"*: what is conducive to his staying alive and his keeping away from mental and bodily disquiet; this is what he takes to heart, this is what he learns.

In short, education, like the instrument it perfects or "forms," is irretrievably involved in action that enhances living. And the villain of these two great essays against dogmatic teaching is the kind of education that imparts a fixed, verbal, authoritarian body of knowledge and does not teach living men to use their wits, to stay healthy in mind and body in a world where there are so many threats to health.

Each man is both himself and a part of nature and society; he walks on his own feet, sits on his own rump, and wants to stay alive and healthy; but his condition is similar to and causally related with other creatures. And his *"jugement,"* his *"sens,"* either faces these plain facts or he and his country lose the substantial, the ultimate goods of life: health, and life itself.

If all this is obvious, it is no less important for being obvious. And if all this is wrong or unimportant, then it is still what Michel thinks and is still what Michel thinks is important, given his own *"conditions et humeurs."* In reading Montaigne's essays we must never forget his little preface *"Au Lecteur,"* where he warns the reader that he is portraying himself in what follows, not trying to start a philosophic fight with others. His essays are personal — his own essays — to be read by other persons or to be ignored, as these persons see fit. He is not courting "the world's favor" by setting up a logically consequential argument or science; he is only presenting these written-down effects of his own *"conditions et humeurs,"* presenting them with vitality and conviction because this is the way he lives: with vitality and conviction. At the same time he is presenting them with a certain ease and detachment. And if all this is not appealing to you, reader, why, he will respect your feelings. He tells you in his preface: "So farewell. Montaigne, this first day of March, fifteen hundred and eighty."

His is a personal philosophy in three respects: it is frankly the portrait of the mind of a particular person named Michel de Montaigne; it talks about the human mind as an instrument, not for finding objective impersonal Truth, but for preserving a given person's own health and life; and it talks to individual persons who may wish to know this particular man. You may find something of use in his words. The provenance, the subject matter, and the audience of a personal philosophy, all are particular human beings whose minds are steeped and dyed with their *"conditions et humeurs"* but who can still achieve enough detachment from their situation to judge how healthy it is.

PART III

Language the Integument

Chapter 5

Language and the Troubles of the World

A. Humanism and language

Ever since we discussed Montaigne's Humanism in the first chapter, we have been coming into contact with his thoughts on language. It is the purpose of this chapter and the next one to give a connected account of these thoughts. Although we have quarreled[1] with the idea that one can summarize Humanism simply in terms of rhetoric, it is an indisputable fact that a doctrine of the pitfalls and powers of language is close to the center of Humanism. It is also plain that such a doctrine is of immense importance in the thought of Montaigne.

Jacques Amyot gave Greekless Humanists like Montaigne the *Lives* and *Moralia* of Plutarch, and he gave these works to them in lucid, robust French. As we have noticed, he believed that Humanism involved the renovation of language, the amplifying, the enrichment, the revivifying of speech, and his translations abundantly illustrated that belief. But he and all the other sixteenth-century Humanists who were not simply bleary-eyed mechanicians felt that this revivification should have two aspects: a close look at past and present ways of speech and a close look at past and present ways of action. They felt that man had a history which he had to take seriously, a funded wisdom which he had to draw from or wither and die. Antiquity was a fat, strong, deeply embedded root to the lively Humanists, a durable and direct contact with the depths of human experience. They saw antiquity not only as a set of patterns of grammatical usage but as a way of life that included such patterns. For people like Erasmus, Rabelais, du Bellay, and Montaigne himself, the history of men and their language was a means, not an end, a means to a richer language and a richer life.

Now this creative, pragmatic historicism took two forms among the more vivid Humanists: attack and example. They were able polemicists and able exemplars. They gleefully saw their task as one of burying the dead forms of life and language and enhancing and celebrating the living forms. In these respects, the Humanist can attack dead and deadly language, and he can write living language; he can try to purge away unhealthy ways of living, and (as we shall be seeing in Part IV of this book) he can devote his life to trying to live healthily. Moreover, he can think continually about the relationships between disease and health, language and life, history and the present.

And such concerns dominate his thoughts on language. In this chapter we shall be considering his attacks; in the next we shall investigate his positive thoughts on speech and his own style. But both as critic and as defender, language will always be of immense importance to him. Moreover, his thinking on this subject will always be guided by the pressures of history and the demands of his own day-to-day life. Language was to him "the interpreter of the soul," and one's "soul" is both a part of history and a participant in present living.

In the twentieth century we have become at least as interested in language as were the Humanists of the sixteenth. The troubles and triumphs that language can occasion fascinate us. It seems to me that Montaigne's remarks on language are as fresh as today's headlines and more durably important. As a troubleshooter and as a good example he speaks to our present needs with extraordinary power. Moreover, some of his insights are strikingly consonant with the thoughts of the boldest philosophers of language of our day. We shall discuss this last point at the end of this chapter.

B. Imagination and its vagaries

IN the "Apology"[2] Montaigne notices that "our speech has its weaknesses and its defects." And he goes further, much further: "Most of the occasions for the troubles of the world are grammatical." Of course the word *"Grammairiennes"* does not refer to straightforward little cut-and-dried rules of gender, number, and the like. The "grammatical" occasions of the world's troubles are not solecisms committed by the ill-taught. On the contrary, they are what schoolboys call "whoppers," and they are committed by the learned, by theologians, for instance, and by princes of dogmatism.

Language and the Troubles of the World

Here, as throughout the "Apology," Montaigne was thinking about such "troubles" as those that arose in sixteenth-century Europe over the meaning of the word *"Hoc"* in Christ's utterance *"Hoc est corpus meum."* Does the word "This" refer to the communion wafer as transubstantiated (and what a learned word *this* one is!) into the substance of Christ's body? Or does it refer to the underlying substance of Christ's body as it *co-subsists* with the underlying substance of the wheat in the wafer and so on? It is this sort of use of language, this highly sophisticated sort of speech, wherein nobody violates a grammatical rule, but wherein somehow people fail to convince each other, that Montaigne was referring to in his remark about the world's troubles. The solecisms that the unlettered man in the "streets of France" might commit are as nothing to Montaigne. Despite or because of them people communicate with each other pretty well in everyday life. In fact, Montaigne insists that the rules of grammar must follow the way words are used in the streets, whatever those ways[3] may be, for it seems to be the case that "those who would combat usage with grammar make fools of themselves." No, it is not the little slips, not the sentences in the mouths of ordinary, unlettered men, that produce these troubles. It is the men who would rather be seen naked than be heard committing a grammatical solecism who create and perpetuate the troubles Montaigne was thinking about. And the defects of their language are not superficial deviations that occur because the speakers have not thoroughly learned the right way of speaking. Those "weaknesses and defects" are the results of mistakes of mind and heart that are deeper than any memorized rules. It is the main purpose of Montaigne's remarks on language to reveal the mistakes of the learned, their mistakes of mind and heart, just as it is the main purpose of the "Apology" to reveal the mistakes of mind and heart committed by the learned, arrogant critics of Raymond Sebond.

The first paragraph in the first version of the essay "Of Glory" goes as follows:

"There is the name and the thing. The name is a sound which designates and signifies the thing; the name is not a part of the thing or of the substance, it is an extraneous piece attached to the thing, and outside of it."[4]

In this essay he is urging men to make a sharp distinction between one's "name" or "fame" and one's private well-being. Still, despite this particular context, this is a thought crucial to Montaigne's philosophy of language. And in the essay "Of Names," in the First Book, he has developed this idea ingeniously. The essay begins with the sentence: "Whatever variety of herbs there may be, the whole thing is included under the name of salad." Whatever differences there may be between things (or between subjects Montaigne handles in a given essay), we can still include them all under one name. A groom can call himself Pompey the Great, and there are at least three Socrates, five Platos, and eight Aristotles in history. Some Aristotles occurred in Greece, some far away from Greece. Sharing a name, must these Aristotles share anything else? Genius, for example, or even intellectual vigor? The answer is, of course, No. What they have in common consists only in certain shapes of "pen strokes"[5] that serve as names for all of them.

It is only by an "unthinking transfer" perpetrated by the imagination of man that anybody will infer from a name to a thing, from the fact that a man is named Aristotle to the conviction that he must have genius or be "essentially" Greek underneath the visible fact of his being, say, a French stable-groom who is a little slow-witted. This is Montaigne's version of the Sceptical attack on Indicative Signs.

This "imagination," which he sometimes calls *"fantasie,"*[6] which confuses the name with the thing named, is for Montaigne the main perpetrator of the troubles that beset mankind. In his last and ripest essay, "Of Experience," he was to write:

"The imagination: in my opinion that faculty is all-important, at least more important than any other. The most grievous and ordinary troubles are those that fancy loads upon us. . . . *God defend me from myself."*[7]

From words and from the emotional fantasies associated in our minds with these words we heedlessly make inferences about things. Carried away by our passion-fed fancy, we create many of our troubles.

What then is this "all important" power called "imagination"? First of all, whatever it is, it is close to thinking: to have an object "vivaciously imprinted upon the soul" is to have something that "illuminates and brings out"[8] the meanings of words. Images vivify our thinking. In fact, sometimes Montaigne simply identifies "Reason" with our "reveries and dreams."[9] But usually he distinguishes the two, all the while insisting on the intimacy of their involvement with each other. *"Jugement"* is a way of seeing the relations between facts clearly enough to allow us to survive and thrive in our environments. It is intimately involved in the visible,

Language and the Troubles of the World 75

palpable facts of our everyday lives. To step in out of the rain or to head homeward for food when one is hungry is an act of judgment. When we are living by judgment we are staying close to our immediate sense experience of the objects that threaten or nourish our everyday existence. Judgment is a practical instrument for dealing with the objects around us, performing a function similar to the one our eyes perform for us when we are trying to cross a busy street. As we have seen, it is often called sense or *"sens"* by Montaigne, and indeed it is a kind of sixth sense, relating us to our environments in a way analogous to the way our particular senses do. It hugs the objects around us, attends to our present feelings of hunger, and so forth, and in general conforms our actions to the exigencies of our environment and our bodies. And as we have also seen, the way Montaigne uses the word "judgment" makes it possible for us to say that a swallow making its nest from available twigs uses judgment, and a man avoiding a precipice or getting in out of the rain uses judgment.

But imagination is something else. Instead of being the servant of our bodily needs and the objects around us, this source of so many of our troubles has a "vagabond liberty"[10] and is as unrestricted as judgment is restricted. In the "Apology" Montaigne talks about a man's imagining as that which "has neither body nor taste. And if it is true that he alone of all the animals has this freedom of imagination and this unruliness in thought that presents to him what is, what is not, what he wants, the false and the true ... from it springs ... the ills that oppress him."[11] The vivacious pictures created by the imagination or fantasy, though they lack tangible solidity, still move us deeply, so that sometimes "we drip sweat, we tremble, we turn pale and turn red at the blows of our imagination; reclining in our feather beds we feel our bodies agitated by their impact, sometimes to the point of expiring. And boiling youth, fast asleep, grows so hot in the harness that in dreams it satisfies its amorous desires."[12]

Imagination operates in both our waking and our sleeping life, casts up images laden with passion, images of objects that may never have occurred or may never occur in the visible, tangible world around us. Judgment adjusts us to the laws of the world around us; imagination frees us, apparently, from those laws, making its own world with its own laws out of the bits and pieces left over in our memories from our encounters with the solid objects of our environment.

There are two kinds of imagination, or two functions of the imagination, according to Montaigne. One is what I shall call the "Poetic." Here the ordinarily experienced objects in the world are illuminated, rendered fresh and fascinating by the images in the mind of the viewer. This is the sort of function of the imagination that Coleridge was talking about when he wrote in the *Biographia Literaria* about

> the power of exciting the sympathy of the reader by a faithful adherence to the truth of nature, and the power of giving the interest of novelty by the modifying colors of imagination. The sudden charm, which accidents of light and shade, which moon-light or sun-set diffused over a known and familiar landscape ... are the poetry of nature.[13]

Montaigne praises a use of language wherein the "sprightliness of the imagination ... elevates and swells the words,"[14] giving vitality to our thought and to our lives. From his earliest childhood,[15] poetry has been able to do this to him, has had the "power to transpierce and transport me."

But poetry does not seek to "persuade our judgment"; it simply "ravishes and overwhelms it"[16] so that we do not judge at all, but simply enjoy our experience as an experience, not as some persuasive, eternal truth. Our experience of it is, so to speak, autonomous, self-contained, intransitive. The support or "proof" of a poem is usually an irrelevancy, a sign of its not having succeeded in ravishing us and therefore of its not having succeeded in its own specifically poetic purpose. The particular words of the poem solve all the problems the poem creates, give all the "proofs" (and of course the word is out of place here) the poem needs; the sounds of those particular words, the particular images in the particular order in which they occur in the poem, the particular ideas embodied in those images and sounds, make the poem unitary, adequate (if it is a successful poem), like a physical force that overwhelms us. Whenever I read this phrase by Montaigne about how successful poetry "ravishes and overwhelms" us, I am reminded of Thomas Mann's statement that Tolstoi used to listen to music with an expression of *horror* on his face.[17] Horror involves having one's attention "glued" to an object, and not only not having to go elsewhere to feel that object's force, but also not being *able,* physically or mentally, to go elsewhere. Sheer, immediate power (not proofs or conclusions detachable or paraphrasable from the poem) create Coleridge's "willing suspension of disbelief" that transpierces and transports us like a physical or like a horrible thing. And this same power is what Plato feared in his Republic. It was one reason for excluding poetry from the Republic.

But there is a milder kind of poetic function of the imagination: the use of metaphor to illumine or vivify ordinary language. We should, Montaigne believes, enrich, stretch, and bend our ordinary words by putting them in fresh contexts. But we must be sure in doing this that we are acting "prudently and shrewdly,"[18] not blurring plain facts or violating ordinary usage, but illuminating those facts and enriching our ordinary use of words. He urges the writer and speaker to borrow from the language of hunting and war, for example, if he would vivify his language; but he cautions us against introducing new words[19] or radically misusing old ones so that the ordinary reader cannot recognize what is being talked about. Ficino, the Italian Platonist, talks about love in a way "too artificial and different from the common and natural one," so that Montaigne's page, who makes love often and apparently well, cannot understand what the philosopher is talking about. Such changes in language smother the facts, do not illumine them.

This brings us to the second kind of imagination, which we shall call the "Assertive" kind. Here the imagination is no longer constrained by ordinary facts or the ordinary rule of language; but old words are radically altered in their usage, and new words are introduced to which no clear meaning can be attached without intricate study. And paradoxically, the use of the Assertive imagination does not often involve metaphor. Frequently it uses a literal, not a literary, language so as to cover up its radical deviation from ordinary usage. But the milder Poetic imagination as it occurs in common talk uses language with obvious metaphoric intent. The metaphors of everyday speech are guiding metaphors, meant to illuminate and organize ("He was a clown") the plainly visible facts that everyday language refers to in its way and can adequately paraphrase. Moreover the Assertive use of the imagination involves us in inferences from our images to facts or statements beyond those images. In metaphysics, for example, we are not being petitioned to suspend our disbelief; we are being petitioned to believe in something that is describable and defensible in various ways other than the way it is now being described and defended. Metaphysical claims are made to persuade, not ravish, and are supposed to be straightforward indicators of The Truth. The Truth is more important than and transcends any particular rhythmic or image-laden expression of it. In metaphysics, in theology, in physics, in medicine, we are not participating in a self-contained, autonomous experience, but are involved in what the Sceptics would call an "indication"[20] that is detachable or paraphrasable from, or goes beyond, any particular configuration of sounds and images.

And it is this kind of use of the imagination that has created so many of the world's troubles. An assertion, or an attempt at persuasion, leads to counterassertions from somebody who does not go along with your special way of using words and wishes to "refute" you with his way of using words; the battles of the books rage on. But though there are a few assertions embedded in poetry (such as de Musset's disagreement with Dante about whether the memory of past miseries is the worst pain or not) there are few battles between poems, although there may be many battles between poets. Insofar as a poet uses his Poetic imagination, he is not involved in disputes; his intentions are frustrated not when he is "refuted," but when he does not "ravish" the reader. But the Assertive imaginers, the arrogant, prosaic ones who would prove their claims, live a life of conflict with each other, of assertion and counterassertion, proof and refutation, quite alien to the autonomous worlds of poetry.

However, the Assertive imagination often occurs in the reader alone, and the text before him may be innocent of it:

"There is no sense or aspect, either straight or bitter, or sweet, or crooked that the human mind does not find in the writings it undertakes to search. In the clearest, purest, and most perfect writing that can be, how much falsehood and lying has been brought to birth! What heresy...."[21]

Of course Montaigne is talking about the Bible, and the heretics are necessarily the Protestants; but his basic criticism throughout the "Apology" and throughout his works is an attack upon anybody who insists on "proofs" based solely on the interpretation of words. Fanatics of all sorts can "prove all sorts of things from the Bible" because their own passions are a part of what they read and determine what words and what meanings of words are important. It is the same story as the one we discussed in the previous chapter: "Je voy évidemment, que nous ne prestons volontiers à la devotion que les offices qui flattent nos passions." We make the words dance to the tune our own private feelings and circumstances play for them. The vagabond, passionate imagination of man can build and populate universes upon the slightest verbal foundations. It is when *proofs* — professedly cogent, universally acceptable, detailed claims — are contentiously presented that this proclivity in man becomes dangerous, an occasion of so many of the world's troubles.

But if a plain, clear language can be a happy hunting ground for Assertive dreamers, what can happen in the readers' minds when the writings themselves are in a "hazy and doubtful style"?[22] Conflicting interpretations and conflicting "proofs" of these interpretations will abound because there simply is no one clear meaning to the language. The writer being confused himself, lost in his own imaginings,[23] leaves ample room, gives ample incentive, for the reader to find a precise, a definite meaning. According to Montaigne, Aristotle is the prince of such dogmatists — the prince of Assertively imaginative men who write in "inextricable obscurity." His Assertive Pyrrhonism[24] leads us to think that something definite *must* be there and stimulates us to commentary, to interpretation, that is, to wanderings in our own imaginations looking for clues or proofs. In this case the Assertive imagination is not simply the product of the reader's feelings but a complicated mixture of the "circumstances"[25] of both reader and writer.

What is it that motivates both readers and writers to use their imaginations? As for the Poetic imagination, Montaigne need not dwell on its provenance. The freshness, the vitality, the joy, it creates, the new awareness of already known but only half-enjoyed facts — the yearning for these creates poetry.[26] But Montaigne is not much interested in this question. It is the Assertive imagination of man that causes the "troubles," that obscures the facts, that creates conflicting claims to knowledge. It is this tendency to take images or names and infer from them facts about the world beyond those images, this tendency to violate natural speech and then assume that the new use of language reveals "reality," that Montaigne wishes to investigate. For in order to clear up troubles you must find out the sources of the trouble.

The first motivating desire that creates the Assertive imagination is the desire for precision. The "luster of a simple natural truth," he tells us in his essay on the education of children,[27] is not enough for us; plain talk is too rough, too broad an instrument for us. Our free imaginations love razor-sharp distinctions between narrower and narrower ideas. The common men who use the rough, simple language of everyday talk have strong stomachs and can take "their meat tougher or in bigger morsels"[28] than many of those whose dreams lead them into sharper distinctions, who need fine, thin morsels because they have tender stomachs. Speaking with all the experience of his sixteen years in active dealing with the law, Montaigne writes in his last essay:

> Why is it that our common language, so easy for any other use, becomes obscure and unintelligible in contracts and wills, and that a man who expresses himself clearly, whatever he says or writes, finds in this field no way of speaking his mind that does not fall into doubt and contradictions? Unless it is that the princes of this art, applying themselves with particular attention to picking out solemn words and contriving artificial phrases, have so weighed every syllable, so minutely examined every sort of combination, that here they are at last entangled . . . in the endless number of . . . minute partitions that they can no longer fall under any rule or prescription or any certain interpretation. "What is broken into dust becomes confused." (Seneca.)[29]

By subdividing subleties beyond the everyday usage of language, men multiply their difficulties. Everyday talk and everyday perceptions have their own "rule or prescription," their own broad but clear criteria for correctness and clarity. It is easy to distinguish salt from sugar or from pepper; but consider all the intricacies you must go through to distinguish the essence of a substance from its own inessential properties. Every person who can use the language can make the first distinctions without effort because the language he learned in youth has made these distinctions quite clearly understood. Its "rule or prescription" is as plain as daylight. But when we get lost in distinctions beyond our ordinary needs, beyond our everyday experiences and language, we get lost in our own imaginings, and we get tangled up in puzzles of our own creation. From these puzzles there is no "rule or prescription" that will help us out.

To insist on precision beyond our needs is as futile as insisting that we know the distance between Bordeaux and Paris *in millimeters:* the borderlines around these cities are too thick, the distinctions between these cities and their environs too vague, to allow us to measure that distance more precisely, say, than in meters. And if one insists on an answer to such a question, endless bickering, arbitrary decisions, and counterarguments are bound to ensue, because people will have to invent special rules for measuring distances in thinner chunks. A mother calls her child "good" at breakfast-time when he is hungry and gentle, and "bad" when both the mother and the son are irritable and tired in the evening. This much is clear to the mother and to anybody who uses plain talk: the child is good when he eats quietly and plentifully, and he is bad when he makes noise and yells instead of eating peacefully. But their philosopher-neighbor comes in and asks what is the *exact* difference between "goodness" and "badness" or between "the good" and "the bad"? He quietly twists her adjectives into nouns and makes a dozen subtle distinctions between emotions, objective facts, purposes, possibly even ethical norms, residing in nature or in God's mind. He wants to lay out with a scalpel all these elements and see in great detail all their interrelations. And if another philosopher should come in who wishes to argue with him for some reason, they get even more entangled in these "vagabond" imaginary distinctions, "like a mouse in pitch," as Erasmus put it.

But what about the mother and her son? Are they waiting breathlessly for a philosopher to give them a more precise understanding of what she meant by "good" and "bad"? Just about as breathlessly as the Mayors of Bordeaux and Paris are waiting to have a passerby tell them the distance between their respective cities in millimeters. They all go about their business of living with the "bigger morsels" of fact that their ordinary language has cut out for them and that long habituation has taught them to digest. The Mayors "know" the distance between their cities well enough; and the mother "knows" when her child is being bad and when he is being good, and she knows this well enough too. They do not "know" these in a way that satisfies every yearning of their imagination; they "know" these in a way that is satisfactory for the rough-and-ready business of day-to-day living. It is the sort of knowledge that is suitable for adjusting to one's environment, for reading maps that tell us how to get to Bordeaux, and for raising children.

Often, and notably in the center of the "Apology," Montaigne puts it this way: the high, "common road" of thought and language is broad and suitable for using to advance toward life's goals, such as health and satisfaction. But when you leave that high common road you find yourself on a hundred little twisty side-roads,[30] and you get lost if you are not wise enough to get back on the highroad. Montaigne quotes the Tuscan proverb "He who grows too keen cuts himself." Artificial words, artificial uses of ordinary words, are all trumped up by the imagination in its search for greater sharpness of boundaries. But the imagination erupts like a wild, sudden upheaval with no "rule or prescription," no path for guidance. This imagination tries to crack the old, solid habits of men but succeeds only in creating greater and greater chaos because it has left behind the regulatory power, the common understanding that those habits contribute. As the Sceptics would put it, in the field of the imagination there are no "criteria" for judging a given claim to be true or false. On the other hand, when we say that this is *salt* and not sugar, or this boy is *good* and not bad in the context of a casual kitchen conversation with the boy's mother, the criteria are plain insofar as we are talking the way a mother talks in such a situation and not the way a metaphysician talks. There are times when the Assertive imagination looks much like insanity, as it might well look to an unimaginative, tired mother being confronted with an analytical argument about the goodness or badness of her boy or about the salt on her table.

There is another yearning besides the analytical yearning of men that stimulates the Assertive imagination. In one of his most perceptive essays on language, "Of Cripples," in the Third Book, Montaigne writes:

> I myself, who am singularly scrupulous about lying and who scarcely concern myself with giving credence and authority to what I say, perceive nevertheless that when I am excited over a matter I have in hand, either by another man's resistance or by the intrinsic heat of the narration, I magnify and inflate my subject by voice, movements, vigor and power of words, and further by extension and amplification, not without prejudice to the simple truth.[31]

This business of being "carried away" by the very excitement of speaking is, Montaigne tells us, only momentary for him: the "first man who catches me up and asks me for the naked and unvarnished truth" gets that truth straight without padding. But one of the great misfortunes of men is that many do not stop short when challenged; instead, they defend themselves, grow more and more eloquent, create a hundred "reasons" to "defend" claims that have been stimulated not by facts but by their own "lively and noisy way of speaking."

In this same essay on cripples, Montaigne gives us some revealing accounts of what it means to be carried away perpetually by one's own lively way of speaking. Part of what permits us to be so carried away is a desire to accept anything we cannot refute conclusively, a desire to affirm *something,* no matter what, providing that there can be no conclusive refutation of our claim. We do this in our drive for self-assertion as a twisted version of our drive for self-preservation. And in matters of the imagination — matters that have long ago left the "rule or prescription" of ordinary talk — all sides are incapable of being proved false conclusively. If there is a rule for using the word "salt," you can prove or refute the claim that this stuff here is salt; but if there is no broadly accepted rule for the use of words like "reality," for instance, then refutation or proof is simply out of the question. Anybody who comes along with a more fertile and slightly antagonistic imagination will be able to pull you into the pitch again. Another way of putting it is that since all sides of an assertively imaginative argument are irrelevant to particular facts, dwelling as they do in the imagination of men, they are inaccessible to refutation or proof on the basis of facts. "The universe is material" can neither be proved nor disproved by pointing to facts or mentioning thoughts; the words have no meaning in terms of such facts; the facts have no purchase on them. Everything is up to our undisciplined, ruleless imaginations. In what Montaigne calls those "verbal and scholastic" arguments,[32] those on one side "have as good an apparent case as their contradictors," providing that all the participants are ingenious in the use of their imaginations. And because men have this yearning to affirm whatever is safe to affirm, the argument continues from all sides.

One of the reasons people yearn to affirm what they cannot conclusively disprove is that they have been taught to be ashamed of admitting ignorance. We are told that our minds have a nobler destiny than that of animals and that therefore we must know more than merely the visible and tangible facts of life that satisfy the other animals. We have been taught (and there is a propensity for vanity in man that makes us capable of being so taught) that it is shameful to answer a question beyond our competence with an "I don't know" or a "Perhaps." And this same vanity, this same conviction that we have what Seneca and the other Stoics called a "divine reason" that soars above facts and above ordinary language, makes us need to argue offensively and defensively about these matters. An attack upon a claim we have made becomes a point of honor. It is a personal attack to which we respond with all our weapons, like true animals.

But for Montaigne arrogance is only part of the explanation for these never-ending battles over unprovable matters. Another part is the dogged amusement these battles give their protagonists. In his ambitious essay "Of Vanity," in the Third Book, Montaigne talks about men creating "altercations fit only for the exercise of our minds."[33] And what he means is that we get pleasure, the joy of ongoing activity, from defending our own position and attacking somebody else's; there is in such defense and attack the pleasure of flexing our mental muscles and using them in new directions. To enjoy the noise of dispute, we bring up subjects "whose essence is controversy and dispute, and which have no life apart from that."[34] In such matters we are assured of a good, long — in fact, an unending — fight, as long as the Assertive imaginations of men continue to work.

These yearnings for precision and for noble contention which motivate the Assertive imagination are various forms of one basic desire — a desire that Montaigne deals with in various forms from one end of the *Essays* to the other. In one of his last additions to his "Apology" he put it this way:

"Man is possessed by an extreme concern with prolonging his being. ... The soul ... being unable to stand on its own feet, goes looking everywhere for consolations, hopes, and foundations in external circumstances where it clings and takes root; and flimsy and fantastic as its imagination may create them, it feels solider in them than in itself, and gladder."[35]

To my mind, this passage (taken more broadly than Montaigne here intends it to be taken) not only illuminates Montaigne's whole complex diagnosis of the sources of our "grammatical" troubles; it is a useful way of describing his whole way of thinking, as well as the whole way of thinking we have been calling "Classical Scepticism." It is a summary in mildly ironic form of his concept of a personal philosophy.

This extreme concern with "prolonging" our being is what makes us use our imaginations in the first place; our distance-receptors, like our eyes and ears, stimulate us to go outside of ourselves, and so do our needs for food and shelter. But there are healthy and there are unhealthy prolongations, and the latter involve "that semblance of intellect" we call "reason."[36] This "reason" is a set of fabrications by our imagination that serves to satisfy our yearnings for precision, affirmation, nobility, and exercise; and this "reason" can be harmful to us. We have a tendency to pass beyond the crude, observable facts when we are "carried away" by these desires, and this tendency triggered by those yearnings makes us able to create a "hundred other worlds" than the one we inhabit in everyday life. With our Assertive imagination not only do we create these worlds but we "know" the causes of a million things that exist in our imaginations and possibly nowhere else.

It is important to see that Montaigne's remarks about language and fantasy are not intended to prove any of our claims about unobservables to be *false*. He is not claiming like a dogmatist that as a matter of fact there is nothing beyond our ordinary experience and our ordinary language. The purpose of all his remarks about what I have been calling the Assertive imagination is to urge us to eschew making inferences of any sort from our imagination or from artificial terminology that cannot be refuted or verified by fact. In the First Book, at the beginning of his essay on the power of the imagination, he says with respect to the imagination, "My art is to escape it, not to resist it." He does not want, for instance, to refute certain particular metaphysical or theological claims by proving their contradictories. We have just been seeing that this is simply out of the question, *ex hypothesi:* you can neither prove nor refute such matters conclusively. He wants us to avoid the whole "unthinking fantasy" that draws people into these endless altercations that have implicit in them no rules for their being settled. He wants us to avoid the tendency to make Assertive claims about matters beyond our language and beyond our perception. We can read poetry about what is beyond us, but we must not infer from the image to the fact beyond the image, from the name to the thing existing independently of our attitudes or images. This way lies the anarchy of mind and society, discourse without "rule or prescription." Here is a "prolongation of our being" that reflects our own passion-laden imaginations more certainly than it reflects any "reality" beyond us.

Now, these distinctions we have been making between "judgment," "Assertive imagination" and "Poetic imagination," and so on are not meant to establish sharp boundaries between "faculties" of the human mind. For the sake of understanding the broad assertions of Montaigne in a small compass I have been acting as if Montaigne felt that these matters admit of rather sharp definition. But he did not think that one can divide man into airtight compartments. In the same spirit that he gladly drops a fanciful story and tells the plain facts, Montaigne finally leaves all these matters up to what he calls the "good nose," the broad judgment, of the reader. He is not, like his beloved Seneca, going to make an "imaginary republic" of the mind with judgment down here and the various sorts of imagination elsewhere. (Look at the ninety-second letter of Seneca to Lucilius for an example of a faculty psychology with wheels within wheels, parts related to parts, as in an "imaginary republic.") Such imaginative precision is contrary to his whole philosophy of language. In the end he wants to say that the plain fact is that people fight endlessly about words and ignore their own "real and essential" life. In the end he wants the reader's olfactory sense, his "good nose," to be sharpened for rotten, purely verbal or imaginative arguments, whether or not he or the reader can give a precise formula for sorting out rotten from sound arguments.

To somebody who finds broad language dealing with "bigger morsels" exasperating, Montaigne is disquieting indeed. But to somebody willing to read Montaigne in his own broad terms, with some temporary refinement from time to time to make the way clearer in some details, his remarks are very useful, very excitingly applicable to those occasions in life when we are getting ready to enter a fight and are wondering whether it will be worth doing.

C. Lies, prayers, and our troubles

THERE are for Montaigne two types of speech importantly related to the Assertively imaginative language of metaphysics: lies, and certain prayers. They are different in several ways from metaphysics, but they involve the same sort of imaginative license that metaphysics involves. Like metaphysics, they spring from a mind not being guided by fact or by the firm conventions of an orderly language. And as in the case of metaphysics, we detect this arbitrariness when we discover a conflict — a conflict difficult to resolve. Montaigne's treatment of these two types of vagaries can serve as a concise summary of his diagnosis and therapy of spiritual sickness.

In "Of Liars," in the First Book, Montaigne gives us a neat example of a liar being crushed between the jaws of an antithesis. A certain ambassador from the Duke of Milan once told King Francis I that the Duke, his master, had executed a man without knowing that this man was indeed attached to his highness King Francis. Actually, most people in the court of France (and the ambassador) knew full well that the dead man was a spy sent by Francis in the guise of a tourist. Now, Francis had a "good nose": he knew where France's advantage lay, and he could smell it out in a minute. And so he pressed the ambassador: "Why did you have the man killed at night as if by stealth?" And that seasoned Italian ambassador, like a schoolboy, said, "Out of respect for his Majesty the Duke would have been very reluctant to have such an execution performed by day." Caught like a mouse in pitch! First he had said that

Language and the Troubles of the World 87

the Duke knew nothing of any liaison between the "tourist" and the French court; now he was saying that the Frenchman was executed at night out of respect for his connection with the court of Francis. I cannot help thinking that Montaigne had in mind both the size and acuity of King Francis' nose when he concluded his story with the sentence: "Anyone may imagine how he was picked up for having contradicted himself so clumsily, and that before such a nose." "Contrary reports"[37] are the key symptoms of a lie, as they are of a metaphysical contention.

Irresolvable conflict is the symptom of human caprice. And this goes for prayers too:

> The miser prays to him for the vain and superfluous conservation of his treasures; . . . the thief uses his help to pass through the risks and difficulties that oppose the execution of his wicked enterprises, or thanks him for having found it easy to cut a passerby's throat. Standing beside the house they are going to scale or blow up, they say their prayers with their intentions and hopes full of cruelty, lust and avarice.[38]

We are back to the central doctrine of the "Apology": when we depart from the steady governance of fact and convention

> we willingly accord to piety only the services that flatter our passions. There is no hostility that excels Christian hostility. Our zeal does wonders when it is seconding our leaning toward hatred, cruelty, ambition, avarice, detraction, rebellion, etc.[39]

Montaigne does not mention it, but Lucian's dialogue *Icaromenippus* contains a passage even more picturesque and even more directly tied in with Scepticism than any of Montaigne's own comments on prayers. In this dialogue a certain Menippus flies up to heaven on a collection of eagles' wings and meets Zeus himself. The king of the gods befriends him and chats with him about various matters, including the fact that nowadays his altars are cold, "colder than Plato's Laws." Then:

> With some talk of this sort, we made our way to the place where Zeus was to sit and listen to the prayers. There were orifices there like the mouths of wells, a row of them with lids to each, and by each a golden chair was set. Zeus stationed himself just over the first hole, and removing the lid, put himself at the disposal of the petitioners. From every quarter of the earth came prayers, as various in form as they were different in tenor. I stooped over, too, I must tell you, and listened with Zeus to the prayers, and they were something like this: Zeus, let me be a king! My onions,

Zeus, and my leeks, help them to grow! Ye gods, permit the speedy removal of my father by death! And these were the words of one: "If I might be my wife's heir! If I might intrigue against my brother unobserved! . . ." One voyager prayed for the north wind to help him, another prayed for the south; and, while the husband-man wanted rain, the fuller wanted sun. . . . In one case I saw even Zeus at a loss. Two men's prayers contradicted one another; but, as the sacrifices they promised were exactly equal, Zeus could not determine which of them should have his wish. In fact, he was in the old difficulty of the Academy, and unable to come to any decision. Like Pyrrho, he was left reserving his judgment, and inquiring.[40]

Like metaphysics, prayers "not being subject to our ordinary reasoning . . . take away our means of combating them." Guided by nothing but our own capricious self-interest, we indulge and aggravate the mobility of our souls, and all in the name of God's will, not merely our own. And what such capricious prayers do to our souls, lies do to our society. In both cases there is anarchy, but both kinds of anarchy, like that of metaphysical speculation, lie in the soul of man; it is the absence of rule or regulation in men's minds that produces all these inadjudicable conflicts. Society simply writes large the vagaries of each of the minds that make it up. Anarchy breeds anarchy.

But as we have noticed in previous chapters, this is not Montaigne's last word on the subject of such vagaries. He is not like some insane "doctor" who thinks that all diseases are incurable. He is confident that language, imagination, and life can be kept from painful chaos, just as an effective doctor has confidence that the human body can function in an efficient way, once the disease is removed.

Now, in part the disease is cured by simply recognizing its provenance and its symptoms. Sextus, the doctor, and Montaigne, the concocter of the preservative called "The Apology for Raymond Sebond," believe that a great deal of good comes from seeing the evil and from simply suspending judgment on all these conflicting claims (the way a sane man would turn his back on a room full of obsessive liars). But this negative, diversionary tactic is only part of the cure: after all, where do we go from here? What does a soul do when it is purged? The answer in all cases is: we go back to comparatively orderly, conventional, action-tested and fact-tested ways. For instance, in our prayers[41] we should talk to God in a distinct, fixed language: "The Jews, the Mohammedans, and almost all others have espoused, and revere, the language in which their mysteries were originally conceived; and any alteration or change in them is forbidden not without reason." When we leave the firm, public language, our words become pebbles in the street, "sports and pastimes," subject to all those accidental movements that can make the preserver of society the destroyer of it. We have seen how Montaigne wanted us to go back to plain talk, instead of talking metaphysics; and as far as lying is concerned, his recommendation is obvious (we shall see later that one of the reasons he will stay away from public life is so that he can avoid lying for the sake of public convenience). And as far as his own prayer is concerned, he uses and advocates a fixed format, the Lord's Prayer.[42] In using it and it alone he keeps his imagination orderly.

Moreover, he advocates that if we must cross the gap between the old language of religion and present everyday life, if we must preach or be preached to, we should do so only with the help of a long, firm church tradition. Only in such a tradition can we find the "rule or prescription" that keeps our lives healthy. Only here can the vagabond liberty of our imaginations be constrained by firm rules of interpretation. And so it is by doubt and affirmation that we keep our speech, our souls, and our society from becoming immoderately "vague, free, mutable, and piecemeal."[43] Our natural condition is vague, free, mutable, and piecemeal enough without aggravating its vagaries.

D. *The modern diagnosis: Wittgenstein*

MODERN "Analytic philosophy" has been coming up with some analyses rather strikingly similar to Montaigne's accounts of the "grammatical" origins of men's troubles. The Logical Positivists of the Vienna Circle and their English representative A. J. Ayer[44] have developed the category of "nonsense" to cover all those remarks which have no relevance to firm *criteria*. All claims which have nothing to do with empirical tests or logico-mathematical calculations are consigned by them to this category. But this group, with its emphasis on formal logic, its great faith in scientific methodology, and above all its lack of faith in the power of ordinary language, is not as close to the spirit of Montaigne as is a group sometimes called "the ordinary-language philosophers." Thinkers like Ludwig Wittgenstein, John L. Austin, and Gilbert Ryle have shared the Positivistic desire to consign criterionless, arbitrary claims to the realm of "nonsense," but they have had greater faith in the language of the man in the steet than have the Positivists, and they have not always insisted on making all our language as precise as the Logical Positivists have done. As Wittgenstein sees it in his *Philosophical Investigations,* there is no one ideal language (like that of formal logic or the exact sciences); rather there are various languages, each with its own rights, its own degree of precision. And each works well:

"Our language can be seen as an ancient city: a maze of little streets and squares, of old and new houses, and of houses with additions from various periods; and this surrounded by a multitude of new boroughs with straight regular streets and uniform houses."[45]

These new boroughs are the languages of the sciences, according to Wittgenstein; they might be the practices of Roman Catholicism, according to Montaigne. But the main point here is that for Montaigne and Wittgenstein the language of the man in the street is of ineluctable importance to philosophy. According to both of them, this language has enough precision, flexibility, and communicative power to do all the jobs we may reasonably require of it — if we use it skillfully (and this use will be the topic of the next chapter). As Wittgenstein puts it in Section 88 of the *Investigations,* to call a sentence "inexact" by some ideal standards of precision is by no means the same as calling it unusable. We can and do use "inexact" language quite successfully without the "help" of somebody who wants to replace it according to his fantasy. The old streets may indeed be a maze, but we find our way through them well enough, if we have any sense.

Another metaphor will help illumine the relevance of Montaigne's thoughts on language to the bold linguistic insights of Wittgenstein. One of the root-metaphors of Wittgenstein's writings is that of illness and normality. What the Positivists (and sometimes he himself) call "nonsense" he often describes as "The sickness of a time."[46] Puzzles (not solvable problems, but hopeless puzzles) are a "philosophical disease" to him, and in Section 255 of his great work the *Investigations* he points out that "the philosopher's treatment of a question is like the treatment of a disease." In all his important works, especially his later ones, this metaphor operates not simply as a picturesque mode of speech but as a guide to his thinking. There are for Wittgenstein healthy ways of life (and to him a language is a way of living) and unhealthy ways; the job of the philosopher is to distinguish these and then to help himself and others to live in

Language and the Troubles of the World 91

the healthy, orderly ways. Criterionless imagining made to look like empirical discovery, pictures in the imagination that are confused with statements of fact — these are the disease the philosopher must learn to recognize and eliminate. When Wittgenstein summarizes his philosophy with the term *"verschiedene Therapien"* — "various therapies" — he is not using a metaphor superficially; he is penetrating to the depths of his method and of his vision of language. According to this vision there are healthy ways of life and there are unhealthy ones; we must expunge one in order to make way for the other. And among these healthy ways is ordinary speech, untainted by pictures that bewitch us into philosophical insanity. For instance, the picture of each human mind cut off from all other minds by a metaphysical wall has occasioned many of the troubles of philosophy. One of the main purposes of Wittgenstein's thought is to cure us of such obsessive, philosophically torturing pictures.

It is not necessary at this stage in our study of Montaigne to point out in detail the important similarities between Wittgenstein's use of this metaphor and Montaigne's use. All we need say in general is that Sextus' purgative and Montaigne's preservative are part of the great tradition that lies behind Wittgenstein's notion of philosophy. A doctrine of philosophy that sees language as a part of life, for good and for evil, is what they share. And also they share the belief that we have available to us, if we will only use it wisely, language that can help keep life orderly, peaceful. Above all, they share the conviction that philosophy's task is to remind men of these things, not to create new castles in the air, new hopeless squabbles, new tortures.

Still another of Wittgenstein's metaphors would help to show the relevance of Montaigne's analysis to modern analytic thought. A language, according to this metaphor, can be fruitfully regarded as a game. Its signs are the pieces in the game, and the accepted ways the signs are used (the accepted ways they are combined with other signs or actions) are the rules of this game. If we speak a given language, we do so within the implicit rules of usage that are part of that language, just as when we play a given game we do so within the rules of that game. When we speak English we say, "I am putting my food on the table," when we are doing one sort of thing with one sort of four-legged, flat-surfaced object. We violate the implicit "rules" of English when we say, "I am putting my nose on the sky," when doing that same sort of thing with the same sort of four-legged, flat-surfaced object. All this a child learns early; he usually learns the rules of his language without being able to formalize them in precepts, but he learns them firmly and effectively nonetheless.

Now if we play one language-game, we find that we must play according to the implicit rules of our game. We do not play bridge according to the rules of chess, nor do we try to mix up the rules of both games when we are trying to play an orderly game. If we try to mix two games without establishing one overarching game that will lay down a "rule or prescription" for our activities, then we shall soon be involved in dispute and chaos. If we play chess, we play chess, and are not playing bridge or some ruleless mixture of the two. Every game we play must have its rules or it is simply not a game; it is chaos.

In the light of all this, what Montaigne is saying is that we should play the language-game of ordinary, everyday life according to the habits, customs, or rules of usage accepted by all those who speak the language spoken "in the streets of France," and we should keep this language-game as distinct as possible from the language-game involved in prayers or ecclesiastical speech. We should avoid mixing up these language-games, since each of them has shown itself by long practice to work very well. Whenever we try to mix them our language becomes "vague, free, mutable, and piecemeal" — subject to our unregulated imaginations. The firm, accepted rules of interpretation of the Catholic Church constitute one "game"; the uninterpreted words of the Bible that we may repeat in prayer constitute another, possibly related to the first; and talk "in the streets of France" constitutes a third. In whichever area we talk, we must always be sure to speak according to firm, though usually broad, rules of usage. At least we should do this if we would bridle our wild, passion-impelled imaginations and live peacefully with ourselves and with other men.

Moreover, remembering Montaigne's attack upon our yearnings for excessive precision and verbal jousting, we must not try to make the game we are playing any more precise than the rules of that game traditionally permit. If we try to do this, we introduce useless, interminable arguments (*Was* that ball pitched exactly 410 millimeters above the base?). Again, if we excite ourselves into ignoring or twisting the rules of the game, just for the sake of winning it or simply in order to keep it going (Now I think I'll make my Pawns all Queens), chaos and anarchy will ensue.

We must keep our games pure (here the Humanists' emphasis on purity of language is influential in Montaigne's thought), and we must play them according to their customary broad but adequate rules. And the reason why we "must" do this is simple: to do anything else is to open up a Pandora's box containing the troubles of this world. It is to bring into being the anarchy to which the fluidity and variety of our minds make us susceptible. Enmity toward such an anarchy is what Montaigne shares with modern Analytic philosophers, as well as some of their ways of fighting it. What they all wanted was a way of thinking which, to quote the *Investigations* again, "gives philosophy peace, so that it is no longer tormented by questions which bring *itself* in question."[47] The modern Analytic philosophers are very different from Montaigne in many ways. For instance, they would not think of themselves primarily as "moral philosophers" nor as men doing self-portraits, let alone as Sceptics with regard to science. Montaigne was all these things and would have been rather impatient, I suspect, with the scrupulous analysis that these modern philosophers engage in. But none of the men discussed in this chapter is the enemy of belief or affirmation. Their only enemy is what we have called the "Assertive imagination." They all try to keep us from using that interpreter of our souls, language, as a means of pitting man against man in dubious battle.

Chapter 6

The Powers of Language

A. Expression and communication

THE most acute twentieth-century Analytic philosophers share with Montaigne an unshakable confidence in the power of language. The modern apologists for science and the sixteenth-century Sceptical Humanist agree that this power can help bring about our troubles as readily as it can help bring about our happiness. They believe that this power can help disintegrate minds and societies, and it can help integrate them into durably progressive, peaceful structures. They do not believe that there is some deep chasm between men's minds, across which we cry to each other in vain. Especially Wittgenstein and Montaigne try in many ways to show how language is embedded in observable action, how indeed it is a kind of action. Wittgenstein calls languages *"Lebensformen"* — "ways of life." Our language is not a set of squeaks and scratches dropping into interpersonal voids; our language, being a part of our actions, is as communicative and powerful as they are. For the ordinary-language philosophers and for Montaigne it is usually no more difficult to tell somebody what you mean than it is to shake his hand or smile at him. Not that these things are always easy! Sometimes such actions are hard to perform, if not impossible. And sometimes it is hard to tell others something or to put it into words for oneself. But the point is that for such thinkers as Wittgenstein and Montaigne, this is not always the case; on the contrary, it is rarely the case, and we can be more or less successful in doing these things. We are not doomed to failure by a metaphysical wall between us, just as we are not sure of success when we want to talk dogmatic "nonsense" (to use the term of the Analysts). We are dealing with thinkers who neither despair of language nor put infinite hope in it.

Between these extremes lies an immense range of possibilities for Montaigne (as for the moderns). We can bring down upon our heads the fabric of society and destroy our own stability, or we can write like a Ronsard or a Petrarch or a Horace. The modern Analytic philosophers see the great beneficent powers of language mainly in terms of scientific progress; the Humanist Montaigne saw those powers in terms of literature and broad philosophizing about ways of life. But they all agree that this powerful instrument must and can be handled with more care and with more effect. In the previous chapter, we saw how Montaigne accounted for the disastrous handling of it; in this chapter we shall be seeing how Montaigne proposed to handle it well. And in the process of seeing this we shall see how great Montaigne felt the powers of language to be.

Of course, the account in the previous chapter[1] implies a broad, positive doctrine of language. It implies that we must not leave the highroad of ordinary linguistic usage, and we must be content with only that amount of precision which a life of successful action requires. It implies that traditional usage is the matrix of language, not arbitrary fiat, not the Assertive imagination. Language is an enduring instrument for helping to secure mental and physical well-being. Montaigne will never depart from this pragmatic doctrine.

Those who underestimate the power of language sometimes think of it as a set of cookie-cutters that are imposed from the outside on the dough that is our mental life. It is as if this mental life has all the ingredients in the right combination before the cookie-cutter descends upon it, and all the cookie-cutter does is give this stuff shape and commercial salability. Perhaps such an external relationship between words and thoughts was what Thomas Gray had in mind when he wrote of "mute, inglorious Miltons" who had all the thoughts and feelings of genius, but simply could not find in their little towns the right language.

But for Montaigne clarity and order in thought and clarity and order in language are one and the same thing. If anybody tells him that he has a head full of many splendid ideas but lacks the eloquence to express them, his answer is brief: "That is all bluff."[2] The mute Miltons may have yearnings, glimmerings of some sort, but "whoever has a vivid and clear idea in his mind will express it, if necessary in Bergamask dialect, or, if he is dumb, by signs." "Splendid ideas" are for him through-and-through expressible, communicable; this expressibility, this communicability, is part of their vividness, their clarity, their force, the way the shape of a hand is part of the hand.

Words then are *"au dedans,"*[3] intrinsic to our vivid and clear feelings and thoughts. But we may not *wish* to divulge our mental life to others. We may have clear thoughts which we suppress; we may keep our feelings to ourselves or within a small circle of friends, or we may publish them at large. Montaigne, for one, has chosen to suppress very little, as he tells us in the Preface.

In the important essay "Of Giving the Lie" he tells us that this book is "consubstantial with its author, concerned only with myself, part of my flesh." In that same essay he assures us that a few times in this book he has lashed out at the public for their sake (and the "Apology" is an obvious instance of this). But, he asks, "If no one reads me, have I wasted my time . . . ?" And the answer he gives is a firm No. He sat down to write his essays in order to give clarity, order, and stability to his own thoughts; he wrote to give himself a firm shape: "In molding a cast upon myself, I have had to form and solidify myself in order to bring out my shape, and the model under the mold has become firmer and has achieved sharper form in the process."

It is of very great importance in understanding Montaigne that we see what is at issue here. He is saying that though language can *communicate* our thoughts to the public, its basic function for him is *expressive*. He had his essays published; but his primary act, not only chronologically primary, but of primary importance to him, was one of keeping the bits and pieces of his mental life from being squandered in that profligate wind, time. He wrote to give a healthful lucidity and order to his mind. And since words do have a deep involvement with the mind of their user, he could hope for success. If others did not read him or if they chose to misunderstand him, he had still set out to put his mental house in order. Like any other animal, he is trying to find his well-being, and like a Humanistic animal he finds it in using words to shape his life.

In the First Book, the essay "Of Idleness" tells us how he retired from public life in 1571 into a castle overlooking a little village about thirty miles from Bordeaux. At first he thought he could simply sit around and let his mind "entertain itself" with any thought that might happen to occur; moreover, he anticipated a solidifying and ripening of his thoughts with every passing hour, just sitting there and thinking. But without having to put his thoughts under the discipline of writing

> I found . . . on the contrary that, like a run-away horse, it [my mind] gave itself a hundred times more troubles than it ever had gotten from others

[in my public life]; it gave birth in me to many chimeras and fantastic monsters ... without order, without pattern ... and so in order to contemplate at leisure their weirdness and ineptitude I began to keep a record of them.

Language can help preserve sanity by ordering one's thoughts so that they can be contemplated in peace and detachment. Of course, for Montaigne communication is vital: he is "hungry" to make himself known for what he really is, not for what rumor might make him out to be. This hunger only the writing *and* publication of the *Essays* could assuage. And so we must not ignore the plain fact that Montaigne went out of his way to publish these essays. In our final chapter we shall say more about the relation between self-expression and communication in Montaigne's writings. We shall find the distinction and connection between the two functions of language of great importance to Montaigne's notion of a personal philosophy.

Now what, more exactly, was the language of the *Essays* designed to do? Certainly it was not designed to prove something about precise, "original essences" which are supposed to be objectively discoverable beneath our gross awareness of things. The essays were written *"premièrement"* to *"mettre en rolle,"* to notice, order, and record his own thoughts and feelings about various subjects. At the same time they would make these thoughts and feelings communicable to others. And this communicative function could be performed easily, given Montaigne's doctrine of language: the same words that express to yourself the shape of your mind can, if you so wish, be published. For Montaigne, metaphysical solitude is a daydream. Knowing yourself and getting yourself known are two sides of the same mold: the rule or prescription of language makes both possible. If you want to be known, write well, take your writings to a good printer, and get them distributed broadly.

B. Essaying a mind

FORTUNATELY for anyone trying to understand Montaigne's use of language, Montaigne, like any Humanist, was very curious about language in general and about his own use of language. As a matter of fact, he is the best authority we have on the subject of his own way of writing. And so, in our effort to see more clearly what he wanted language to do, let us look at the way he used the key word *essai*. He used it very carefully, very self-consciously, and he used it in a very revealing way. What *was* the *essai* supposed to express and communicate? We have, in effect, answered this question in the previous section; but let us make the answer more specific.

The word *"essayer"* means to try out something in order to grasp or understand it. The first passage I want to point out comes at the beginning of the famous essay "Of the Education of Children," in Book One.[4] But look at the context first, because a great deal of injury has been done to the long strands of his thought by taking snippets from it. He had opened the essay with an implicit comparison between his writings and a son he might have, say a "mangy or hunchbacked" son. Now a father, whether of essays or sons, will be able to see defects in his offspring, if he is not blinded by paternal affection. But even if he can see defects, "the fact remains that the boy is his," and, Montaigne implies, he is now going to criticize as well as acknowledge his paternity of these "reveries" of his. Among the faults in his writings is the fact that they spring from a man "who has tasted only the outer crust of sciences," who is, in fact, as far as the objective sciences are concerned, a dilettante. He has glanced at many subjects (like medicine, jurisprudence, mathematics, and the metaphysics of that "monarch of modern learning," Aristotle), but has looked thoroughly into none.

Why, he could not even examine a child on the content of an early lesson. And if somebody forced him to judge the child in some way relevant to that lesson, all he could do would be to generalize broadly from the lesson. (I could imagine him asking, as he put it, "rather ineptly," with reference to a simple astronomy lesson, "Isn't the world vast, and aren't we small?") All he could do, he tells us, is examine the boy's *"jugement naturel"*[5] by asking him to comment on that "rather inept" generalization.

Now comes the phrase we were getting ready for. Montaigne is talking about how much he loves poetry because it is compressed within rigid metrical requirements, the way sound is compressed in a trumpet, and so it comes out more violently, hits you harder than loosely flowing, wandering language. Then he drops the metaphor of compression and picks up the related metaphor of *weight,* downward pressure. Implicitly what he is saying is that what he reads in books serves as a sort of weight for making his own attitudes come forth "sharper and stronger":

> As for the natural faculties that are in me, of which this book is the essay, I feel them bending under the load. My conceptions and my judgment move only by groping, staggering, stumbling, and blundering; and when I have gone ahead as far as I can . . . I can still see country beyond, but with a dim and clouded vision. . . .

And so the weight of the books of other men helps him to use his own muscles, his own "natural faculties," but not in the triumphant way that poetry uses meter or that a trumpet uses its channels.

An essay is not itself an acquired "scientific" fact that can be memorized from a textbook or from any book. It is the reasonable expression of a man's own reaction to facts or to any book or work of art that he comes across. Unlike a memorizable fact, it is an inconclusive reaction, one that involves "groping, staggering, stumbling, and blundering." It involves the feeling that one does not understand everything, that one is constantly readjusting his "muscles" or his own powers in order to find some stable relationship with his world. But one never achieves that adjustment, never reaches a resting place: there is always "country beyond." There is always more readjustment, more pushing onward toward one's own goals. An essay is active, as against passively mnemonic; it is "of universal scope," rather than precisely detailed; it is inconclusive, rather than final. It acknowledges no "monarch of modern learning," no authority more final than the powers of the essayist himself. In short, it is broadly personal. It essays the *"facultez naturelles qui sont en moy"* in action and is not impersonally or objectively factual. *Who* you are and *how* you are, not what you have or what you know, is being essayed.

Let us look at another passage, still in Montaigne's first published version of the First Book. This one is to be found at the very beginning of the tiny essay on Democritus and Heraclitus. The essay opens:

> Judgment is a tool to use on all subjects, and comes in everywhere. Therefore in the tests [*essais*] that I make of it here, I use every sort of occasion. If it is a subject I do not understand at all, even on that I essay my judgment, sounding the ford from a good distance; and then, finding it too deep for my height, I stick to the bank. . . . I do not see the whole of anything; nor do those who promise to show it to us. Of a hundred members and faces that each thing has, I take one, sometimes only to lick it, sometimes to brush the surface, and sometimes to pinch it to the bone.

And then he makes a remark that is a bridge between the "Apology" and his notion of what man *can* know:

> I would venture to treat some matter thoroughly, if I knew myself less well.... I [give] ... myself up to doubt and uncertainty and my ruling quality, which is ignorance.

Finally, he explains why such inconclusive activities are worth putting into words: "Every movement reveals us." In short, he is not mainly concerned with the depth of the ford that he is probing; he is content to probe it from a good distance and then to stay on the bank if it looks too deep. He is not recommending himself to us as an ontological oceanographer. He is primarily presenting *himself* in the act of judging various subjects, and he can reveal himself in each particular judgment as well as in a whole essay taken as a single argument. He is telling us that he wishes to present a man looking at the universe, not the universe pure and simple. He is revealing a particular *"jugement"* in action.

Consider some possible translations of the word *essai*. The word "trial" is sometimes used to translate it, but this word does not plainly convey the tentative nature of an *essai,* at least as Montaigne uses the French word. A trial is final, though the judgment of the judge or jurors is, except in the highest courts, subject to revision; we think of trials by ordeal or by fire, or trials of strength as having something of finality about them; and even in court-trials the "judgment" of the court is, on that level at least, final, other things being equal. The word "test" has connotations of finality as well, plus an air of precision in many of its uses. The word "experiment" has its difficulties too, but is useful, implying as it does tentative searching, and often searching not for one particular result, but for any or all the capacities or powers of the object we are experimenting with. To experiment with an acid, for example, would be to investigate its behavior under a variety of circumstances, under different temperatures, in various containers. Here, as in Montaigne's essays, we are interested in these external circumstances mainly insofar as they tell us something about the stuff that we are experimenting with: in this case, Montaigne's mind.

But the word "experiment" reminds us of systematically varied factors in a laboratory; its connotations of precise, even quantitative analysis make it a misleading term to apply to our Humanist's writings. We can say in general that an essay resembles a trial, a test, and an experiment insofar as these words refer to an active exploration of the powers something has.

A good working translation for his word *essayer* is a phrase that carries with its swinging sound, some idea of trial, test, or experimenting without having enough detailed meaning in modern English to be misleading; the phrase is the English verb "to essay" or the noun-form usually adopted by translators, "essay." What Montaigne is "essaying" is his own capacities or powers; he is making his "judgment" act or react in order to give comprehensible shape to its powers. He is doing new things with it in order to display its inherent limitations and peculiarities, but he is doing all this in an unsystematic, inconclusive way, taking whatever subject comes along, because the subject is not the main thing he is looking for. Montaigne had a "greedy appetite for new and unknown things,"[6] not only because he enjoyed diversity but because diversity brought out the properties of his judgment more fully. Essays are the form self-knowledge takes in a shifting world.

C. Two kinds of order

By displaying in use the groping, changing judgment of the same man, all the essays of Montaigne, and notably the major ones, exhibit a tension between change and stability, between diversity and unity, between spontaneity and control. Aside from a unity of purpose or subject matter, there are various dominant metaphors that unify many of them; the most complex and omnipresent of these is the image of conflict or change. (Consider the "Apology" and "Of Repentance.") But it takes experience and a rather keen eye for ideas and metaphors to see at an early reading the unity of many of Montaigne's essays. In part this is so because Montaigne deliberately avoided putting in connective words or phrases. But whatever his techniques, the result is what Montaigne called *"descousu."*[7] He wants each chunk to be a whole entity.

The *Essays* do not give what their titles promise; digressions often drown any principal idea; there is often only a physical proximity of groups of words with each other. He wants to arrest the attention of the reader and to keep him awake: "Who is there that would not rather not be read than be read sleepily or in passing? *Nothing is so useful that it can be of value when taken on the run.*" (Seneca.)[8]

But getting or maintaining attention is not the main reason for the sometimes baffling variety of ideas and incidents and metaphors that he shoots in our faces in most of his longer and many of his shorter essays. Communication for Montaigne, especially the communication between man and man, involved an *empathic* or sympathetic awareness of the movement of a mind. Montaigne's pen moved the way his mind moved, often jumpily, sometimes logically and coherently, and he wanted the reader's mind to move just that way. He wanted the reader (himself, or somebody else) to think his way for a little while, and in doing so to get a direct acquaintance with that way. He did not want the reader to understand him only in an objective way; he wanted the reader to get the feel of the way his mind moved, and thereby to understand him without categories, without any claims to objectivity or precision — by direct acquaintance. He wanted the reader to get from the essays not *"la science"* of Montaigne, but as he put it in the Preface, *"la connoissance"*: familiarity with him. This is the way he "knew" Etienne de la Boétie, the best friend he ever had; this is the way he wanted to be "known" by those of his readers who would give him their attention; this is the way he wanted to know himself.

He wanted many of his sentences to be understood alone, not as part of an argument, but as the direct, immediate expression of insights or feelings. Each such remark, each epigram, has its own kind of obviousness and therefore its own kind of appeal to his "judgment," as we noticed in a preceding chapter.[9] If each moment reveals us, or at least if certain moments can reveal us for what we are, so can each sentence or each phrase, if it is well molded and if it is carefully set off from the surrounding text so it jumps out at you. Self-contained *sententiae*, individual judgments, are at least as important — each on its own — as the conclusion the whole essay is trying to substantiate. Montaigne insists that we respect the autonomy of the moment, the distinctness of the individual phrase. For him such moments, such sentences, do not readily blend into wholes. Each is an organism: it contains within itself its own best excuse for being.

A man is not a logical unity; he is a set of individual moments spread out in the time between his birth and death. And if you would understand him you must see him in these terms. Montaigne believed that any man's most trivial actions reveal him. Do you want to know Alexander the Great? Watch the way he plays chess or the way he talks and drinks at table. Is every sinew of his soul strained? Or is he detached? And watch his reaction when he wins or loses. Watch these moments closely, and you get a deep insight into this man. In such moments, his habits and temperament appear plainly. And to construct airtight logical arguments on paper is to hide — not reveal — the variety and disparateness of these moments. As Northrop Frye puts it in his *Well-Tempered Critic*:

> The use of discontinuous aphorisms suggests to the reader that here is something he must stop and meditate on, aphorism by aphorism, that he must enter into the writer's mind instead of merely following his discourse. What one says is surrounded by silence, as though a hidden context of mental activity lay behind every formulated sentence.[10]

It is this mental activity, surrounding each aphorism like silence, that Montaigne is communicating to us in his baroque essays, rather than an impersonal topic and a tight argument that almost make us forget that we are thinking and feeling men living from moment to moment, changing, swerving. A tightly knit argument is a stiff mask over the face of the man who offers it. And Montaigne is not presenting a mold of the face that men artificially prepare to meet the faces that they meet. He is presenting a mold of his personality, down to its guts.

Finally, the reader of the *Essays* who spends much time looking for a single conclusion or "point" in every essay will miss a great deal and will often get very little for his pains. In "Of Some Verses of Virgil," for example, he will come up with a very thin generalization or he will get quite befuddled looking for an informative one. He will not enjoy a tree in that amorphous forest. You fail to read Montaigne well if you always look for an important unifying idea and try to explain away his individual *aperçus*. To spend much time looking beneath the surface for abstract unities is in some instances to miss the palpable substance of the *Essays*.

They are intended to give you an acquaintance with someone who loves "the poetic gait, by leaps and gambols.... Lord, what beauty there is in these lusty sallies and this variation, and more so the more casual and accidental."[11] For an accident is a mixture of circumstances, and a mixture named Michel is what he is portraying. As we have seen so often, the universe for Montaigne — and this includes his mind — is full of changes, uncertainties:

"I confess, I see nothing, even in a dream or a wish, that I could hold myself to; variety alone satisfies me, and the enjoyment of diversity, at least if anything satisfies me."[12]

The essays are iconic; and what they portray is a shifting part of a shifting world. His pen must move the way his feet move in this world. He is portraying a particular living man, not a neatly articulated, anonymous skeleton.

And yet, Montaigne *is* often out for bigger game than separate little maxims or reactions to maxims and stories. A man can have a direction, and an essay can have a *"bout d'un poil,"*[13] a bit of hair to hold it together. The wildest poetry sometimes needs some pressure, some discipline, in order for it to come forth strongly, as does air; an essay can have a burden to carry, a ford to probe, a quotation to turn around and examine. Montaigne himself tends to get sluggish and muddled when he has no sense of direction.[14] He is fully aware of the difference between spontaneity and wildness, change and chaos, diversity and utter disorder. And many of his essays communicate that awareness with their bit of hair.

Sometimes the title points out the shape or direction of an essay; at other times the title refers only to an unimportant occasion that happened to give rise to the essay (see "Of Some Verses of Virgil," in the Third Book). Sometimes an essay acquires what unity it has by a rich interplay between a dominant idea (like the idea of vanity as ignorance of one's limitations in "Of Vanity") and a large, overarching metaphor (like that of traveling in that same essay). But whether it be the title, an idea loosely related to the title, a metaphor, a quotation, or more than one, the ideas in a given essay may "follow one another, but sometimes it is from a distance, and look at each other, but with a sidelong glance." Montaigne is not simply careless, though he is usually free from overrestrictive plans.

Before turning to more special aspects of Montaigne's style, it would be useful to make one more point — a point implicit in this whole section. The *opposition* between a unified essay and a disunified one can be misleading. There are many sorts of order, many sorts of unity: there is the kind of unity and orderliness a whole essay can have, and there is the kind of orderliness an individual epigram or insight can have. Looked at from the point of view of the whole essay, Montaigne's writings can often be described as "disorderly"; but if we look at each epigram we often find a single, lucid view of the whole world or of a given subject.

What looks like disorder when one thinks of the essay as a whole becomes a set of separately revealing perspectives, each of which unifies its "subject." Montaigne said: "Each man bears the entire form of man's condition." Many of his separate epigrams do this; they are microcosms, revealing the world or some subject ordered in a little space. They are judgments "of universal scope," though they occupy a small space and may not fit into the other judgments of a given essay.

And so the whole argument of this section can be rephrased: there are two ways Montaigne used his judgment to give order to his mental life: through each individual epigram, and through a total essay made up of more or less loosely unified epigrams. He spoke in a moment, and he spoke in a more or less unified sequence of moments. And so in an important but loose sense of the word "order," epigrams as well as unified essays expressed the "order," the clarity and unity, of his judgment.

D. *The style of Montaigne*

WHEN Montaigne is in Paris he speaks like a Parisian, not like the Gascon he is.[15] When he was young and wrote Latin verse, each new production "clearly revealed the poet I had last been reading."[16] And now, he sees that some of his first essays *"puent un peu à l'estranger."*[17]

Montaigne does not try to destroy this tendency in himself, though he may shake it up a bit and weaken its hold on him. After all, he is not trying to reform man; he is trying to portray one, imitativeness and all. But Montaigne has other traits that have rendered his imitativeness harmless. One of them is his lack of memory. For instance, he tells us at the end of "A Consideration upon Cicero" that he simply forgets the steps of ceremony, the oft-repeated words and phrases that people use around him. Such fluent, rote language simply cannot come out of his mouth; he neither remembers them nor feels the desire to do so.

And this brings us to another trait that more than counterbalances his imitativeness: he has a way of talking, a way of acting, whether in Paris, Bordeaux, or his own castle, that is "of a form all my own," despite any tendencies to superficial imitation. When somebody is entering his castle or leaving it he is as barren of courtly language as a stump. A person entering his castle or approaching him in the streets of Paris can read his feelings right off, not through a haze of empty phrases.[18] His manner, no matter where he is, is "disorderly, abrupt, individual."[19] He stands at his door, or anywhere, not with the old, empty words on his lips, but with his own feelings in his heart. And he has a deep confidence that they will simply shine forth and be seen in their individuality, in their immediacy.

What happens when such a man is standing at the door of his home saying good-bye to someone he cares for deeply, but is unable to bow with a flourish or offer those fashionable, courtly long promises of eternal servitude and respect? What does he do to express his feelings when he can neither remember nor want to remember the monkey-tricks? He uses what he has, these eyes, these lips, this head, his own everyday words, with his own felt warmth residing in them. With these he speaks to his friend in a language not worn thin of meaning by mindless repetition, not impersonal by virtue of having been said carelessly by so many different persons, but a language intimately his own and abundantly clear to anybody interested in understanding it.

And what has he done with his face and with the language of everyday speech that has invested them with his own individual, personal meaning? Has he twisted that language or that face into shapes absolutely new, absolutely unheard of, and thereby individual? Hardly. On the contrary, he has used the same sorts of expression that men customarily use in such circumstances, and he is speaking plain, very unspectacular French. But what has happened to create *his* "style"? He has slightly varied, he has slightly altered, that face and that colloquial speech, stretched them and added to them. Perhaps he gives a little sigh; perhaps he withholds one and simply looks with a warmth deeper than gesture at the person he is addressing. Perhaps he utters a playful threat or a promise that both parties know will be kept. He has bent, by just a little, but enough, the shape of his face, the shape of his language, so that they fit the shape of his soul at that moment and so that the person he is addressing sees and knows this.

It is Montaigne's contention that the same sort of bending, the same sort of stretching, is what we do with language in our writing when we struggle to give it more weight, more penetration, more power to say something faithfully, fully, and freshly. It would not be wise to do so by making an ass of oneself with wild grimaces or unheard-of speech: Montaigne would not give language fresh "unaccustomed movements," as he puts it, by abandoning ordinary speech in favor of radical innovation.

Such innovation expresses and communicates only the asininity and self-consciousness of the innovator, and not the richness or individuality of his thought and feeling.

Montaigne summarizes this notion of slight but crucial changes by using one of his most frequently recurring metaphors — the travel metaphor. He had used it with strong effect in the essay "Of Vanity" and also at a crucial point in the "Apology," when he adjured the personage to whom he addressed the essay[20] to "stay on the highroad." In talking about linguistic style, as in talking about living-style, he uses the same figure: speaking of the ostentatious, imprudent innovators, he writes, "They are bold and disdainful enough not to follow the common road, but want of invention and want of discretion ruins them." All you can see in such people is an absurdly extreme originality that seeks not effective communication, but seeks only to "strut gorgeously in ... novelty."

We are back to the "Apology," to the theme of moderation, of the *juste mileu,* the golden mean between extremes, the recommendation that we walk upon the well-traveled road that lies between the extremes. But there is a new theme now implicit in the metaphor of following the common road: the road is wide; there is room for special ways of walking, for movements toward one extreme or the other, for individuality, and for changes within the life of the individual. If you look back at the "Apology" you will find that he never says that men must not change, that they must be rigid in their following of "usage." On the contrary, his whole theme there is mobility in all nature, man included. And though in his writings he sometimes falls into contradictions, this is one point he will never reverse. What he says in summary of the whole practical impact of the "Apology" is this: "Our faulty condition should make us behave more moderately and restrainedly in our changes."[21] We change everything that comes into our hands, just as our hands are changing. The point is that we must avoid the extremes, the wildness, the unruliness, that Montaigne found in his personal life before he wrote the *Essays,* and in public, religious differences of his time. Danger does not lie in change itself; it lies in a wild, vagabond imagination that leads us to changes which destroy the peaceful orderliness of our personal and social well-being and leaves us wandering and colliding outside of *"la route commune."* It is our lack of prudence that is dangerous. Absolute stability, if there were such a thing in nature, would be a death like no death we know, and Montaigne never advocates it or even envisages the possibility, either with respect to customs and institutions or with respect to language.

Of course, Montaigne tells us, in the language "used in the streets of France" many penetrating phrases and metaphors have long ago begun to lose their color with too much handling. Still, many of them have the right "savor" to somebody who has a "good nose." Here is that phrase we have encountered so often — the phrase that Montaigne loves to use for unpremeditated judgment, for choosing not "for reasons," but just because something feels right or smells right at the time, because something is obviously (*évidemment*) the case at the time.

Still, there are some deliberate moves one can make in this business of "stretching," "bending," or invigorating one's language. Montaigne tells us that when his French cannot capture what he is driving at, he sometimes turns to Latin. It should be remembered that it was as late as 1539, during the reign of Francis I, that the tribunals of France were instructed to replace their Latin with French; we are talking about a time when Latin was very close to the modern in the minds of educated men, and even in the minds of rough, soldierly men like Henry IV.

But Montaigne tells us of another way he uses to make his language more expressive of what he is, and this way indicates his esteem for laconic action:

"There is nothing that might not be done with our jargon of hunting and war, which is a generous soil to borrow from. And forms of speech, like plants, improve and grow stronger by being transplanted."[22]

He had used this metaphor of transplanting at the beginning of the essay "Of Books," in the Second Book, when talking about what he got from Latin and Greek authors.[23] There he had discussed the fact that he wanted to "confound" these quotations with his own words and thoughts, so that if you wanted to criticize Plutarch you would have to give him "a fillip on my nose," so closely would the plant and the new soil — Montaigne — be involved with each other. And the same holds in regard to transplanting the language of "hunting and war." He would make that language part of himself by changing it.

Montaigne always admired what he once described as language that is *"sec, bref, signifiant . . . masle et militaire."*[24] You will find, especially in the first Book of the *Essays,* but also elsewhere, many signs of Montaigne's admiration for action without verbosity, honor without long explanations, vigor, healthful out-of-door living, all those things that he associated with the military life and with hunting. The essay "Of Cannibals" is a good example of this. Despite his refusal to hunt and his hatred of fractricidal war, he saw in war and hunting, and in the language they used, many important virtues. Soldiers and hunters use a language whose metaphors and phrases are embedded in action, in suddenness, in a kind of heavy, male impetuosity. For them talking is for the sake of living, and not for the sake of talking alone, as it so often was in the parlors of France.

And the language of hunting and war is a bold-mouthed, even a coarse-mouthed, language from time to time. It is the language of men talking with men, and it deals with hidden parts of the body unashamedly, just as it deals with sex. Montaigne likes women in private,[25] but in public they are too afraid to talk about what they are not at all afraid to do in private — the sexual act, defecation, and such. They are not too sensitive to talk about killing or robbing or betraying, but they are too sensitive to talk about what they themselves know to be "natural ... necessary, and just."[26]

Montaigne hates this perpetual concealment of the natural and the right activities of human beings. When you are in the army, and you want to get up and piss, you get up, and if the occasion requires, you explain to your companion that you are going to do just that. If you are in the company of ladies, you say: "Pardon me; I'll be right back; I must talk to somebody in the next room." Or if you are not an out-and-out liar, you simply leave without saying anything about what you are going to do. You certainly never get up and say: "Pardon me, Madame; I am going to take a piss." At least you don't say this if you are in your right mind and want to remain in mixed society. To Montaigne this concealment of the truth is a perfect symbol[27] of language being used as if the bodily actions of its users were on one planet and the words on another. The fact is that bodily actions are the very life of language.

Montaigne can describe — with a quotation from Horace — his own penis as a "real flash in the pan,"[28] because it rises up with a little vigor about three times a week and manages to "bustle about and swagger with the same fierceness as if it had some great and proper day's work in its belly" when actually all it has is "one inch of wretched vigor" in it; the poor thing will be "too sudden"[29] as well. He can open "Of Vanity," one of his most ambitious essays, by comparing his own essays to the excrements of a certain gentleman he knew who "gave knowledge of his life only by the workings of his belly; you would see on display at his home a row of chamber pots, seven or eight days' worth." And then he can add without a break, "That was his study, his conversation; all other talk stank in his nostrils." That last touch is Montaigne, at least one aspect of him; and so is his whole easygoing comparison between the contents of those chamber pots and his own essays, which are "some excrements of an aged mind, now hard, now loose, and always undigested." But he can end that same essay with one paragraph (in Frame's translation)[30] that is as majestic in its vision and its language as any passage I have ever read.

Now, Montaigne is not simply trying to shock; he is not a boor. He is simply showing what he is and why he is that way. And in talking about concealed, natural actions he does more than try to violate hothouse sensibilities. He points out that in some cases, like that of love-making, half-concealments have a place, but only because they reveal more to our stimulated imaginations. He thinks that a Martial who turns up the skirts of Venus as high as her eyes, or any other man who insists on telling everything *without taste,* quite quickly "satiates and disgusts us."[31] No, again: lying concealment and perpetual coarse-mouthedness are the extremes which each man with a "good nose" must move between. As to Montaigne, his nose is rather that of a soldier than of a courtier.

Toward the end of the "Apology" Montaigne starts talking about philosophers who will turn a dozen somersaults in public, even without breeches, for a dozen olives, or who will stand on their heads on the table with their legs apart (in the age of togas), or who will fart or have farting contests with each other. When Montaigne does this, he does it because he feels like doing it, because his "good nose" lets his mind bring these things in for examples.

But he also brings them in because kinesthetic verbs, the words that display action, are his dear love. "My philosophy," he tells us, "is in action, in natural and present practice."[32] This is what he was thinking of when he wrote about those "lusty sallies," those delectable present moments in his writing.[33] Remember the great traveling metaphor in "Of Vanity," where he tells us that his pen and his feet go the same way. Look back at the passages that were quoted to show the way the word "essay" is used in his writings. The first talks about his judgment as "groping, staggering, stumbling, and blundering" and "bending under the load"

The Powers of Language

of books he has read. The second describes judgment as a tool for "sounding the ford from a good distance" while one stands on the shore. And in that same passage he speaks of his essays as taking each subject "to lick it, sometimes to brush the surface, sometimes to pinch it to the bone." An essay is for Montaigne usually a set of pictures of actions like a walk, a climb, or a probing.

Let me offer one more quotation: the last few sentences of the "Apology" in all the editions of it published during Montaigne's lifetime.

> To make the handful bigger than the hand, the armful bigger than the arm, and to hope to straddle more than the reach of our legs, is impossible and unnatural. Nor can man raise himself above himself and humanity; for he can see only with his own eyes, and seize only with his own grasp.
>
> He will rise, if God by exception lends him a hand; he will rise by abandoning and renouncing his own means, and letting himself be raised and uplifted by purely celestial means.

This is a summary of the "Apology" as surely as is any laborious conceptual analysis of it; no, more surely, more in the "style" of Montaigne, the man who loved the language of action as much as he hated the cruelty and killing that some men perpetrate with their actions. Here is an instance of how his eloquence is achieved by using metaphors involving silent action.[34] When he is not using such images, he is very often using transitive verbs to arouse the sensation of action in the reader, the feeling of spontaneous, vigorous, unashamed life.

Language as it appears on the printed page is a stable thing; it is not life, nor is it an image of life. It is only the movements and the shapes that the human mind experiences when confronted with that stable thing that makes it possible for piles of still, black ink on hard, white paper to become life or to become like life. Montaigne felt all this very strongly, and he used all his powers to embody in ink on paper the movements, sometimes patterned, sometimes random, of his mind. Control and spontaneity, pattern and variety, were the two kinds of naturalness he had found in antiquity[35] as well as in his own mental life. He would express them both, using kinesthetic metaphors, the language of war and hunting, sudden changes of direction in his ideas, and broad, unifying ideas. His was a way of thinking and feeling somewhere between "sleepy idleness" and "painful busyness," though closer to the latter because he was a physically active man. Montaigne said in his essay "Of Presumption,"

"I do not have my tools catalogued and arranged; and I know about them only after doing something."[36] If we would know him, if we would become acquainted with him as he is displayed in these essays of his mind, we should not try to make of him an "imaginary republic" whose powers are all labeled and precisely related to each other; we should let our thoughts move with his in their patterns and in their self-contained, individual patternlessness and then look back *"après l'effect,"* after the metaphors, after the sharp breaks between ideas, and after all the other expressive elements of his "style" have done their work. We should look back with the awareness that though we cannot catalogue all the powers he has exhibited in action, we are acquainted with them, the way a person becomes acquainted and intimate with another person in the progress of a friendship. There is much that one can say *"en proposition"* about Montaigne after one has read his essays, and there is much that Montaigne has said about his way of living, much that he has explicitly laid out *"en proposition,"* after he has seen himself in action and read his own words. But his judgment can be fully understood, at least the way Montaigne wanted us to understand it, only *"après l'effect,"* only after we have participated in the pace of his own thinking. And even then we shall not be able to give a precise, neat map of his soul, for it is not, it seems, a neat soul "at bottom" or anywhere else. It is a changing thing, only broadly describable, and it is as important to get to know it by acquaintance as it is by description. "Friendship" and "acquaintance" are deeply related terms in the thought of Montaigne; *"l'amitié"* and *"la connoissance,"* involve knowledge *"après l'effect,"* in action and after action.

In short, Montaigne *shows* us what he is and what he is not at least as much as he *tells* us *about* his judgment. With images of action, with mental jumps and zigzag motions, he shows us the abruptness, the mobility, the male, active force of his judgment. And he also shows us in the plainness of his vocabulary the respect he has for the "rule or prescription" of ordinary usage, of day-to-day life. He shows us both his unique self and what he feels to be the human condition in general. His essays are to a great extent iconic, as their Preface tells us: they portray a man (with both of these last words emphasized — a particular one, and man in general); they reveal him directly, not merely through abstract categories. They are essays of his mind, not merely descriptions of it. There are plenty of descriptions of his way of thinking in the *Essays*, but you read the *Essays* poorly if you do not see how much Montaigne's style reveals the man, how much Montaigne's way of talking reveals his mind. In the book you are now reading, I am primarily describing that mind; in *his* book he is presenting it more directly.

I do not mean to say that there is a sharp final distinction between showing and describing; but there is a useful distinction. When Montaigne tells the reader to notice his manner as well as his matter, his style as well as his subject matter, he is being most fully himself. He is a Humanist profoundly aware of the deep relationship between one's language and one's life. In this chapter we have emphasized his style, what he showed of himself in his language; in the next we shall be emphasizing the way of life he described and advocated. But manner and matter cannot be separated in the *Essays,* though they may be tentatively distinguished from each other for the sake of a more aware reading of this rich book. What the *Essays* boil down to is this: here is a certain man, impulsive within limits; he is one man, but also he is deeply involved, intermixed, with society and nature. This is what his language shows us; this is what his language also tells us.

PART IV

The Fruit of a Personal Philosophy

Chapter 7

The Scar of Montaigne

Montaigne called his age "a sick age,"[1] and sometimes he described France as a "worm-eaten and maggoty body,"[2] dead and decaying. In our first chapter we saw how full it was of fanaticism in the name of gentle Jesus, "dissimulation and lying"[3] in the name of truth (remember the King's secret), and bloodshed in the name of order. Now a man who believed that his judgment was an instrument for keeping him in good health had to take a stand vis-à-vis such an age. The stand Montaigne took was to draw a sharp distinction between his personal or private life and the maggoty body of which he was a citizen-part. But this distinction was not a separation: he would do whatever he could to relieve the public disorders of his time — disorders that were always threatening to hurt his own life. More, in the first essay of the Third Book (*"De l'utile et de l'honneste"*) he insisted that these two distinct aspects of his life remain distinct, but face each other often, judge each other. In this essay and elsewhere he insisted that he would judge the publicly useful by the standards of his own conscience (even though he knew that his conscience was born of habituation and temperament, not immaculately conceived in the Sovereign Good);[4] and he also insisted that his private life be judged for its public utility — within limits.

But the distinction between the public and the private is more important to Montaigne than any relationship between them: his main business in life was his own conduct, not the conduct of his nation; his judgment was able to take care of him, with luck — more able to do so than it was able to take care of his nation. This is one of the summary and basic insights of Montaigne's *Essays*. Consequently the distinction between the public and the private looms larger there than does any account of the relationship between the individual and the state. The purpose of this chapter is to explore Montaigne's reasons for making that distinction and in so doing to see what that distinction was.

A. Freedom, ease, and stability

MONTAIGNE's ruling qualities were a love of freedom and a love of ease.[5] And he felt that by "penetrating, intimate mortgages and commitments" in the public service he would allow his freedom and his ease of living to be destroyed. It is as simple as this: he sharply distinguished public life from his own private life in order to be free and at his ease. But this simplicity goes very deep: to the bottom of his personality and his philosophy.

He tells us in "Of Presumption" what we noticed in our first chapter, that he was raised *"d'une façon molle et libre,"* in a pleasant, orderly way, awakening to music, speaking only Latin, and suffering no punishment. His early education was, in short, an "easygoing" one, as he tells us in that same essay. And since education does so much to make us what we are, it made him "soft and useless for serving others, and no good for anyone but myself." It developed in him "a soul all its own, accustomed to conducting itself in its own way." It made him "extremely idle, extremely independent, both by nature and by art." That is, he was by temperament inclined to seek his own pleasure, and he was raised to do so; now having done much rationalizing after the fact of his upbringing and temperament,

> if I am not lured to it by some pleasure, and if I have any other guide than my own pure free will, I am good for nothing. For I have come to the point where except for health and life, there is nothing for which I am willing to bite my nails, nothing that I am willing to buy at the price of mental torment and constraint.

Now, these "ruling qualities," love of freedom and love of ease, amount to much the same thing for Montaigne. Freedom for Montaigne has nothing to do with the metaphysical puzzle as to whether or not all our choices are caused. Freedom for him involves both an absence of unpleasant, alien pressures from other individuals and a presence of easy, clear, rule-abiding courses of action. Freedom for him is not an absence of order or of rules; it is an absence of chaotic, external interference, and involves the easy guiding pressures of habit, of tradition. For Montaigne the deepest kind of slavery is the painful chaos of the human mind and heart — a chaos that consists in the absence of rules and the presence of painful external interference. A man is free if he does what pleases him, and doing this requires habituation or order so that he can accomplish what he wants. More, it requires not having a thousand external wills or a thousand unbridled desires pulling and pushing him in a thousand directions. Orderly, pleasant autonomy is freedom for Montaigne.

And such pleasing autonomy is for Montaigne present only in a private life, a life involved primarily in managing one's own affairs. A dedicated public life requires a kind of man "more obedient and suppler" than this person who all his life "had hardly anything to manage but my own affairs," as he puts it in "Of Presumption." And Montaigne has another trait, closely related to his laziness and love of liberty: he is not adroit, not agile, though he is the son of a physically and mentally nimble father. And his lack of adroitness is, again, "by nature and by art," something he was born with and raised with and also something he wants to retain. As he says in "Of Presumption," "Even as in roads I like to avoid the sloping and slippery sides, and cast myself into the beaten part, even the muddiest and boggiest, from which I cannot sink lower, and seek security there." The old and the stable pleases him, and (as he says also in "Of Presumption"), "The worst thing I find in our state is instability." Mentally and physically he is "thick-set" and stubborn, likes to follow his accustomed ways; and he can find all sorts of reasons that will defend this basic trait of his, like the dangers and difficulties involved in radical changes at this time in France's history.

But a committed public life is the enemy of all these traits in his personality: it destroys his freedom, his ease, and his stability. It requires obedient, sacrificial, supple men.

For instance, it requires that a man live in a realm of language and thought where simplicity is as difficult as it is rare. The public man must live not primarily according to himself, but according to the views of many other individuals and many factions. Others bring him problems, and others have various interests in their solutions. The committed public servant is like a man walking in a crowd: he cannot readily walk in a straight line to his own goals; he must step aside here, stop there, pull in his elbows, all according to those other wills and physical presences he serves.

His will leans so heavily upon the wills of so many other people that he must move the way they let him move, and he must also see the same act from a thousand points of view other than his own. He must subtilize, fragment his own plain language to accommodate all these points of view. Once[6] in his dealings in public affairs (these lines had been written between 1585 and 1588, after Montaigne had finished his second term as Mayor of Bordeaux) he tried to use his own "ideas and rules for living," plain and incircumspect as they were, for public purposes. He found them "inept and dangerous for such matters."[7] The public service required a language more subtle and more supple than the language of private life. In private life a man decides to do something because he thinks it is right; and though there may be some complications in his decision, the decision is mainly a matter of his own life. In private life he finds it easier to think in broad, plain moral and expediential terms than when so many other lives are directly involved. We have seen where the subtilization of language, the too great refinement of plain speech, leads us. It leads us away from an orderly kind of thought where the criteria for making decisions are comparatively plain and obvious into a way of thinking where there are no criteria for deciding what is right or what is wrong. It leads us to disorder. In private life it is simply wrong to lie or cheat or kill. In public life, well, consider de l'Estoile's remarks on the rightness of eating children, or consider the "justifications" leaders and others committed heart and soul to public positions found for the St. Bartholomew's Day Massacre of 1572, or consider America's dropping of the atomic bomb on Hiroshima and the hopeless debates about its "rightness." The ties that bind society together, the persuasive communications between men, are snapped, and we are left with bickering, misunderstanding, pain. The plain highroad of speech that each man can walk — with difficulties, true, but with comparatively manageable ones — is pulverized for the completely dedicated public servant; he must walk in the thicket. Montaigne is too jealous of his freedom, of his ease, and of his own accustomed ways to walk in thickets.

B. *The two laws of man*

BUT given his predilections for freedom, ease, and stability, how will he "stay out of it"[8] as far as public life is concerned, and how will he stay out of it without cutting himself off from it completely? How will he arrange it so that his private life continues to face and judge the public life of his nation? What does it mean to avoid *intimately* engaging one's thinking in public life, either as a follower or a leader?

He will do all this by offering to his sovereign only "limited and conditional services." He will not enter into public duties immoderately, feverishly. He will keep his own conscience and his own desires "a law unto themselves."[9] His actions will follow the public law and usually follow what the sovereign deems useful to society. But — and here is where the "limited and conditional services" come in — when an action threatens to compromise his conscience he will not let a feverish attachment to his sovereign melt that conscience into a different shape. He will avoid the act without engaging the sovereign or anybody else in hopeless argumentation about his position. And if the public utility plainly demands it for the survival of the state, why, he may then do it — but he will try his best to avoid it, will call the act "wrong" until the end, and will remember its wrongness *as* wrongness, unrationalized, unsubtilized, until the day he dies. In this way his "will and desires" will remain a "law unto themselves," and his bodily actions will continue to receive *their* law "from public regulation."

Bitterness, feverishness of any sort, these are a sign that we are confusing and indeed destroying these two "laws":

"We must not call 'duty,' as we do every day, an inner bitterness and asperity that is born of private interest and passion; nor 'courage' a treacherous and malicious conduct.... It is not the cause that inflames ...it is...self-interest."[10]

Coolness in and toward public action: this is Montaigne's preferred way of avoiding this particular mixture that adulterates the human heart, or at least would adulterate his conscience in his own time. Montaigne got along comfortably (and this word which summarizes all his "reasons" for privacy in one notion is the one he uses — *"commodément"*) with both of the two hostile parties by keeping his "most personal manner" (*forme plus mienne*) in the negotiations, amidst the divisions and the subdivisions that were tearing France to pieces in his day.[11] He always made it clear to both sides that here stood "a tender and green negotiator, who would rather fail in my mission than fail to be true to myself." And both sides, because his principles remained unsubtilized, unrationalized, incircumspect — in fact, crude and unpolished — both sides knew where he stood. He was a Catholic born and raised, "attached to the general and just cause only with moderation and without feverishness." There have not been many, Montaigne says, who have, like him, "passed between one party and another with less suspicion and more favor and privacy [*privauté*]."¹² He was open, plain-spoken, in stating his reasons for doing or not doing something. He was constantly revealing his *"naiveté,"* constantly revealing the broad, plain lines of his conscience. Cool toward the public issues, open in revealing his own stand on these issues, he preserved the *naiveté* of his moral language, of his moral judgment, and he preserved his own special usefulness to the princes of his time and to his nation.

To Montaigne it is obvious that we "have a soul that can be turned upon itself; it can keep itself company; it has the means to attack and the means to defend, the means to receive and the means to give."¹³ It is by using these means that Montaigne wishes to keep his conscience crude and plain.

And as for the mayoralty of Bordeaux, which involved his passing between two parties that were both powerful there at the hub of the civil wars of France, he says that the Mayor and himself have always been two "with a very clear separation."¹⁴ The man would continue to think and talk in naïve, gross, unpolished moral categories and would continue to act coolly. He had heard it said that we must forget ourselves for our neighbor, "that the individual was not to be considered at all in comparison with the general." But this he would not follow, out of laziness, out of a desire for freedom, but also out of a conviction that this way lay moral and social chaos, the breakdown of our customary ordinary language and morality. In keeping his language and his morality intact he was able to be a Mayor "without departing one nail's breadth from myself, and to give myself to others without taking myself from myself."¹⁵ In short, he was able to perform his public duties while keeping his conscience not only intact but also *in the open* for all those who would look at it.

After all, what is required of us in discharging public duties is our actions, not our passions. We are *doing* something for the public; it is not necessary for us to fragment ourselves and *be* a many-headed being for the many-headed public. Indeed, passion, violence of feeling, Montaigne feels,¹⁶ palsies men's hands, fills their minds with impatience and unnecessary frenzy, and makes them suspicious of the people, both allies and opponents, with whom they deal. It is a kind of intoxication, and like intoxication it is murderous of efficient performance, murderous of useful, orderly action, and murderous of relations between man and man.

And so, because he wants to preserve his freedom and his ease as well as the orderly working of the state, Montaigne will be cool, self-centered, often stepping back into this "back-shop" all his own to face his conscience on his own terms. But the basic reason Montaigne gives for living this way is that such a way of life is easy for *him,* free according to his notion of freedom. His job on this planet is to live a life that is excusable to others, hopefully even useful; but most importantly, his job is to live a life that pleases him. And a crude, incircumspect conscience pleases him, is full of freedom and ease for him; and it is also excusable, even useful, to others in wild times like his.

In every government, Montaigne is convinced, there are duties which are vicious; there are vices, like murder in cold blood, that "are employed for sewing our society together."[17] In every government men are needed who will ignore or annihilate their consciences for the public welfare and will do so without a qualm, swiftly, like a butcher or a soldier, and without a backward glance. Montaigne gives warning to every man he serves: he is not one of these.

The easy way for him is to "follow common usage in language, which distinguishes between things useful and honorable, so that it calls dishonorable and foul some natural actions that are not only useful but necessary."[18] But not only is it easier to follow common usage in language, to obey one's conscience; it is also "less hazardous." Violate your conscience, and you risk punishment at the hands of your commander, who may distrust you for your lack of honor, may indeed choose to sacrifice you as a shifting, pliable person in order to expiate his own feelings of guilt. Exactly this happened, says Montaigne,[19] in the case of Mohammed II, who had his brother, a rival to his power, executed by having one of his officers pour water down his throat so fast that he choked. Then, in expiation of his guilt, Mohammed willingly gave the murderer into the hands of the dead man's mother, who in the presence of Mohammed had the murderer's stomach opened and his heart torn out of his warm body and thrown to the dogs. Montaigne has found it not only easier for him but less risky to refuse to violate his own conscience; he has found that he is always understood, always respected, or at least never suspected of dangerous opportunism.

It is important to see that Montaigne is *not* saying: "I shall never violate my conscience for the public welfare." He is too much aware of the pressures that especially a sick and strife-ridden state can put on a man.

All he is saying is: do everything possible to save your conscience, to avoid doing the act that will violate it. He may act against his conscience when the public utility of that violation "is very apparent and very important."[20] But he will do everything he can to avoid doing the act or to avoid letting it be done; and when it is done he will use no "pretext of reason"[21] and will not call his act honorable. No. Public utility in such cases will always be one thing, honor quite another, which will never be confused with it, at least in Montaigne's mind. And this eternal refusal will be his last stand in defense of his personal ways of thinking. All he will be able to say about such an action is that it was useful, nay, "very important." He will never say or think that it was honorable or right. Here is where he will draw the line; here is where he will maintain the "clear separation" between his own "will and desires" and his public actions. Here is where he will maintain the integrity of his conscience, though it be painful to do so. In the long run it is the easiest way for a man like him, who finds his ease and his freedom under a "rule or prescription" that is intimately his own. His hand may be, perforce, enlisted in such public services, but never his soul.

Now, Montaigne is not presuming to speak for all men: *his* conscience has inertia; *his* personality is such that when he violates either gradually or dramatically the dictates of this conscience, he loses his valuable ease and freedom; others may — indeed, for the successful operation of a state, some people *must* — have pliable, blind, or non-existent consciences. But for Michel Montaigne "there is no remedy. I frankly tell them my limits." And this is where Montaigne stands, not without some self-congratulation, of course, but certainly without bitterness toward the other sorts of persons or toward the governments that find vicious measures necessary.

Well, at least most of the time in the *Essays* Montaigne displays no bitterness toward the "others." At the end of the crucial essay on the useful and the honorable he bitterly attacks those who would identify personal honor with public utility. Talking about Caesar, he says:

I abominate the rabid exhortations of that uncontrolled soul:
> When weapons flash, no pious sentiments, though you confront your fathers, you must feel; No, slash their venerable faces with the steel.

Let us take away from wicked, bloody, and treacherous natures this pretext of reason. Let us abandon this monstrous and deranged justice.

Here he speaks not simply as one particular person with his sort of sturdy conscience and his sort of temperamental attachment to that conscience;

here he speaks for all men: whoever uses the words of morality as pretexts covering up vicious deeds — whoever violates a way of thinking developed in his childhood and calls that violation by sweet, empty moral names — is as "monstrous and deranged" as the terms he uses. Such a man's unruly imagination is masquerading under words (like "justice") which when plainly used keep us at peace with ourselves and with each other; and such moral terms are being used by "that uncontrolled soul" for doing the publicly necessary in the name of the honorable. Toward this, Caesar's betrayal of conscience by cruel fanaticism, Montaigne can show no forbearance, no forgiveness. There was too much of it happening in his own day, destroying France and Frenchmen, destroying men's bodies and men's orderly minds. In this outburst of bitterness against Caesar's words, Montaigne avoids acknowledging the public utility of such fanaticism as far as making good soldiers is concerned; and by not even mentioning this utility, he reiterates his conviction that public utility is still one thing and personal goodness or personal honor quite another. His feelings here toward those who subvert conscience are different from what they usually are: they are bitter, not forbearing; categorical, not local or based upon his own temperament. But the point he is making is still the same: conscience and public utility are different things, and we confuse them at our peril. Elsewhere he said *he* would not confuse them, being the kind of person he is; here he is saying: let no man confuse them, neither Caesar nor anyone else.

But again, the differences are minor; the main point is the same in all passages about conscience and public utility. And besides, Montaigne in the passage I have quoted opens with the first person singular, "I abominate...." He has thereby shown us how he is aware that he, one particular man, is speaking up for himself, for his own views. We cannot expect him always to treat his own point of view *simply* as one among many, especially when the issue is fanaticism, the violation of man's language, of man's thought, of man's feelings, and of man's very flesh and blood, a massive violation that lasted throughout his lifetime and that was always happening nearby.

C. *Mens sana in corpore sano*

BUT more should be said about Montaigne's reasons for not dedicating his soul to the public weal and for not being "nonchalant about what lies at our feet, what we have between our hands, what most concerns our use of life," as he puts it in "Of Presumption." What has been said thus far can be looked at in a somewhat different way; as we were reminded at the beginning of this chapter, Montaigne felt that his judgment was an instrument for keeping his "health." In a society like his (he often leaves it open whether this applies to all societies or not) total commitment to public service would undermine his health, and so his judgment tells him to abstain from such service.

He had memories of his father, the former Mayor of Bordeaux:

> I remembered in my boyhood having seen him old, his soul cruelly agitated by this public turmoil, forgetting the sweet air of his home, to which the weakness of years had attached him long since, and his household and his health; and truly heedless of his life, which he nearly lost in this, engaged for them in long and painful journeys.[22]

Montaigne admired this "kindly and public-spirited soul," but from a distance. When, after a more than token refusal to take the job of Mayor of Bordeaux, Montaigne addressed the *jurats* or municipal council of that city, he warned them that he would not let the public affairs of the city "weigh so heavily on my will as their affairs and their city had formerly done on him."[23] Some men are willing to live in the market-place in the service of the community. Some men are willing to sacrifice the peace and freedom of their private lives for the good of society. In fact, if you look at most of the precepts we learn by heart in our history books and from our parents, you will find that they "take this course of pushing us out of ourselves."[24] Alas, these are wasted on Michel the son. He shrugs them off his shoulders by noticing that the wise men who make history "preach things as they serve, not as they are." Let them attach *themselves,* let them mortgage *their* very souls, to public utility.

Montaigne will grant and, indeed, will insist in his essays, as in his actions in sixteenth-century France, that "he who lives not at all unto others, hardly lives unto himself." The rules or prescriptions of society are our rules or prescriptions, as far as language, as far as law, as far as the institutions we were raised in are concerned; and if we fail to give them allegiance we fail ourselves as well as them. We fail ourselves not only in the sense that our disorderly imaginations take the place of plain language and conscience, but also in the sense that we contribute by our neglect to the destruction of those institutions that keep us living in a peaceful community. Both inwardly and outwardly to betray or neglect society is to betray or neglect ourselves.

But the fact remains, at least for Montaigne, that "the main responsibility of each of us is his own conduct; and that is what we are here for."[25] Any man who abandons "healthy and gay living of his own to serve others thereby" takes, to Montaigne's taste, "a bad and unnatural course." The substantial goods, the real goods, the natural goods, are the goods that one's health of mind and body offers, at least for such a man as Montaigne.

And so Montaigne will lend a hand, his coolly considered actions, to the public, but not his heart or his guts or his mental and physical repose. And he will not only part company from, but he will also pity those who would not distribute their money to others, but who give most of the time of their lives to others.[26] Here, he says, where avarice would be "really" useful to us, we are sacrificially generous. The soldier climbing the wall and risking his life and the soldier on the other side passionately eager to hold out against him (while leaders on both sides are relaxing over a glass of wine) — these phenomena are as deplorable and sadly humorous to Montaigne as the pedant with the runny nose and bleary eyes coming out of his office at midnight who has given up the joys and the health of living to make a pedantic point to the learned public. Montaigne had a friend who, in working for his prince, "nearly drove himself out of his mind by too passionate attention and devotion to the affairs of ... his ... master."[27] But the prince, being a friend to himself and solicitous of his own well-being — as well as of the well-being of his country — maintained a "great nonchalance and freedom" throughout the same dangerous and complicated affairs. Montaigne finds only admiration in his heart for the prince and no admiration at all for the gentleman, Montaigne's friend, who had enslaved himself body and soul and had destroyed his own health for a cause he could have handled better if he had remained self-possessed.

Montaigne once heard that as Mayor of Bordeaux he had been accused of pursuing his duties "too weakly and with a languishing zeal," and he says that these rumors are not far from the truth. But this is the nature of the limited and conditional services he gives to the public. And he summarizes his attitude frankly and with a touch of irony as follows: "Certainly, had an occasion arisen, there is nothing I would have spared for their service. I bestirred myself for them just as I do for myself."[28] If he had been forced by unavoidable public necessity he would have given anything for the welfare of the people of Bordeaux; fortunately he was not forced into self-sacrificial actions on their behalf. As it was, he tried to keep peace in a turbulent city with as much assiduity (but not a whit more) as he exercised in keeping peace in his own private life. As Mayor of Bordeaux, he would abandon the subject that was dragging his private self onto the stage, and he would do so as soon as possible. He is one of those who can avoid passions much more easily than moderate them, once their claws are in.[29]

We have witnessed this avoidance-tactic in Montaigne's way of life on cognitive matters, and now we are witnessing it in practical matters. The great scholar Villey has said[30] that Montaigne discovered *la diversion* late in his development. An awareness of his deep Scepticism and of what Scepticism is shows that this is not the case.[31] Just as he would avoid an Assertive imagination on matters of truth, he would avoid that same *"desreiglement de nostre fantasie"*[32] in matters of everyday and public action, especially if that imagination endangered his own health of mind and body.

There is a story (whose main source is a letter by Montaigne himself, dated July 30, 1585) about the conclusion of his services as Mayor of Bordeaux. There was a plague in that city at the time, and Montaigne turned down an invitation to go back to it to help inaugurate his successor's term of office. Commentators in the nineteenth century were appalled at this refusal to be courageous in the public service. But Montaigne's action was quite plainly in line with his solicitude for his own health, except when the public necessity *unavoidably* demanded sacrifice. And public necessity was by no means involved in a ceremony inaugurating a new Mayor's term of office. This "coolness" to a "duty" which would jeopardize his health and which was not plainly "important" for the public welfare, far from being an exception to anything Montaigne has ever said about public service and private welfare, is a striking and exact example of everything he has ever said on these subjects. A man must have, he believed, a friendship for himself, and this is his primary obligation, *except* when the public welfare is quite plainly and importantly at stake; then he must bow to it, but only then. It should be noticed here that Montaigne was a vigorous, alert Mayor of Bordeaux. This also is consistent with his words on the public utility.

Just as it may be said that the unruly, "vagabond" imagination of man is what Montaigne is trying to avoid by eschewing contentious claims about universal or public Truth as well as by evading too long and too deep an involvement in public actions, so it may be said — speaking roughly — that what he seeks by this avoidance is health. Health for Montaigne, whether it be the health of the individual or the health of the nation, is one of the overarching metaphors of the *Essays* and one that he uses as frequently in referring to the condition of France with its "diseases," its "symptoms" of those diseases, and its "public death" as he does in referring to the condition of the mind and body of the individual. He even talks about the *"plus sain"*[33] of the parties, implying in the context that he is neither of the feverish League nor of the feverish Huguenots.

Health for Montaigne is essentially moderation, the avoidance of extremes by means of "maintaining my accustomed state without disturbance.... I believe nothing more certainly than this: that I cannot be hurt by the use of things that I have been so long accustomed to."[34] Moderation that avoids feverish fanaticism on the one hand and inhuman and unrealistic indifference on the other, like a body that is neither feverish nor frozen — moderation that comes from avoiding wild departures from accustomed ways — is crucial to all the reasons we have been examining for Montaigne's withdrawal. Basically for Montaigne it is the images of our overwrought brains that have endangered the health of individuals, parties, and nations. The admiration he had for the cannibals — despite, *not ignoring,* the horror of their acts in eating their fellow men — was an admiration for direct, plain, unsubtle living, for living without infinite refinements and without consequent arbitrariness of language and thought. These men sought to preserve their health of mind and body, rather than involving themselves in the verbal niceties and brutalities of civilized men. They lived and died strongly, grossly, in big, broad outlines, in full awareness of the exigencies of life around them. Their way was not Montaigne's way, but their way was in many ways healthier than the unruly way Frenchmen were living in Montaigne's century.

And so Montaigne's reasons for retreating to home truths and to a predominantly private life amount to one: when our passionate imagination blurs or destroys the plain (what Sceptics called "evident") facts of public utility and personal well-being, we lose our health, as men and as nations of men:

"Health is a precious thing, and the only one, in truth, which deserves that we employ in its pursuit not only time, sweat, trouble, and worldly goods, but even life; inasmuch as without it life comes to be painful and oppressive to us."[35]

And health essentially involves the customary, peaceful, easy working of man and the state. All of this Montaigne saw writ large in the events of his day, but he saw it inscribed also in his own *"conditions et humeurs."*

D. *The scar*

MONTAIGNE's reasons for drawing a clear line between public and private life may be looked at from still another point of view, one often suggested, sometimes discussed at length in this book: his Scepticism, that is, the doubting or negative aspect of his Scepticism (we have seen that Scepticism has another, more positive pole, to which the other reasons given in this chapter have some relevance). From this point of view, Montaigne would take his private life most seriously not because he chose to do so for reasons of freedom, ease, integrity, or health in general; he would concentrate on his private *"arrière-boutique"* (as he calls it in "Of Solitude") because his personality in combination with his Sceptical philosophy made it *impossible* for him to be such a committed figure. For such as him, public affairs are full of doubt, and decisions concerning them leave (as he puts it in "Of Presumption")

> ... a fine field open for vacillation and dispute:
> As when an even scale with equal weights is pressed,
> Neither side rises, neither falls; it stays at rest.

Of course, all this is another way of talking about the disorder involved in thinking about the public weal in any but a traditional, conservative way. But in noticing the role doubt plays in Montaigne's choice of the private as against the committed public life, we see how deeply rooted this choice is in Montaigne's thoughts on the nature and limitations of human judgment. And we see more: we see how deeply these thoughts are mixed in with Montaigne's own *"conditions et humeurs,"* his own personality. When we see that doubt is at once a philosophic principle for Montaigne and a personality-trait, we see clearly just what it means to have an explicitly personal philosophy, expressing a local mixture, and we see this in the form of a key doctrine of Montaigne's personal philosophy, the defense of a private way of living.

Again we turn to the crucial essay "Of Presumption," in the Second Book. Toward the end of it, a couple of pages before his remarks on "judgment" or "sense" which we have discussed at some length in our chapter on that subject,[36] we find an interesting passage. One day, he tells us, he saw King Francis II of France presented with a self-portrait which another king, René of Sicily, had drawn, and Montaigne asked himself: if René could draw his own portrait with a pencil, why could not he, Michel, draw his with a pen? Now the exact reasons and timing involved in his deciding to write essays of himself as a self-portrait are still matters of scholarly debate, but the fact that his *Essays* were in the end written as such a portrait and not as a landscape of universal truth is a certainty to which much of this book attests and which is contested, as far as I know, by no scholar.

And so these essays are a self-portrait. Right after asserting this, he goes on to say: "So I do not want to forget this further scar . . .: irresolution, a most harmful failing in negotiating worldly affairs." And then he adds that he does not know how to make a decision in *"entreprinses doubteuses."* In such affairs Petrarch's Sonnet 135 applies to him: "Nor yes, nor no, sounds in my inmost heart." In such affairs he can follow decisions others make; he cannot make them himself. Then follows a long statement which (1) summarizes the Scepticism of the "Apology" in a little space (balance-scales, doubt, and all), and (2) shows that his scar has to do with political or public affairs in particular. It is here in *"affaires politiques"* that Machiavelli or anyone else can state a solid argument that will still produce "answers, rejoinders, replications, triplications, quadruplications, and that infinite web of disputes." Here reason shows itself to be a "two-edged and dangerous sword" in even the best of hands — even in the hands of a Socrates. Justifications on all sides are as plentiful as blackberries in season.

In making political decisions, Montaigne says, "I keep doubt within myself," and when necessity demands that he make a choice, either he will cast dice and abandon himself to fortune and to the slight inclinations or circumstances that may sway his mind into a decision, or he will simply follow the old ways of doing things. In neither case will he endanger the whole fabric of society by trying to make a radical improvement. But he prefers not to undergo the pain and confusion of having to make such decisions; he prefers to leave such "uncertain choice" to "some man who is more sure of his opinions and wedded to them than I am to mine, whose foundations and grounds I find slippery."

How familiar all this is to anyone who has studied the "Apology"!

He is still using his Scepticism to defend a private way of life — the way of life of a passive follower. But now he is speaking far more personally than he usually does in the "Apology." Here he is making Sceptical doubt on political matters a plainly visible part of his portrait; it is not an impersonal epistemological doctrine, but a scar on his face; irresolution on important political matters becomes not merely a generally plausible position, as it is in the "Apology," but a way of living characteristic of Michel de Montaigne in particular. There must be others, born political leaders, who are decisive, resolute; *they* would violate their consciences and their thinking for the public good. Michel de Montaigne is not one of these.

But just how impersonal or "epistemological" is the "Apology"? Here is the most ambitious "proof" Montaigne ever produced, and yet notice this paragraph from it:

> My behavior is natural.... When the desire to tell it seized me, and when, to make it appear in public a little more decently, I set myself to support it with reasons and examples, it was a marvel to myself to find it, simply by chance, in conformity with so many philosophical examples and reasons. ... A new figure: an unpremeditated and accidental philosopher!

This is a Sceptic's sort of irony. He notices that everything he asserts in this "public" essay is a rationalization, a special way of revealing what he is, his behavior, his *"meurs."* In the essay "Of Presumption" he will be more explicit and tell us that he is by temperament and condition a follower, a man reluctant to take the initiative in changing public matters. But here in the "Apology" he says much the same thing in broader terms: when he tried to articulate and render plausible his way of thinking and acting — his *"conditions et humeurs"* — he found in Scepticism a method. And elsewhere in world literature he found many ideas that would rationalize his personal incapacity to make public decisions. What a novelty — or is it? — a philosopher whose arguments do not spring from The Truth, but from an accidental confrontation of his own behavior or personality with a lot of classical texts!

What Montaigne shows in that little passage in the "Apology" is that he never left behind his awareness that claims to knowledge — even claims to doubt concerning knowledge — are in the end personal claims, whatever else they may be as well, and no matter how broad, how universal they may look. All his arguments in the "Apology" (marvelously!) support his way of life, give his scar a publicly plausible shape. And that scar even shows up in his domestic life: "I make little choice at table, and attack the first and nearest thing, and I change reluctantly from one flavor to another." The more you study the *Essays* the more you find similarity between the behavior of the man who wrote them and the beliefs or "philosophy" of that man. And Montaigne's awareness of that similarity is exactly what he warned us about in his Preface, where he said that he is presenting us with a personal portrait, not a public truth. This is exactly what the word "essay" means: a way of revealing a man's mind. And all this is beautifully exemplified in the essay "Of Presumption," where the conclusion of an elaborate argument appears as a scar on Montaigne's own face.

The point of all this is that he was using arguments, personal descriptions, everything he could get his hands on, to reveal himself for what he was. He was presenting no claim to The Truth about public matters, either theoretical or practical; he was presenting himself as a man in many postures, in many situations or encounters, all of them *his,* Michel's, with his name on them.

And so, like everything else Montaigne defends, a private way of life — one devoted to his own health primarily and to the health of his nation secondarily — has in the end no justification more persuasive than this: Montaigne prefers it, in fact requires it, being the kind of person he is; and he can find lots of "philosophical examples and reasons" to rationalize his personal requirement. His defense and description of the private life are parts of his self-portrait, aspects of a personal philosophy.

Chapter 8

Personal Philosophy and Privacy

M<small>ONTAIGNE</small>'s *apologia* for privacy crystallizes his personal philosophy. In it his general beliefs about judgment, language, custom, and nature get a specific meaning and application. Here his particular personality (for instance, his love of "freedom" and "laziness") transforms those general beliefs into a program of action, a way of living, a way appropriate to a man like him living in times like his.

But if privacy has this important function in the *Essays,* it must be understood for what it is and not confused with other notions somewhat like it. The word "privacy" has many sorts of usages or meanings, and if we would see clearly the practical upshot of Montaigne's personal philosophy, we in the twentieth century must distinguish Montaigne's use of the words *"privé"* or *"particulier"* from other uses adjacent to it.

A. Absolute privacy

I<small>N</small> twentieth-century philosophic circles it has become fashionable to speak of the "privacy"[1] of human awareness. The word is used to refer to the unavoidable, absolute isolation of one person's experience from everybody else's experience. This way of using the word "private" is comparatively new, but the idea it expresses is quite old. From Protagoras and the Sophists through Plato, Descartes, the British Empiricists, and Kant up to present-day philosophers, men have defended, or tried to refute, the belief that each person is fundamentally, irretrievably walled up within his own consciousness. In twentieth-century philosophy, when we defend a "private world" we ask such questions as "Are there other minds?" "Is there an external world?" and "Is there communication between minds?" And we need philosophers, so the story goes, to help us cross this abyss or to help us get along without trying to cross it.

In the *Essays* Montaigne says things like *"Moy, je tiens que je ne suis que chez moy."*[2] And at the end of the "Apology" he says, "We have no communication with being." Elsewhere[3] he talks about the fact that "our soul must play its part, it is at home, within us, where no eyes penetrate but our own" and "Strangers see only the results and outward appearance . . . they do not see my heart, they see only my countenance."[4] But in their context these statements *never* mean that in principle, forever, we cannot communicate with each other. *"Parfaicte communication"* can occur between dear friends, as it did between Montaigne and La Boétie (see the essay "Of Friendship"); and degrees of good communication do occur, as we have been seeing in our chapters on language. The success of communication depends on, among other things, whether we stay within the "rule or prescription" of some custom-sanctioned language.[5] The choices men make and the accidents of circumstance determine just how much communication there is between men. But the main point we should notice is that for Montaigne the question one addresses oneself to is not *whether* communication can occur, but *how we can go about making it better*. As has been suggested, his problems are practical, not metaphysical or purely theoretical. The solutions to his problems pay off in actions, not in metaphysical systems or detailed epistemological analyses.

When he says, "I exist only in myself," he means that he is trying to take care of himself, that he can keep secrets or often avoid contact with certain other people, and that he can use his own judgment without leaning mindlessly upon other people or upon books (remember his friend who could not tell whether he had an itchy backside unless he looked up "itchy" and "backside" in the dictionary). When he talks about a soul where "no eyes penetrate but our own" he is not saying that we have thoughts that cannot be communicated to others, though those thoughts be clear; in our chapters on language we saw how intimately one's own thoughts are involved with common language for him: if one has clear thoughts in mind one can communicate them. If you have it in you, it can come out. And so when he talks about strangers seeing only "the results and outward appearance" he is not saying that all men are forever cut off from him; he is saying that it takes intimacy, deep, persisting friendship, choice and happy circumstance, to bring about communication of any profound sort. He is also saying that quite often these conditions do not obtain, and we keep feelings and thoughts to ourselves. Whether there are "universals" that haunt two minds (or a mind and an object) and make communication or knowledge possible never concerns

Montaigne. For him there is only the plain fact that sometimes we manage to understand things and get our thoughts and feelings across and at other times we do not. Indeed, as we have so often noticed, when you get so "deep and subtle" about human communication and knowledge that you are talking about metaphysically separate worlds and universals, you create squabbles and misunderstandings that destroy the communication you were trying to explain.

As for Montaigne's statement that "we have no communication with being," the main point of this and other such remarks in the "Apology" and elsewhere is that the hidden "essence" of things around us is something we had better not get into arguments about, since we do not seem to be equipped to settle such arguments. It is important for an understanding of his vision of man and the world to see that according to him we are parts of a world, and this involvement with the world around us is obvious if we do not fuddle it by following our vagabond imaginations. We are involved in this world by birth and through our need for material sustenance. And habituation in its various forms — language, custom, education — helps bind us to our fellow men.

There is a plain relationship between the creatures of this world: the relationship of action. We are active creatures trying to find the best and longest lives possible in a world of other such creatures. In such a universe, wherein the mind of man is an instrument that obtains for him security and contentment when he is lucky and it is working well, the notion of an absolutely isolated consciousness is an irrelevancy, not even something to be attacked.

In some ways Montaigne is an early Pragmatist, a precursor of Peirce, James, and Dewey, a proto-Darwinian thinker to whom action, successful striving for survival and satisfaction, is the highest, the main upshot and content of mentality. Ideas for him are made clear and life is abundantly lived not in isolation from the human or non-human world around us, but in an active give-and-take (what Dewey called "doing and undergoing") with this world.

B. Introspection

Nor is Montaigne that first cousin of the isolated mind, the "introspectionist" thinker. Some of his remarks, if taken out of context, can mislead one into thinking that he practiced "introspection," that he "looked into" himself in a way analogous to the way the psychologist Titchener and his followers observed their own "mental contents." Montaigne could say things like "We have a soul that can be turned upon itself."[6] But the *"âme contournable"* he was talking about was not the passive observer of an interior movie-show of sense perceptions and feelings. It was not a reporter who simply records, describes, and categorizes what he sees while carefully avoiding the "stimulus error" and trying hard to avoid confusing his own artificial, scientific language with the language of common sense or physics. When he talked about a "soul that can be turned upon itself" he was talking about "a private life [wherein we] now pat ourselves on the back, now punish ourselves." He was saying that we should think about ourselves in plain language, should think about how healthfully, how unhealthfully, we were acting; he was reminding us that "we owe ourselves in part to society, but in the best part to ourselves." He was not asking us to squint our eyes and "look" at an inward peep-show in order to describe it and categorize it under various headings. The judgment that he was essaying, as we have seen in so many different ways, was not an instrument for snapping a picture of pure entities; it was a practical instrument, there to help me to act well in my environment, in a world of mixtures.

Montaigne can describe his own experiences brilliantly in such essays as "Of Practice." But such description always involves external objects or "stimuli," and it is never an end in itself for him, never proto-psychological or purely scientific. He does it as an aid for living in the everyday world of action on things and with other people. The experience and attitudes he so sensitively writes about are put down because they may be immediately "useful to me and may also by accident be useful to another."[7] For instance, after some brilliant descriptions of his own feelings when he had been struck down in the road by a heavy horse, he writes:

"This account of so trivial an event would be rather pointless, were it not for the instruction that I have derived from it for myself; for in truth, in order to get used to the idea of death, I find there is nothing like coming close to it."[8]

And he goes on to quote Pliny, who said that each man can educate himself if only he studies himself closely. Montaigne is not trying to produce a pure, detached, descriptive science of the consciousness of man or even of himself; he is trying to educate himself for living well and long by studying closely but common-sensically his own reactions in various circumstances. As I have suggested,[9] he is getting to know himself the way one could get to know an acid by studying its reactions in various circumstances.

But still, even this sort of analogy implies a descriptive science with all its specialized methods and vocabulary. This sort of "know-what" is not what Montaigne is trying to present:

> I do not attempt to arrange this infinite variety of actions, so diverse and disconnected into certain types and categories.... The scholars distinguish and mark off their ideas more specifically and in detail. I who cannot see beyond what I have learned from experience, without any system, present my ideas in a general way, and tentatively.[10]

And this statement is crucial; he has not forgotten his basic doctrine that our minds may not give us neat, precise essences, The Pure Truth; he is saying that our "judgment" can be trained and used for giving us rough, broad rules of thumb, *know-how* for living better and longer. The *Essays* are efforts *à tastons,* tentatively made and recorded, and never with the excessive precision, order and detachment of the *"scavans,"* the would-be knowers of The Truth.

This is the broad, pragmatical way Montaigne continued to his dying day to think about the uses of this *"âme contournable"* of his. He wrote some things in the way of personal confessions and broad generalizations about nature that the cautious, impersonal Greek Sceptics would never have written; but he never violated their basic conviction that we are here to act vigorously and if possible successfully upon our environment. He never left far behind their belief that our "knowledge" need not go beyond what is required for the satisfaction of this need to act, and to act well.

The awareness of this need, assumed by both the Greek Sceptics and Montaigne to be basic, removes Montaigne also from the camp of the Romantic "introspectives" like Chateaubriand's René, with his melancholic immobility. Consider this paragraph from *René* and compare it with, for example, Montaigne's essay "Of Solitude" or any of his remarks on the subject of human sequestration. René is speaking:

> Alas! I was alone on this earth. A secret lassitude took over my body. This disgust with life I had felt since childhood now returned with new force. Soon my heart no longer fed my thoughts, and I felt everything in my existence through a deep sentiment of boredom.

What a difference between this and the voluntary, active, pleasure-seeking solitude of Montaigne!

Privacy for Montaigne was not some ineluctable condition describable only in ultrarefined philosophical, psychological, or literary language; it was a chosen way of living vigorously, easily, and gaily within the broad prescriptions of ordinary language. It was an easy way of living amidst physical things and other people; it was a way of seeking one's own health and happiness in a very real and pressing world of things that are *"grossiers et apparens."*

C. Aloneness

ANOTHER kind of sequestration should not be confused with Montaigne's sort of privacy. It has to do with everyday choices, with plain speech, and with obvious external, physical conditions (not super-refined spiritual ones), but it is still not to be identified with the privacy he chose.

In the essay "Three Kinds of Association" he calls this sort of withdrawal *"solitude locale."* And what he is talking about is physical sequestration, being separated from other people by distances or walls. Here the topic is everyday, observable facts: people sometimes choose to be alone in their gardens, in their bedrooms, in their privies. But though all this is common-sensical, though the subtleties of the pedantic or morbid imagination that conjures up ontological, epistemological, or emotional abysses are not at work here, Montaigne will not identify what he calls *"solitude réale,"* the privacy he wants, with mere spatial or physical isolation. For him, privacy is not so simple a matter as being alone.

The privacy he wants can be had in physical seclusion *or* it can be had in a crowd. Sometimes he says that what he wants *"se jouyt plus commodément à part";* at other times he says that the privacy he seeks is best achieved in a populous place where he is driven back into himself.[12] Local solitude — aloneness — is neither a necessary condition of "real solitude" nor a sufficient condition of it. It is neither a vital part nor an adequate guaranty of privacy. Men who find solitude of place frequently do not find privacy: "These men have only their arms and legs outside the crowd: their souls, their intentions are more than ever in the thick of it."[13] By being fearful or ambitious they are frequently trying to please others more than they are trying to please themselves. And on the other hand, Montaigne's kind of privacy can be found in a crowd, even in a Mayor's office.

The richness of his notion of privacy as compared to the notion of mere physical sequestration is well summarized in his statement that "the solitude that I love and preach is primarily nothing but leading my feelings and thoughts back to myself, restraining and shortening not my steps, but my desires and cares, and not so much the press of people as the press of business."[14] Privacy is not simply a matter of bodies or feet or space; mainly it is a matter of actions and reactions in accordance with desires and thoughts. If it is not a deep and subtle matter involving absolutely isolated spirits beating their spaceless wings upon the void, neither is it a mere matter of bodies sequestered from bodies. In the end, for Montaigne, privacy, whatever else it is, does not involve such abstractions as pure spirit or pure body; it is richer than any of these, and yet it is a more common sort of thing than these. It requires neither deep and subtle metaphysics nor a disregard of plain experiences like friendship, love, ambition, and cowardice. It is a voluntary, not metaphysically inevitable, condition of a whole human being, body and soul, as he is revealed by plain but sensitive talk.

D. *Privacy and publication*

WE have been seeing that for Montaigne essaying one's personal, private life means revealing one's judgment to anyone who may ("by accident") be interested. But if he liked privacy so much, why did he want to publish essays of himself?

He asked this question himself in the essay "Of Repentance": "Is it reasonable that I, so fond of privacy in actual life, should aspire to publicity in the knowledge of me?" This could be interpreted as a merely biographical question: Why did this man publish his essays? As much as possible we have avoided speculation on the personal "causes" of the essays and have simply quoted passages from them that suggest an answer to that question. For instance, Montaigne says that he is not one of those men of "private, retiring, and inward natures. My essential pattern is suited to communication and revelation; I am all in the open and in full view." What Montaigne tells us in his essays is that he is a man who loves his privacy but is hungry to make himself known, or rather he is a man hungry to be known correctly, for what he is, not by way of rumor or public image. But how does one rescue this whole project from self-contradiction, given the double fact that Montaigne loved, needed, and defended privacy while he loved, needed, and defended publicity?

To answer this question, all we need to do is to point out the distinction between two meanings of the word "privacy" (or "publicity"). As Montaigne's question itself suggests, there is privacy *"en usage,"* Behavioral-privacy, and there is privacy *"en cognoissance,"* Acquaintance-privacy. In ordinary speech — in the speech used "in the streets of France" — there is privacy of behavior on the one hand and privacy of verbal communication on the other. Everyone knows that it is one thing to live a private life and that it is quite another to keep that life unverbalized and unpublished. A hermit can write a book; and the fact that he publishes it does not in itself make his solitude paradoxical or sham; he may prefer to keep away from direct involvement with the pace and servitudes of social or public behavior, while at the same time he may wish to announce this preference and its fruits to anybody who cares to read what he has to say. Here is a case of Behavioral-privacy and Acquaintance-publicity that is perfectly "reasonable." It is similar to Montaigne's case, which he tells us about early in the *Essays*:[15] he was a man whose behavior was modest as far as actually uncovering his private parts was concerned (in fact, he felt that he was too constrained in this respect for a soldier); but he was nonetheless "bold-mouthed" with regard to talking or writing about his own private parts, as we have seen. Nowadays one can have a private phone and still have the number published in a telephone directory. And so it goes. Behavioral-privacy and words that *"me rendre public en cognoissance"* are quite consistent with each other.

But after one has resolved any apparent contradiction or paradox, there is a further question whose answer takes us more deeply into Montaigne's notion of privacy. The question is: how do Behavioral-privacy and verbal Acquaintance-publicity help enhance each other? It is easy to say that the two are perfectly consistent and can be defended at the same time. After all, in logic, consistency is a very weak relationship between statements. "The moon is made of purple cheese" and "My nose is forty-five yards wide at the nostrils" are two mutually consistent claims, false as they are in fact and unrelated as they are in meaning. Any two statements that could be true at the same time are "consistent." But what do Behavioral-privacy and Acquaintance-publicity have to do with each other, given that you can have one and still have the other? In substance, Montaigne's answer to this question is that a behaviorally private life is a life that can be essayed in words and deeds, can be made public *more readily* than can a committed public life.

We have already seen how the clear separation between private conscience and public utility keeps a man transparent, makes a man known for what he is. To put it one way, his moral language — the language he talks and thinks and lives by — follows a plain "rule or prescription." It is understandable by others raised within roughly that same sort of tradition. The subtleties, the changes of an opportunistic moral vocabulary, are absent from such a man. You know where he stands because you know what he means when he talks about right and wrong. This is the way *you* learned to talk in childhood, even though you may have tried in your many-faced adulthood to forget this "green" and coarse way of talking. In general, you know what to *expect* of a man who keeps his own conscience intact and operative; and in knowing what to expect of him you know him, because this is a good part of what it means to "know" people. A feeling of familiarity, affection, and the like may be misleading, even blinding: we "know" people in much the same way we know horses or trees or metals, by knowing what they have done and what they will do and what they will not do under various particular circumstances. A man whose conscience is his own, a man who plainly states and shows in action what he will not do and what he will do, is a man we can "know." This is the whole spirit of what Montaigne means by *"cognoissance."*

But as we have noticed in the previous chapter, there are forces in public life that cause men to be "taken to be other" than they actually are. The man who is a committed public servant is hard to know if you do not know all the circumstances involved in practical, political action. And he is not only not known; he is misunderstood, mis-taken: one has false or irrelevant notions about him, not simply no notions at all. The public man is behind a mask, and people see the mask, not the face; they take the mask for the face. Now Montaigne is a man who has a "mortal fear" of having this happen to him — a fear that is the underside of his "hunger" to be a person who can be known.

One of the reasons why in public life the mask is seen and not the man is that in public life one is seen only in extraordinary circumstances, at certain times or in the course of certain kinds of events. The acquaintance the public has with its leader, for example, is sporadic, usually infrequent. Private acquaintance is continuing, usually regular. And another reason why a public man is mis-taken is that when he is seen or heard from he is involved in events that are as much a product of a thousand other major causes as they are a product of his own will or desires.

As for this indirectness of the knowledge we have of a public man, Montaigne has this to say in his essay "Of Glory":

"What is there more fortuitous than reputation? *Truly Fortune rules in all things she illumines or obscures all things according to her pleasure rather than the truth.* To make actions be known and seen is purely the work of fortune."[16]

For Montaigne, an "accident" or something that happens by "chance" is the upshot of an unexpected event. A man plans to conquer the world, but dies in his bed; a man walks down the street firm in his control of his financial destiny, having been assured by his admiring doctor-friend that he is in excellent health; but the omnipresent tile on the roof, which philosophers have been talking about for centuries, falls on his head, addling his brain and his life. Paths of causation he has no knowledge of cross a man's road continually, sometimes frustrating, sometimes supporting his plans. The sum-total of such paths Montaigne usually calls "Fortune," in accordance with the way we generally use the word. A man once threw a stone at his dog and killed his mother-in-law;[17] well, perhaps in some cases "chance decides matters better than ourselves," as Montaigne and Menander say. But for better or for worse, all men are subject to these unknown, unpredicted forces; that this is the case is one of the things Montaigne means when he exclaims that our condition is "amazingly corporeal."

But the public man is more subject to such forces than the private one; or rather the forces that come to bear on him serve to obscure his own personality more than do the forces that come to bear upon a man in private life. In his little essay "Of War Horses," Montaigne advises a man to use "the shortest weapons" because he can best answer for them. A public man is too dependent on other men and the circumstances and accidents of their lives. It is, Montaigne says,

> more sensible to rely on a sword that we hold in our hand than on the bullet that escapes out of our pistol, in which there are many parts — the powder, the flint, the lock — the least of which, by failing, will make our

fortune fail. You strike with little certainty the blow that the air carries for you.

Your own actions speak more of you when your instruments are simpler and your dependencies fewer. If you would best express yourself in your actions, you must use not only swords instead of pistols but short swords instead of long ones, because a short sword does not depend for its speed and accuracy upon the air that carries it. The public man is intimately involved with and profoundly dependent upon the most complicated, shifting instrument in the world: other men.

In private life, on the other hand, though there are, of course, accidents, the man usually shines through them and makes himself known to his intimates. Montaigne's most intimate friend, Etienne de la Boétie, of whom he speaks so movingly in his essay "Of Friendship," was known to Montaigne so well that Montaigne could say of him:

"Not one of his actions could be presented to me, whatever appearance it might have, that I could not immediately find the motive for it. Our souls ... revealed themselves to each other to the very depths of our hearts."[18]

Accidents served only to reveal more deeply the man to whom they happened. This was because not many men, not crowds, not history, were involved in their relationship to each other. Here were two men facing each other in the comparative simplicity of private life.

There is another reason for our not being known through our public life: any man can put up a "brave appearance," can counterfeit virtue, for example, if he appears only sporadically and for short periods of time before those who are trying to know him. To judge or to try to understand a man from these extraordinary, glamorous, or ignominious appearances in public is like admiring the philosophic power of a man because he played the part of Socrates in a successful play.

And so Montaigne will write his privatistic essays as a continuing register of his thoughts and feelings. The pen, he believes, is the shortest sword of all, and in his hand it is the most direct and spontaneous expression of his soul. By means of it he will reveal himself not in sporadic poses, not "passing from one age to another, or, as the people say, from seven years to seven years, but from day to day, from minute to minute."[19] Of course chance will change him, his bodily conditions, his passing states of mind; and he will show all these changes, and the intentional changes too, in this continuing register of his mind. But because he wants to make himself known (to himself as well as to others) for what he is, he will talk hardly at all about his sporadic public life. And he will talk about it only if the subject reveals a personal trait — a trait that has something to do with preserving his health of mind or body.

But if the political leader is masked, so is the dogmatist. More, they are both hidden for the same reasons. The dogmatist presents himself to the public at a few carefully selected moments of his life. And he presents himself in a way quite different from the way he presents himself to an intimate friend or to himself. He dresses his mind up in "therefores" and rigid, artificial structures of reasoning, covers himself with a rigid logical mask. By doing this he makes knowledge of himself indirect and very difficult to ascertain. He is in the same sort of condition as the behaviorally public figure; he remains, as far as acquaintance with him is concerned, in private. And what of the fierce controversies, the elaborate misunderstandings that isolate one dogmatist from his enemies without hope of real communication? All this is summarized in one of the last remarks in Montaigne's last essay "Of Experience":

> Come on now, just to see, some day get some man to tell you the absorbing thoughts and fancies that he takes into his head, and for the sake of which he turns his mind from a good meal and laments the time he spends on feeding himself.... His ideas and aspirations are not worth your stew. ... Between ourselves, these are two things that I have always observed to be in singular accord: supercelestial thoughts and subterranean conduct.

These people who "want to get out of themselves and escape from the man" hide themselves — hide their *conduct* — from themselves and from their fellow man. They concentrate on their fancy-full thoughts, while their thoughts dwell in one place and their everyday actions dwell in another. But Montaigne cannot endure to be hidden, and so he avoids a committed life in the public service, whether that service be political or whether it be "scientific."

And because he confines his attention to his own conduct, as he tells us at the beginning of "Of Repentance,"

> no man ever treated a subject he knew and understood better than I do the subject I have undertaken; ... in this I am the most learned man alive ... no man ever penetrated more deeply into his material, or plucked its limbs and consequences cleaner.

He is saying that no man has used so many means, and used them with such ongoing *"fidelité"*[20] as he has, in order to reveal himself for what he is. Others are obsessed with certain subject matters and fail to notice themselves in all postures, in all situations. He is a man who spends his time "taking stock of myself so continually, so carefully."[21] Everything he has said in these essays is an essay of himself, of his judgment, and consequently a line in his self-portrait, whatever else it *may* reveal of "Reality" or "Truth" about the universe.

And so, Behavioral-privacy, being concerned with himself as the most interesting and immediate entity in the universe, has given him Acquaintance-publicity. But, as we have noticed in so many connections, communication is not the same as *"la science,"* precisely sorted out, categorized, final knowledge. It is rather *"la cognoissance,"* flowing, changing acquaintance with a particular man seen from all sorts of points of view — physical descriptions of himself, descriptions of his way of thinking, his purposely imprecise assertions about man and the world, and so on. He has not given us a system to be memorized or refuted; he has offered us a friendship to be enjoyed, used, rejected, or ignored, as each of his readers sees fit."[22] Certain *"apparens et grossiers"* generalizations emerge from this friendship (and we have been considering them in this book), and also certain rather precise local facts (like the fact that he has a mustache, is small and rather thick-set, has a loud voice, and likes to scratch the inside of his ear). But he has not been trying to present conclusions; he has simply been revealing himself in action.

Montaigne felt that the essays were "consubstantial" with himself, a *"membre de ma vie,"*[23] an extension of his life, an immediate effect of his personality. And just as it makes no sense to ask whether an effect is false with respect to its cause, or whether a grimace is false if it was indeed directly caused by pain, or whether a man is speaking falsely when he is being candid and scrupulous in describing and giving voice to his own feelings, so it makes no sense to ask if Montaigne's essays are false. They are among the effects of his personality, and unless we can cast doubt on Montaigne's candor or scrupulosity in writing them we must accept them as "true" of Montaigne, at least at the time he wrote them down.

Near the end of the essay "Of the Art of Discussion," in the Third Book, Montaigne says, "I who am the king of the matter I treat . . . [I] owe an accounting for it to no one." If what he was after was The Truth about, say, all men, then he would "owe an accounting" to all men, for he would be speaking about their lives, would be claiming to be revealing the nature of their lives. In fact (he goes on in the same passage), he does not always believe in the objective truth of what he writes, insofar as what he writes is dealing with other matters than himself. But he puts down these "sallies of my mind which I mistrust" like a good historian who tries "to relate common beliefs, not to regulate them." He presents these *"boutades"* of his mind as sallies of *his* mind, as part of the history of his mind, not part of a lesson on The Truth for all men. This is what he is saying in that powerful opening of "Of Repentance" when he writes, "Others form man; I tell of him, and portray a particular one, very ill-formed." One could translate *"un particulier"* with "a particular one," but one could also translate it "a private man." If we did the latter, we would be emphasizing not Montaigne's uniqueness as much as the modesty, the limitedness, of his chief purpose in writing these essays. He is not primarily trying to teach the public about the truth that concerns *them;* he is trying mainly to reveal his own personality. Whether or not they can use these essays is their affair, not his, and subject to the obvious fact that personalities differ in many ways. And as we have noticed,[24] this pragmatical modesty is central to his way of philosophizing; it is basic to his notion of personal philosophy.

And this disarming modesty makes it somehow irrelevant to try to apply Sceptical doubt to the essays, to put them into antithesis with opposing reasons and differing temperaments. All we can do is accept the portrait as the best one we have of Montaigne (and certainly we have none better). Perhaps it is the best one we have ever had of any man. And we can say, as he said of his own personality, *"Mes-huy c'est fait"* — "That's the way it is." There he is in these *Essays,* a fact. There are different sorts of men; but this book, the *Essays,* would not "contradict" the portraits of these other men; it would be a portrait of *"un particulier,"* different from them and not ambitious enough to go about "contradicting" them.

The "prince of dogmatists," Aristotle, would have been in a similar position if *his* basic claim had been that his writings expressed his own personality, his own temperament and ideas. But Aristotle contended, Montaigne says, that he was giving *"la vérité"* — *the* precise truth — not about his own personality, but about the universe, man included. He therefore "owed an account" to his fellow men. And so Aristotle's claims can be — and were — put into antithesis with other claims about The

Truth. The universe can be cross-questioned, and other men can study themselves and their fellows and come up with conflicting reasonable notions of what the "original essence" of man and the universe are. But there is something cognitively disarming about a man who claims only to be voicing his own opinions, expressing his own temperament, essaying his own "judgment." He can change his mind, but we cannot contradict him unless we want to call him a liar or a hypocrite. And I am not one of the very few readers who find it plausible to do this. At any rate, whether or not he was a liar or a hypocrite is a problem beyond the scope of this book.

In the end, what Montaigne manifests in these essays of his judgment can be called his own "style" or way of living. In saying this I am not using the word "style" in a narrow sense, to refer only to some mannerisms of writing or acting that are external to the "substance" of a work or a man, as a vase would be external to the flowers it holds. I am using the word far more broadly than this, as Montaigne uses it at the end of his little essay "A Consideration upon Cicero" when he says:

"I have naturally a humorous and familiar style, but of a form all my own, inept for public negotiations, as my language is in every way, being too compact, disorderly, abrupt, individual."

Here and elsewhere in the *Essays*, *"stile"* or *"façon"* is not a matter of mere externals or trappings. It has to do with the way a certain man acts and reacts, no matter what the circumstances. In this sense of the word you do not learn the style of a man by reciting his titles or his profession. To manifest his style Montaigne will not simply report that he was Mayor of Bordeaux for two terms and an unofficial mediator in the religious wars. To reveal his style he will tell us how *he* acted in these impersonal functions.[25]

And so whenever he mentions his public actions he is careful to display in the foreground his way of satisfying himself first, his way of doing what is "easy and near" for him, with his free and lazy nature. Instead of telling us that he once helped get Henry III to equalize the tax burden upon the people of Bordeaux, he tells us about the way he performed his functions:

"Some say about this municipal service of mine ... that I went about it like a man who exerts himself too weakly, and with a languishing zeal; and they are not at all far from having a case."

To essay one's personal style is to emphasize one's personality.

Montaigne was acutely aware that when you speak of a man strictly in terms of his functions or services to others, (1) you make a specialist of him and therefore cut him off from all other specialists, and (2) you leave out what he is to himself, personally. When you speak of a lackey or a mule-driver you talk only in terms of boots and mules and specific actions performed on these (as Montaigne puts it, in hiring a lackey you do not worry about his chastity, unless, of course, his promiscuity might get in the way of his polishing your boots). But an occupational specialty (what he calls a *"marque particulière et estrangere"*[26]) does not reveal a man as a *man* (*"par mon estre universel"*). As a *man,* one's actions have some relevance to the actions of all men, whether they be lackeys or Mayors. Montaigne was trying to reveal a member of a *species,* a part of *nature.* He was trying to give meaning to his little phrase "each man bears the whole shape of the human condition." And to speak of a man only as a lackey or a Mayor is to speak of him too exclusively, by a *"marque"* too *"particulière"* for a man like Montaigne. He saw himself as a member of a broad community: nature. He wanted to leave the essays *open* as far as their relevance to other men was concerned, open to all men, no matter what their occupations.

And yet (2) he wanted to keep his essays of himself *personal.* He did not want to speak of functions that did not reveal *him "jusqu'aux entrailles."* He was essaying his *own* personal actions in these essays, but such actions that any man might do, no matter what his external function might be. In short, his essays reveal the style of *a man,* with an emphasis on both these last two words, a particular member of the species Man.

The notion of *"stile"* or *"façon"* springs from the depths of Montaigne's philosophy. In his essay on the taste of good and evil, he talks about an oar that looks bent when seen in water, and he says, "Il n'importe pas seulement qu'on voye la chose, mais comment on la voye." It is not enough to look at the subject matter that a man treats; one must consider *how* he sees that subject matter, the medium in which it appears. And Montaigne's style is the medium in which the various subjects he treats appear.

We are back to the Sceptic's notion of mixtures. The subjects and events Montaigne encounters in his essays are not important in themselves for him: they are not essences to be treated impersonally, through no medium whatsoever. Take the oar out of water and you are still seeing it through air. Montaigne's way of thinking is itself the medium through which we see all those subjects and events mentioned in the titles of his essays (and so many other subjects and events irrelevant to those titles!). What he is presenting in his essays is an encounter, a mixture, of a particular man and an event or subject (like the encounter of water and oar or air and oar).

Still another way of saying that Montaigne is manifesting his *"stile"* or *"façon"* is to point out that the upshot of the *Essays* is not a *method*. Style is a personal way — a way one cannot pass on to others by way of strict, precise rules of procedure, as one does in teaching a profession or craft. To have a style does not necessarily involve having clear, fixed categories or rules that can allow others to imitate that style readily. Method, on the other hand, is a way of doing something that is not one's own personal way. Any good cookbook gives us a method, a recipe; and so does Descartes' *Discourse on Method* (as well as all his other formal works). But Montaigne's *Essays* present us (by way of their written style, by way of their descriptions of the man's mental and bodily characteristics, by way of the man's arguments or rationalizations of these characteristics) with a totality not so readily detachable from their author as a method or a recipe is.

Still — and this has been one of the main points of this book — style *can* be communicated. You learn it not by learning "rules," but by watching a man in action in various sorts of circumstances. By doing this you get a *"cognoissance"*; it is not a "science" of the man, but you do get to "know" him. You may not be able to summarize him in neat categories, but you get to know his way of doing things, as you would get to know a friend by watching him in action, not by memorizing rules.

And what you do with what you learn is very different when you are learning a style from what you do when you are learning a method. To learn a method is to learn a procedure, with a beginning, a middle, and an end — a procedure you must follow mechanically, scrupulously, without leaving out a step. But it is essential to Montaigne's personal philosophy that he leaves it up to each reader to have enough "wit to pick out and put to use what happens before [his] eyes, and to judge it keenly enough to make it an example."[27] He offers these essays, assuming that each reader will use his own judgment and will use or reject whatever he reads here; he assumes in revealing his style that the reader will remember always that the reader's business is his own conduct, his own way of using what he encounters. An impersonal way of attaining a specific goal asks the reader to perform in the more or less fixed patterns of an efficient lackey or cook. Personality, choice, are peripheral if we are dealing with a method. But Montaigne does not offer a mechanism; he offers a cup, the *Essays,* containing a mixture of what he calls "the practice that has guided me so far" with his judgment on this practice. The reader can sip of the cup himself, or he can turn his back upon it, or he can simply look curiously at it in order to become acquainted with this *"comique et privé"* man.

And so the *Essays* manifest the style of a particular man, not his purportedly impersonal conclusions, nor a professional role, nor a method. And the kind of "style" they manifest is much the same sort of thing that J. Robert Oppenheimer was thinking about when he wrote in *The Open Mind:*

> It is style which complements affirmation with limitation and with humility; it is style which makes it possible to act effectively, but not absolutely; it is style which . . . enables us to find a harmony between the pursuit of ends essential to us, and the regard for the views, the sensibilities, the aspirations of those to whom the problem may appear in another light; it is style which is the deference that action pays to uncertainty.[28]

Style is what a man can offer who does not claim to know The Truth nor The Way to it, but who does wish to live, to think, to feel, and to act vigorously. It is a particular way of living that can be communicated by a particular way of writing or speaking. It can be communicated by what a man *says* and by what a man *shows,* by what a man talks about and by his way of talking about it.

In this book we have been trying to become acquainted with the broad patterns of his verbal and vital style. As a Humanist, Montaigne was concerned with ways of using language and ways of living; as an essayist, he manifested both of these activities in intimate involvement with each other. He wrote the way he lived: his pen moved the way his feet moved, modestly but firmly seeking his own well-being. And in doing all this he made himself as public as any other man who has ever lived, down to his guts.

And so, the answer to the question that opens this section, whether it is reasonable that a private man wish to make himself public, is Yes. For a man like Montaigne, it is very reasonable; indeed, for a man like him, only a dedicatedly private man can hope to make himself known for what he is. The public figure, like the impersonal dogmatist, fails to do so, or perhaps does not even try.

E. Conclusion

EARLIER[29] we noticed that a philosophy is "personal" if its provenance, its subject matter, and its audience have to do mainly with particular personalities, particular mixtures of circumstance and temperament. The personal philosopher asserts — explicitly, and by his emphasis on style — that this particular man, living when he is and being what he is, is the origin of this book, not Pure Reason, and not Pure Truth. He points out also — again, explicitly and by his emphasis on style — that ultimately his own judgment is what his writings are about. He is not trying to settle great questions as much as he is trying to understand his own mind by essaying it in words. Finally, he is quite content to assume that some men will find his essays useless or wrong; and to such men he is willing to say what Montaigne says in his Preface, *"A Dieu donq, de Montaigne"* — "And so farewell, from Montaigne." The elucidation of these three aspects of personal philosophy has been our basic concern in this book.

But we have also been concerned with the upshot of a particular man's sort of personal philosophy. The portrait Montaigne paints in his *Essays* is that of a privatistic man, whose scar is this: ineptitude at taking the lead in vast public "causes," irresolution in dealing with doubtful enterprises whether they be political, religious, metaphysical, or all three. And the living tissue in which this scar is embedded is his friendship for his own mental and bodily health. Achieving this well-being is his main job in this life, not taking the lead in the dubious enterprises of the Assertive imagination.

His age was one of vast variety that sometimes issued in mental and physical destruction. His temperament was that of a man who loved independence and ease; and he managed ("Marvelously!" he would say, with a Sceptic's irony) to find lots of reasons for living his most intense life in a back-shop all his own.

This in brief is the portrait he paints, scar and all. And it is up to you, the recipient of this pen-portrait, to ask and answer for yourself the question: Is this indeed the portrait of a scarred face, or is it the portrait of a face with a beautiful line? The appropriate reading of any personal philosophy demands that we pose and answer such a question for ourselves, *and* that we give our best reasons for the answer.

I believe that whatever your response to this question may be, your effort to respond to it will reveal that you too are a mixture of private and public concerns, a mixture different enough from others and similar enough to others to profit from candor.

APPENDIX

Montaigne and Descartes

Introduction

From time to time in this book we have touched upon the differences between Montaigne's personal philosophizing and Descartes' methodical philosophizing. It would be useful to explore a bit further the profound differences between these two ways of examining life. Such an exploration, though brief, could help bring out more plainly the traits of personal philosophizing. These two Appendices, then, are offered as heuristic devices to make Montaigne's approach more understandable. Their purpose is not to "refute" or denigrate Descartes' beautifully wrought philosophy as much as it is to reveal more clearly the rich but profoundly unfashionable philosophy of Montaigne.

In reading these two Appendices, we must not forget that Montaigne lived in the century of the French religious wars and that his friend Henry IV had considerably pacified France by the time Descartes was attending the Jesuit school of La Flèche. In fact, the heart of the dead king was brought to La Flèche while Descartes was a student there. But more important than all this, Descartes was a creative force in the century of scientific genius, the century of Galileo, Kepler, Newton, Torricelli, Snell, Boyle, Vesalius, and Harvey, to name a few. The century in which Descartes grew to maturity was one in which the explanatory and practical power of precise, mathematical science was achieving enthusiastic, even feverish, acceptance in many intellectual circles in Europe. In the seventeenth century the conviction was afoot — and in many cases triumphant — that man did not have to lean on Aristotle's coarse, non-mathematical, heuristically narrow logic to understand nature. Nor did he have to lean on the Church's dogmas. To understand the world, all men needed was mathematically controlled reason and observation. Any contrast we draw between Montaigne's and Descartes' doctrines must be seen against the background of this deep difference between their intellectual milieux: Montaigne matured in a century of hopelessly conflicting dogmatisms; Descartes matured in a century of infinite scientific hope. The way they used doubt and the way they used language, for example, were profoundly affected by this difference. I leave it up to the reader to decide what sort of century *we* are living in.

Appendix A

Montaigne's and Descartes' Doctrines of Language

Even a casual reading of Descartes' *Discourse on Method* reveals that the heart of his method is his effort to forge a special language "almost like" the language of mathematics, but independent of the details of mathematical analysis as well as independent of the vagueness of ordinary language. The method is a way of making language as lucid, perspicuous, precise, and unarguable in its claims as arithmetical calculation. And it is also a way of making language far broader — that is, more powerful — than the rather restrictive symbolism of mathematics proper.

To do all this Descartes: (1) distinguishes everyday living and thinking from special philosophic or scientific concerns (he gives us a provisional morality in one part of the *Discourse* and in another gives us a method whose rigorous standards differ diametrically from the rather credulous maxims of the provisional morality); (2) sets up standards of evidence, precision, and order that will determine what kinds of claims are admissible into his special philosophic language; (3) uses those standards, in Part Four, to solve those fundamental problems which he knows will be "so metaphysical and so unusual that they may perhaps not be acceptable to everyone"; and (4) applies those same standards to the various fundamental problems of physics with which he deals in the treatise to which the *Discourse* is an introduction. In short, Descartes seeks to create a mode of thought or speech that is not relative to the various and changing conditions of gross, expediential everyday life — a mode that is independent of ordinary talk, absolutely cogent, unambiguous, lucid, and fundamental.

And yet here we come to a curious point about his philosophy. He has no doctrine of the pitfalls of precise language. He simply assumes that we can recast chunks of our old vocabulary and syntax, putting together ordinary words in fresh, compelling ways, and that we can do this as straightforwardly and uneventfully as we do it in, say, assigning letters in algebraic calculation. He assumes that we can stipulate precise meanings outright for such words as "I" or "me" or "existence," as if there were no relevant pressure born of our having learned these words, of our having used them throughout most of our waking, rational lives. Montaigne had a profound respect for ordinary ways of talk, wished to vivify and make them more flexible by borrowing metaphors from hunting, for example — by writing epigrammatically whenever possible, and so on; but all these stylistic ameliorations were done out of respect for the great possibilities of ordinary language and were *not* done out of a conviction that ordinary language is a pretty inadequate tool, crying for absolutization. But Descartes, in his reply to the Fifth Objection, says that "names have been conferred on things for the most part by the inexpert, and ... for this reason they do not always fit the things with sufficient accuracy." And so, in order to augment their "accuracy," he will "emend" the usage of such names ("soul," "mind," "thinking," and so forth), as if one can do so without stepping outside the "rule or prescription" of ordinary talk and without setting up "imaginary republics" that are supposed to reveal the "original essence" of men, but actually succeed only in creating endless bickering.

This assumption — that you can stipulate into being a language that is as fresh and unexceptionable as one's clear and distinct mathematical intuitions — is one that Montaigne not only would not have dreamed of adopting but that he denied from one end of the *Essays* to the other, as we saw in our chapters on his philosophy of language. Language, like man himself, is a product of a long history of influences and activities for Montaigne, and it is tantamount to insanity to act as if this were not the case. The "rule or prescription" of ordinary talk is something quite similar to the rules or customs of human society with regard to morality and religion. To violate them, to act in flat disregard of these rules or prescriptions in matters of language, is as dangerous to our thinking, Montaigne says throughout the *Essays,* as revolution and immorality are dangerous to society. All such radically new departures are not really independent of the past; they are *violations* of it, and as such they entail

Doctrines of Language

chaos and punishment. In our talk, in our thinking, we are as much involved with our past and with society as we are in morality and religion. In fact, customs and laws do not exist in society apart from our language and thinking; they inhabit and inform that language and thinking, at least if we would communicate with others; and when language breaks down, so does social order.

We have seen that there are certain pitfalls involved in using language, and all of them amount to using language "so metaphysical and so unusual that they may perhaps not be acceptable to everyone," as Descartes puts it at the beginning of the Fourth Part of the *Discourse*. They all amount to stepping outside of any criterion, standard, rule, or prescription for deciding what a given word means and what it does not mean, or when it is used truly and when it is not. The whole of classical Scepticism involves the assertion that starting with a language outside the accepted, "reasonable," or common ways is a sure path to antithesis, endless bickering, with no criterion, no standard for settling the passion-laden tricksterish disputes of "reason." You can tell "salt" from "sugar"; but telling "body" from "mind" so that all will concur is something else again. We are operating, in using these last words, outside the rule or prescription of plain talk; in the first two quoted words the criterion is built in, from usage. In trying to get some sort of agreement or understanding on the last pair ("body" and "mind") you enter a forest of antitheses, because you have left the "highway" of plain, broad, vague but comfortable usage.

And this is what happens to Descartes. Take the word "I," for example: he jumps from the word being used in one way (italics are mine), a way we plainly understand — "I remained the whole day shut up alone *in a stoveheated room*, where I had complete leisure to occupy myself with my own thoughts" — to the same word used in a different way — a way involving queer, "artificial" words: "I was a substance, the whole essence or nature of which is to think ... that for its existence there is *no need of any place nor does it depend on any material thing*." This jump from one use of the word "I" to its apparent opposite, from a spatial, dependent self to a non-spatial, independent one, is one way of getting into a chaotic relationship with your language.

And this departure from "rule or prescription" occurs because of the yearning on the part of some men for "original essences," for great precision, for subtlety *in ordinary language*. They try to have their bigger morsels and subtilize them too, try to use the same words we use in ordinary speech and still achieve mathematical, extraordinary precision with them by putting them to extraordinary uses. They break up the "bigger morsels" of plain talk by making razor-sharp "distinctions" (to use Descartes' word) between the parts that are mixed together in plain talk. They do this by taking an ordinary word (like "I" or "mind" or "thing") and by contriving "artificial phrases" (to use Montaigne's expression) with an "endless number of minute partitions that ... can no longer fall under any rule or prescription or any certain interpretation." It is this desire for precision beyond the rules or prescriptions of plain talk or of everyday sugar-finding that is for Montaigne one of the most powerful motives for concocting artificial phrases from plain words.

Salt will always be different from sugar (until some metaphysician gets a hold on these poor little words) by criteria available to anybody who talks the language. But when you try to use ordinary language with a precision beyond that of these vague, broad criteria, your subtleties, your razor-sharp distinctions, rupture the relationship between your language and the "language spoken in the streets of France." The vital relationship between our words and our lives, the solid tie that related these words adequately to our needs and habits, is broken, and we become "mice in pitch," involved in endless squabbles, with no "rule or prescription," no customary criterion to decide anything for us.

Such squabbles, as we have noticed, are fostered by the tendency of men to continue to accept something that they believe in simply because it cannot be refuted conclusively. Men will often not see that the reason their belief cannot be refuted is that it is as the air, invulnerable, too confused to be labeled definitively with the word "true" or the word "false." They do not often see that truth or falsity in ordinary talk involves our having understood enough of what has been said to flatter it with such words. (Is "Lamps sing pomegranates yesterday tomorrow" worthy of being called either "true" *or* "false"? And yet there are men who will defend a claim almost as hard to verify as this partly because they have never found anyone who can prove it false.) Some claims have not been refuted only because they are too irrelevant to any acceptable criterion of truth or falsity to be called either true or false; and yet, again, there will always be men who will continue to defend them as true because they cannot be proved false. The so-called fallacy *per ignorantiam* (it has not been proved that angels do not sing Bach; therefore, they do sing

Bach) is not as infrequent as we might think when we are looking at it in its nakedly implausible form.

But whatever the underlying desires, or the mechanisms used, in pushing language beyond its broad, customary highways, the effect is the same: to set up a radically new language *in the midst of current usage* is to blow up the town. It is not simply reforming one's own building; it is not simply tearing down one's own foundations and building afresh. It is a revolt against one of the basic tissues that hold society together: language, or broad, ordinary ways of thinking.

And so for Montaigne the whole notion of a new "method" that abuses the vocabulary of the language "spoken in the streets of France" is as subversive as a theological or civil war (as a matter of fact, as Montaigne knew, such linguistic innovations were in the sixteenth century among the basic causes of the religious civil wars of France). There is only one thing to do with such a notion: do not try to refute it; simply avoid it and talk plain talk, the way you learned to talk and the way you have succeeded in talking thus far in your life. Go back to the rough ways of ingesting "bigger morsels," good for rougher, healthier stomachs; turn your back on the refined methods, and do not be so sharp or you will cut yourself — not to speak of all those around you.

Again, as I have often said, all this does not mean that Montaigne believed that there was only one language in which man could legitimately talk or think. We discussed this in our early chapter on language: ecclesiastical language was perfectly suitable if it had a long tradition and a special domain that would determine the criteria for its correct or incorrect usage. And in his remark about Copernicus, Montaigne suggests that the language of physics or mathematics may be a complete and consistent way of talking about such matters. Trouble comes when we *confuse* languages, and when men, as Montaigne puts it in the "Apology," "accept medicine as they do geometry," when they confuse languages so that no one set of rules or criteria applies. This, he might say, Descartes tried to do: he confused the precise language of mathematics with the rough, "big morsels" talk of everyday discourse about myself, things, and so on.

Now, the key test of whether such a confusion has occurred is in the controversy that issues from a certain way of talking. Descartes tells us in his letter that serves as a preface to the French edition of the *Principles* that what he wants in the foundations (the metaphysics) of his scientific philosophy is to offer truths which, "being perfectly clear and certain, will remove all subjects of dispute, and thus dispose men's minds to gentleness and concord." He wants to present a philosophy that will not be captious and produce "heresies and dissensions." By Descartes' time Galileo and Copernicus, despite their troubles with religious authorities, had shown the scientific community that in the language of mathematical physics they had found such a way of presenting truths. Anybody speaking mathematical language was led to assent to their propositions or to add to them or correct them in a way agreed upon by all. Their language was *cogent,* not captious; it removed subjects of dispute and disposed men's minds to assent by the sheer force of its rule-abiding arguments. It is this sort of language that Descartes wanted to create for metaphysics, for dealing with "original essences" or "principles."

But look at any fairly complete edition of the Objections and Replies that Descartes got involved in when he had his *Meditations* sent out to the learned world. The Haldane and Ross edition is judicious and representative. The *Meditations* had given up the autobiographical style of the *Discourse* and were plainly claiming to be the truth for any orderly and attentive mind. Now, it is not the fact that there was argumentation, that there were objections and responses, that makes these exchanges indicative of conceptual or linguistic confusion. It is the fact that no criterion, no rule or prescription either explicit or implicit, is agreed upon by all participants. And so there is no visible hope of ever finding a way to reach agreement or even understanding.

If there is any such criterion proposed by Descartes it is the criterion of clarity and distinctness, or to put the same point a bit differently, self-evidence, obvious, transparent truth. But from one end of the Objections and Replies to the other, not only do "subjects of dispute" multiply like some prolific underwater animals, not only do we see no sign that the ways of talking and thinking that are being employed by either party "dispose men's minds to gentleness and concord" (look at Descartes' responses to the materialist Hobbes, with their withering phrases like "all this is quite self-evident"), but Descartes' central criteria for resolving disputes, for determining "self-evidence," are sometimes seen to be understood only by Descartes himself! Most strikingly in the Third Objection and Replies, but everywhere else in this barrel of pitch that Descartes and his critics are involved in, claims that the proof of the antagonist "has been already satisfactorily refuted" abound and are ignored by everybody but the speaker of the claim.

Doctrines of Language 165

At one point in this mass of antitheses labeled "Third Objection and Replies" Descartes informs Hobbes:

"No one can be unaware that by mental illumination is meant clearness of cognition, which perhaps is not possessed by everyone who thinks he possesses it."

In effect this says that there is no agreed-upon criterion for deciding whether our so-called "criterion" is met. Upon reading this admission that there is no applicable criterion for distinguishing the true from the false, the self-evident from the false, and so on, the Sceptical Montaigne would close the book. Descartes' "criterion" simply does not operate as such, does not help to clarify or resolve disputes when it itself is subject to dispute, when one may "think" he meets it, but somehow does not, according to Descartes.

Reread Montaigne's last essay, "Of Experience," before and after having read attentively the Objections and Replies in the Haldane and Ross edition, and you will find a hundred little summaries of those antithetical arguments. For instance, Montaigne will say that our

> disputes are purely verbal. . . . "A stone is a body." But if you pressed on: "And what is a body?" — "Substance." "And what is substance?" and soon, you would finally drive the respondent to the end of his lexicon. We exchange one word for another word, often more unknown. I know better what is man than I know what is animal, or mortal, or rational.

Solemn words ("clearness of cognition and that nature which puts me in possession of the idea of God"), artificial phrases "explaining" other artificial phrases ("The distinction between essence and existence is known to all") — all of these, because there is no real operative criterion for their correct use, as there is in most mathematical argumentation,

> can no longer fall under any rule or prescription or any certain interpretation. *What is broken up into dust becomes confused*. (Seneca.)

By using the common language for subdividing subtleties and difficulties

> they lengthen them, they scatter them. By showing questions and cutting them up, they make the world fructify and teem with uncertainty and quarrels, as the earth is made more fertile the more it is crumbled and deeply plowed.

The protagonists are like children

> trying to divide a mass of quicksilver into a certain number of parts. . . . The more they press it and knead it and try to constrain it to their will the

more they provoke the independence of this spirited metal; it escapes their skill and keeps dividing and scattering in little particles beyond all reckoning.

But whatever metaphor or diagnosis Montaigne may offer to describe and account for those intricate objections and replies that have exercised philosophers for centuries now, the upshot of it all is the same: there is no applicable criterion for resolving difficulties and misunderstandings. There is what the Sceptics call "Antithesis."

What then has happened to Descartes' great ideal so gallantly and imaginatively borrowed from the ideals and practices of the mathematics and physics of his day? Where is that discourse that "will remove all subjects of dispute, and thus dispose men's minds to gentleness and concord"? It is realized only in the realms from which it was borrowed by Descartes: mathematics, physics, the exact, rule-abiding sciences, where when you break something down according to unequivocal rules you can put it back together to everybody's satisfaction according to unequivocal rules; where, as Descartes puts in the *Discourse,* "a child, . . . who has been instructed in Arithmetic and has made an addition according to the rule prescribed . . . may be sure of having found as regards the sum of figures given to him all that the human mind can know." True lucidity, true distinctness, are not based upon optical metaphors, but upon rules or criteria that actually constrain all minds.

As we have been noticing here, Descartes neglected to face in dealing with his *lumen naturale* the fact that he was working with a social force, language, and a force deriving its rules or criteria from long, complex, vague social usage. When he wrote in the Second Part of the *Discourse,* "My design has never extended beyond trying to reform my own opinion and to build on a foundation which is entirely my own," he failed to see that his and all other minds are deeply involved in society — at least as far as using language or "thinking" is concerned. The Objections and Replies are the result of that failure, and the following weary reply to Hobbes has served as a symbol to me of that failure. It is a short reply, and here it is in its entirety:

"When it is said that we cannot conceive God, to conceive means to comprehend adequately. For the rest, I am tired of repeating how it is that we can have an idea of God. There is nothing in these objections that invalidates my demonstrations."

He ends by making a judgment against Hobbes's objection without any reference to clear and distinct ideas that others might scrutinize. He simply assures us that he, Descartes, knows that "there is nothing in these objections that invalidates my demonstrations." And one finds the same weariness, the same despair of applying the criterion of clarity and distinctness in the *Discourse,* in the Sixth Part where he says that as far as objections to his system are concerned he has no hope of "deriving profit from them." He is reduced to saying that "hardly ever have I encountered any censor of my opinions who did not appear to me to be either less rigorous or less judicial than myself." On this same page, in the Haldane and Ross edition of his works, he asserts that no other man, no matter how great his intelligence, has understood his, Descartes', philosophy, just as Descartes wrote it. And he begs the readers "never to believe that what is told to them proceeded from myself unless I myself divulged it."

Appendix B

Montaignian and Cartesian Doubt

Any complete treatment of the differences between Montaignian doubt and Cartesian doubt would have to be a complete analysis of both their philosophies, so crucial is doubting in their writings. But here we can indicate some of the differences.

First of all, there is a difference between the ultimate goals of their doubting. Descartes' original title for the *Discourse* was *The project of a universal science that could raise our nature to its highest degree of perfection . . . proving the universal science that the author proposes.* Sometime after March, 1636, Mersenne, Descartes' learned friend, persuaded him to tone down the title, which finally became: *Discourse on the method of rightly conducting one's reason and of seeking truth in the sciences.* Also in the *Meditations,* the goal of all his philosophizing was a "Universal Science," involving certain conclusions about the universe and a method for proving these conclusions and for finding more truths. Such a science he wanted for many reasons: it could make belief in God and the conclusions of the mathematical sciences rationally unassailable; it could directly improve the lot of mankind by perfecting the very important science of medicine; and so on.

On the other hand, the title page of the Bordeaux First Edition of Montaigne's *Essays* (1580) reads as if the presentation of the author himself is the main point of the *Essays* (and of course, as we have found, it is):

Essais
De MESSIRE
Michel Seigneur

de Montaigne
Chevalier de l'ordre
du Roy & Gentil-homme
ordinaire de sa Chambre

Remembering the publishing customs of the time, which dictated some such designation for the writings of a nobleman, and also Montaigne's ambivalent pride over his titles (see the last dozen pages of "Of Vanity"), we are still being told by this title that what we are going to witness is the "essaying" of an individual, Michel de Montaigne. And as we have seen in so many ways, the little Preface "To the Reader" (which also appeared in the First Edition, as well as in all subsequent complete editions) bears out the title, as do the essays themselves. Phrases in that Preface like "it is myself that I portray" point to the ultimate goal of the book. Here not the construction of a science, but the portrayal of a particular person is the ultimate goal.

And the subject matters of these two philosophies (if subject matter can be usefully distinguished from their ultimate goals) are profoundly different. Descartes' subject matter is the universe itself, as studied through a science capable of giving us a thorough understanding of it. For Montaigne, it is always man we are dealing with, and one particular man in this book, a man full of idiosyncrasies, whatever his affinities with other men may be. For Montaigne, in trying to understand the basic structure of the universe we only "entangle our thoughts in generalities . . . and we leave behind our own affairs and Michel, who concerns us even more closely than man in general."

There are moments in the First Part of the *Discourse* when Descartes protests that the Treatise to which the *Discourse* is the introduction, *Le Monde,* was written "only to show in what manner I have endeavored to conduct my own [Reason]." For instance, early in that Part he tells us that here he will be setting forth "my life as in a picture," relating "a history, or if you prefer it, a fable." At such moments he offers his thoughts as a cup from which men may drink if they so choose, a fable that men may learn from if they can or will. And such passages are in the spirit of Montaigne. But the emphasis of Descartes' writings as a whole is, as the title of the *Discourse* suggests, not upon self-revelation, but upon proving ("*rendre preuve*"), not upon himself as a *"domestique et privé"* individual, but upon a universal science of God, nature, and man. His is not a personal philosophy, though sometimes he lets us see that he is aware that a particular person is writing it. As for his motives in being so modest in these passages, we shall not speculate here.

Whatever the biographical reasons, the fact is before us: the primary subject matter of Descartes' philosophy is *"la vérité,"* precise, cogent truths about the universe; the primary subject matter of Montaigne's philosophy is a particular man, himself, in the act of essaying himself in words. The functions of doubt in two such different philosophies could not help but be different.

Now, let us turn to those functions. Early in the *Discourse,* Descartes makes a move that is a classical Sceptical one; talking about his mental development, he tells us: "I could not ... put my finger on a single person whose opinions seemed preferable to those of others." A Montaigne would nod his head at this situation and then turn his eyes away from the subject, as would a Greek Sceptic; but not Descartes: he goes on immediately to tell us that "I found that I was, so to speak, constrained myself to undertake the direction of my procedure." After putting down his first Sceptical phrase, instead of recognizing the balancing of criterionless claims, Descartes goes right ahead with the same sort of enterprise that Aristotle and others had failed to carry off. And he goes right ahead because he is convinced that previous claimants to deep knowledge had committed "extravagant errors." Instead of speaking in terms of the *suspension* of judgment, he speaks in terms of *adverse* judgments, error, falsity. Here in brief is the difference between a "Sceptic" who talks about *error* and goes about finding The Truth and a Sceptic who *suspends judgment* on, avoids claims about, The Truth.

But we have not gone far enough into the differences between these two uses of doubt. For Descartes there is a deep difference between the life of reason and the life which searches primarily for bodily comfort and the like. In the life of reason one gives oneself entirely to the search after Truth; in the life of practice or action one seeks comfort and the prolongation of life. The whole purpose of separating the Second Part from the Third Part, the Provisional Morality from the Method, in the *Discourse* is to keep these two different ways of life from ruining each other by getting in each other's way: excessive rational demands can lead us to reject customs, practical needs of all sorts, and in short, can destroy us and society; on the other hand, being concerned with the vague, shifting requirements of everyday life can destroy the rigorous requirements of the rational life. And so he will make a dramatic separation — temporary, he hopes, but now quite real — between the methodical use of his *lumen naturale* and his practical everyday moral existence. This split between thought and action runs across all the works of Descartes, even those letters wherein he emphasizes everyday life.

And his kind of doubt is the dramatic — and at the same time convincing — way he achieves this separation. His kind of doubt involves a principle that would be deadly to practical life, but purificatory, bracing, to the life of reason. And here is the way he summarizes it in the *Discourse*:

"I . . . [will] reject as absolutely false everything as to which I could imagine the least ground of doubt [*Je rejetasse, tout ce en quoi je pourrais imaginer le moindre doute*]."

In order to expunge from his intuitions any hint of habit, custom, or prejudice or any (as he puts it in the *Meditations*) "ancient and commonly held opinions [that] still revert frequently to my mind against my inclination," he decides to reject anything that he could even in his wildest dreams imagine to be false. If he gives to merely probable beliefs any degree of assent he will be in danger of letting them get mixed in with his intuitions, of "deferring to them," of letting them to some extent become "masters of my belief." To avoid this danger of impurity, this danger of heteronomy with respect to society and the past, and in order to maintain the utter autonomy of his natural light, Descartes is willing to err on the side of overcautiousness. He will wipe out any possibility of his giving assent to these received and customary opinions by using a strong and sweeping prejudice against them all: he will

> for a certain time pretend that all these opinions are entirely false and imaginary, until at last, having thus balanced my former prejudices with my latter, my judgment will no longer be dominated by bad usage or turned away from the right knowledge of the truth.

He is straightening the growing twig by "for a certain time" bending it in the direction opposite to its present bent. Or, as he puts it in his responses to the Seventh Set of Objections to the *Meditations,* he is spilling all the apples out of the basket so that he can look them over one by one just to be sure there are no rotten ones, and so that then he can put the sound ones back. The habits, the customs, that Montaigne found to be our second "nature" and part of us, part of our innermost being (though he often advocated that we reexamine them so as to be sure they were really instrumental to our health), Descartes wants to reject as false. And he is assured that there is no practical, everyday danger in this project, because he is plainly (though only for the time being) divorcing philosophy from living: "I cannot at present yield too much to distrust, since I am not considering the question of action, but only of knowledge."

Much has been written about this hyperbolic, methodical doubt that helps Descartes to lay the first stone of his foundations. But here I shall try only briefly to compare it to Sextus' kind of doubt, which is essentially Montaigne's, and show where their use of doubt differs importantly from it.

First of all, Descartes' provisional code of action is similar enough for our purposes to the Sceptic's Practical Criterion: both the classical Sceptics and Descartes "put aside" the actions and the motives for action in everyday life; they accept them, not because they are "true," but because it is obvious that one must live, that one must be allowed to live by society in order to do anything involving the search for truth. The Academic Sceptics had called this obviousness the *"eulogon,"* the "reasonable"; Montaigne had called this aspect of man that guides him in action *"sens"* or *"jugement."* Descartes had no one name for it (he sometimes called it "spontaneous inclination" or the "instruction of nature"). But the classical Sceptics and Descartes shared with Montaigne the notion that doubt is not something one brings to bear on everyday practical public and private life, on "living experience."

But classical doubt involves antithesis, the balancing of a belief by an equally likely or reasonable opposing belief; and then after this has been achieved, it involves turning one's back on the set of antitheses with the words "I determine nothing" or "No more this than that." For Montaigne and Sextus, it is always possible that one of the set will be true; we simply do not have a criterion for deciding which one is true and which false.

On the other hand, as we have noticed, Descartes' notion of doubt is hyperbolic, extreme (because he wants to separate very sharply action from contemplation, the "common life" from "the search after Truth," to use the words of the first paragraph of the Fourth Part of the *Discourse*). And Descartes has from the beginning a criterion for rejecting as *false* any given belief: if it can be supposed, dreamed up, imagined, that that belief could be false. The classical Sceptics had no such criterion. All they could do was oppose beliefs and show how that trickster reason could make plausible arguments on both sides of its mouth. But all of this indicated nothing about which of the beliefs was false. Antithesis showed that on some matters "reason is such a rogue." For the Sceptic, doubt involved only suspending judgment; for Descartes it involved making a judgment or at least feigning to make it. The cautious Sextus never proposed a criterion for rejecting a proposition as "absolutely false"; the whole point of his Scepticism is that we have not found such a criterion as yet.

And there is a second, related difference between Descartes' spilling out of the apples and the Sceptics' weighing antithetical claims against each other. The Sceptics usually felt that the only doubt worthy of the name was reasonable doubt. That is, you usually do not oppose beliefs to imagination or suppositions; you oppose beliefs to beliefs; you suspend judgment on the "real" (non-evident) shape of the tower, not because it looks round and you can *imagine* or *suppose* it to be otherwise, but because it looks round from a distance and looks square from close at hand. You must have reasonable grounds for doubting a given belief; you must have an opposing belief that is as probable as the one you are trying to doubt. When Sextus presents unreasonable opposing beliefs, he is usually joking, at least in my opinion.

In short, Descartes' kind of doubting is a perfect instrument for stripping away, for excluding, beliefs on the slightest grounds (or no "grounds" or reasonable arguments at all), and for excluding them decisively, sharply. The Sceptics had to find counterreasons to *balance the scales* against a given indicative belief, and when they managed to do this there always remained the possibility that one of the claims they had suspended judgment on was true. Descartes did not have to find counterreasons against a given proposition; he could simply imagine or suppose the opposite, and the proposition he wanted to get rid of was whisked away into the blackness of falsity. Degrees of probability — grays — could never occur in his dubitative scheme; there were only black and white, cleanly, sharply cut off from each other. One could swiftly and finally detach the black from the white the way one detaches the husk from an ear of corn and throws the husk away, or the way one detaches the skin from a banana. The result was a separation between the "doubted" (false) claim and the undoubted claim — a separation that is "complete" (as Descartes describes the distinction of mind from body in the reply to the First Objection). Doubting for Descartes was not a way of balancing probabilities against each other, as it was for the Greek Sceptics and even for Montaigne; it was a *separative,* exclusive procedure, suitable to a Method dedicated to discovering clear and distinct *"parcelles"* or simple intuitions that are as distinct from other intuitions as 1 is from 2.

Consider an example of how this happens in the *Meditations*. In the First Meditation, Descartes says that there are many things, like the fact that these hands and body are mine, "of which we cannot reasonably have any doubt." He would indeed, he says, have to be "insane" if he would claim to have reasonable or seriously defended doubts about whether his body was there now. And so in the Second Meditation he "supposes," he "imagines," "a certain genius which is extremely powerful, and, if I may say so, malicious, who employs all his power in deceiving me." And given this purely imaginary condition, this sprite whose existence Descartes never lifts a finger to defend or justify, he will "exercise my imagination" and come up with the assertion: "I am not a collection of members which we call the human body." After having *supposed* the existence of such a deceiving sprite, and after having *imagined* that the sprite was deceiving him about his own body, he *concludes* from this supposition and imagination that it is *false* that he has a body now, though he feels it and sees it. In this way he neatly separates the thinking thing, the mind, from all other things, and not by "reasonable" doubt, nor by suspending judgment.

Now, I am not here contesting the utility of hyperbolic super-Sceptical doubt when you want once and for all to get rid of rotten apples or when you want to straighten out your sword-blade. All I want to do is show how readily that hyperbolic doubt slices off, separates off, the thinking thing that is doing the doubting from the body and the bodily actions that in the "lassitude" of "my ordinary life" (see the end of the First Meditation) I think of as really my body and really my bodily actions.

But for Montaigne, as for Sextus, doubt is not an instrument primarily designed to isolate simple constituents, simple entities and relationships (*rapports*) between those entities; it is not an instrument for finding theoretical truth of any sort, simple or complex. For the classical Sceptics, doubt is a gross, practical instrument, designed to allow us to live more tranquilly in an everyday life of mixtures. It is not an instrument of theoretical analysis, but an instrument of practical avoidance. It is not used to separate reason from everyday life — however temporarily;

it is used to turn our attention — if you will, our "reason" — to everyday life by way of a suspension of judgment on certain other matters.

In the hands of Montaigne doubt is a way of achieving relief from the personal and public chaos and eternal busyness of dogmatic squabbling; it is a way of satisfying his own needs for freedom and ease. In his personal philosophy it is what he needs, with his particular *"conditions et humeurs,"* in order to live the way he wants to live. It is, like everything else in his philosophy, a *"membre de ma vie,"* a part of his everyday life in much the same way that his hands are *his* members, part of his body. In short, doubt is personal and practical for Montaigne. For Descartes it is the main tool for cutting out the *"fondements,"* the basic truths of a Universal Science.

To put the difference in a slightly different way: the primary function of doubt for Descartes was to find assertions that were universally cogent, guaranteed certain; the primary function of doubt for Montaigne was not to secure certitude, but to enhance his own life. Both kinds of doubt were concerned with criteria or guarantees of certitude, and both kinds of doubt were concerned with enhancing life. But the all-important difference between them is one of emphasis, and this difference is what distinguishes the personal philosophy of Montaigne from the disinterested metaphysical and analytical philosophy of the Modern era. Differences of emphasis can indeed be immense.

Notes

N.B.: In the following Notes, the abbreviation "Pl." refers to the Pléiade edition of Montaigne's *Essais,* edited by Albert Thibaudet (Paris: Gallimard, 1950). The abbreviation "Fr." indicates *The Complete Works of Montaigne,* translated and edited by Donald M. Frame (Stanford: Stanford University Press, 1948).

Chapter 1: Montaigne's Century

1. Nancy Roelker (ed.), *The Paris of Henry of Navarre* (Cambridge, 1958), p. 193.
2. Duc de Lévis Mirepoix, *Les guerres de religion* (Paris, 1950).
3. J. W. Allen, *A History of Political Thought in the Sixteenth Century* (London, 1960), p. 344, *passim.*
4. J. W. Thompson, *The Wars of Religion in France, 1559-1576,* (Chicago, 1909), p. 429.
5. Mirepoix, *op. cit.,* p. 251.
6. G. H. Sabine, *A History of Political Theory* (New York, 1946), p. 400.
7. Mirepoix, *op. cit.,* p. 270.
8. Pl. 1114.
9. Fr. 800.
10. P. O. Kristeller, *Renaissance Thought* (New York, 1961), p. 11.
11. *Ibid.,* p. 13.

Chapter 2: Doubt and Man

1. P. Villey, *Les Sources et l'évolution des Essais de Montaigne* (Paris, 1933), Vol. 2, p. 152.
2. *Ibid.,* p. 143.
3. *Ibid.,* p. 142.

4. Fr. 36–37.
5. P. P. Hallie (ed.), *Scepticism, Man, and God* (Middletown, Conn., 1964).
6. *Ibid.*, p. 41.
7. *Ibid.*, p. 86.
8. *Ibid.*, p. 38.
9. *Ibid.*, p. 44.

Chapter 3: Men and Mixtures

1. See "Of Cannibals" in Book I of the *Essays;* see J. H. Parry, *Europe and a Wider World, 1415–1715* (London, 1949), and A. P. Newton (ed.), The Great Age of Discovery (London, 1932).
2. Fr. 761.
3. See J. Coppin, *Montaigne, traducteur de Raymond de Sebond* (Lille, 1925).
4. See P. Villey (ed.), *Essais* (Paris, 1930–31), notes to Vol. 2.
5. c.a. Sainte-Beuve, *Port-Royal* (Paris, 1953–55), I. III, Chap. iii; see F. Tavera, *L'idée d'humanité dans Montaigne* (Paris, 1932), Chaps. VII and IX.
6. Fr. 419.
7. Fr. 324.
8. Pl. 627.
9. Pl. 572.
10. Fr. 429.
11. Fr. 430.
12. B. Jowett (ed.), *The Dialogues of Plato* (New York, 1937), Vol. 1, p. 405.
13. Fr. 453.
14. P. P. Hallie (ed.), *Scepticism, Man, and God* (Middletown, Conn., 1964), p. 48.
15. Fr. 454.
16. Fr. 328.
17. Fr. 457.
18. *Supra,* pp. 5–6.
19. Fr. 354.
20. Fr. 402.
21. Fr. 378.
22. Pl. 643.
23. Pl. 563.

Chapter 4: Common Sense and Habit

1. Fr. 331.
2. Fr. 39.
3. Pl. 507.
4. Fr. 345.
5. Pl. 515.
6. Fr. 177.
7. Fr. 177-178.
8. Fr. 498.
9. *Ibid.* (Italics mine).
10. *Infra,* pp. 101-105.
11. Fr. 37.
12. Fr. 499.
13. Fr. 85 ;*"jugement"* Pl. 146.
14. Fr. 582.
15. Fr. 86.
16. *Ibid.*
17. Fr. 772.
18. Fr. 77.
19. Fr. 80.
20. Fr. 11-18.
21. Fr. 111.
22. Fr. 100-101.
23. Fr. 101.
24. Pl. 175.
25. *Ibid.*
26. *Ibid.*
27. Fr. 111.
28. *Ibid.*
29. Fr. 100.
30. Fr. 102.
31. *Ibid.*
32. Fr. 102.
33. Pl. 192.

Chapter 5: Language and the Troubles of the World

1. *Supra,* p. 10.
2. Fr. 392.

3. Fr. 667.
4. II, 16.
5. Fr. 204.
6. Pl. 317.
7. Fr. 833.
8. Fr. 665, Pl. 977.
9. Fr. 791.
10. Pl. 79.
11. Fr. 336.
12. Fr. 69.
13. Chap. XIV.
14. Fr. 665.
15. Fr. 171.
16. Fr. 810.
17. H. von Kleist, *The Marquise d'O* (New York, 1960), Preface by Thomas Mann.
18. Fr. 665.
19. *Ibid*.
20. *Supra*.
21. Fr. 442.
22. *Ibid*.
23. Fr. 816–818.
24. Fr. 376.
25. *Supra*, pp. 40–44.
26. Fr. 171.
27. Fr. 125.
28. *Ibid*.
29. Fr. 816.
30. Fr. 419.
31. Fr. 786.
32. Fr. 789.
33. Fr. 730.
34. *Ibid*.
35. Fr. 414 (I prefer my translation here).
36. Fr. 425.
37. Fr. 23.
38. Fr. 235.
39. Fr. 323–324.
40. S. T. Irwin (ed.), *Six Dialogues of Lucian* (London, 1894), p. 22.
41. Fr. 232.
42. Fr. 229–230.

43. Fr. 232.
44. A. J. Ayer, *Language, Truth and Logic* (New York, n.d.).
45. L. Wittgenstein, *Philosophical Investigations* (Oxford, 1953), p. 8.
46. L. Wittgenstein, *Remarks on the Foundations of Mathematics* (New York, 1956), p. 57.
47. L. Wittgenstein, *Philosophical Investigations,* p. 51.

Chapter 6: The Powers of Language

1. *Supra,* pp. 72–86.
2. Fr. 125.
3. Pl. 204.
4. Fr. 107.
5. Pl. 177.
6. Fr. 723.
7. Pl. 207.
8. Fr. 761.
9. *Supra,* pp. 60–61.
10. N. Frye, *The Well-Tempered Critic* (Bloomington, Ind., 1963), p. 87.
11. Fr. 761.
12. Fr. 756.
13. Pl. 784, fn.
14. Fr. 736.
15. Fr. 667.
16. *Ibid.*
17. Pl. 980.
18. Fr. 186.
19. *Ibid.*
20. Fr. 419.
21. Fr. 424.
22. Fr. 665.
23. Fr. 296–297.
24. Pl. 721.
25. Fr. 644.
26. *Ibid.*
27. Fr. 440.
28. Fr. 676.
29. Fr. 671.
30. Fr. 766.
31. Fr. 671.

32. Fr. 639.
33. *Supra*, pp. 102–103.
34. See F. Gray, *Le style de Montaigne* (Paris, 1958), p. 262. There are few color-metaphors in the *Essays* and very few visual descriptions of landscapes. I was pleased to find, after I had written this chapter, that Floyd Gray agrees with my emphasis on the importance of movement-images in Montaigne.
35. *Supra*, pp. 15–17.
36. Fr. 480.

Chapter 7: The Scar of Montaigne

1. Fr. 759.
2. *Ibid.*
3. Fr. 760.
4. Fr. 83.
5. Fr. 759.
6. Fr. 758.
7. *Ibid.*
8. Fr. 727.
9. Fr. 603.
10. Fr. 602.
11. Fr. 600.
12. *Ibid.*
13. Fr. 177.
14. Fr. 774.
15. Fr. 770.
16. *Ibid.*
17. Fr. 600.
18. Fr. 604.
19. Fr. 606.
20. Fr. 607.
21. Fr. 601.
22. Fr. 769.
23. *Ibid.*
24. *Ibid.*
25. Fr. 769–770.
26. Fr. 768.
27. Fr. 771.
28. Fr. 781.
29. Fr. 780.

30. P. Villey, *Les Sources et l'évolution des Essais de Montaigne* (Paris, 1933) Vol. 2, pp. 402–403.
31. Fr. 68.
32. Pl. 1131.
33. Fr. 89, 156, 277, 516, 760, 800.
34. Fr. 827.
35. Fr. 580.
36. *Supra,* pp. 53–61.

Chapter 8: Personal Philosophy and Privacy

1. P. P. Hallie, "The Privacy of Experience," *The Journal of Philosophy,* June 22, 1961, pp. 337–346.
2. Pl. 707.
3. Fr. 472.
4. Fr. 474.
5. *Supra,* pp. 86–93.
6. Fr. 177.
7. Fr. 272.
8. *Ibid.*
9. *Supra,* pp. 100–101.
10. Fr. 824.
11. Fr. 176.
12. Fr. 625.
13. Fr. 182.
14. Fr. 625.
15. Fr. 11.
16. Fr. 471.
17. Fr. 164.
18. Fr. 140.
19. Fr. 611.
20. Pl. 900.
21. Fr. 504.
22. Fr. 827.
23. Pl. 751.
24. *Supra,* pp. 130–133.
25. Fr. 781.
26. Pl. 900.
27. Fr. 828.
28. J. R. Oppenheimer, *The Open Mind* (New York, 1955).
29. *Supra,* p. 68.

Critical Bibliography

This is by no means a complete list of the works relevant to this book. But if the reader wishes to explore or contest any of my main claims, he will find works here that will help him to do so. And if he wishes to look closely at the details involved in handling the *Essays* (like the important differences between the successive editions) he will find books and articles here that will help him. Frequently there are critical remarks after an entry; these may help him to select what he needs from a vast amount of material.

Bibliographies

ENGLISH

STRAWN, RICHARD R., and SAMUEL F. WILL. "Michel Eyquem de Montaigne," in Vol. II of *A Critical Bibliography of French Literature*. Syracuse: Syracuse University, 1956. Pp. 155–187, 314. (An excellent critical bibliography; on the whole, the best in English, despite omissions of some useful French articles.)

TANNENBAUM, SAMUEL A. *Michel de Montaigne: A Concise Bibliography*. New York: Samuel A. Tannenbaum, 1942. (A handy key to the literature on Montaigne, with many mistakes, however.)

FRENCH

CIORANESCO, ALEXANDRE. *Bibliographie de la littérature française du seizième siècle*. Paris: Klincksieck, 1959. (Non-critical; very helpful on French works; classified, and easy to use.)

PLATTARD, JEAN. *Etat présent des études sur Montaigne*. Paris: Etudes Françaises, 1935. (A useful little bibliography, with an analysis and a synthesis of the whole field as of 1935).

Editions of Montaigne's Essais

ENGLISH

COTTON, CHARLES (tr.). *The Works.* Revised by W. C. HAZLITT. 10 vols. New York: Edwin C. Hill, 1910. (Only a fair translation.)

FLORIO, JOHN (ed. and tr.). *The Essayes of Montaigne.* New York: Modern Library, 1933. (Often misleading, though always colorful; first edition, 1603.)

FRAME, DONALD M. (ed. and tr.). *The Complete Works of Montaigne.* Stanford: Stanford University Press, 1948. (Reprinted in 1958, this is the best translation into English of the works of Montaigne and has been the sole English edition referred to in this book; there is a three-volume paperback edition published by Doubleday in their Anchor Books.)

IVES, GEORGE B. (tr.). *The Essays.* Introductions by GRACE NORTON. 4 vols. Cambridge: Harvard University, 1925. (Bowdlerized and incomplete.)

TRECHMANN, E. J. (ed. and tr.). *The Essays.* 2 vols. London: Oxford University, 1926. (A fine translation.)

——— (ed. and tr.). *The Diary of Montaigne's Journey to Italy in 1580 and 1581.* London: Hogarth, 1929.

ZEITLIN, JACOB (ed. and tr.). *The Essays.* 3 vols. New York: Knopf, 1934–36. (The most thoroughly annotated edition in English.)

FRENCH

ARMAINGAUD, ARTHUR (ed.). *Journal de Voyage.* 2 vols. Conard, 1928–29.

GOUGENHEIM, GEORGES, and PIERRE-MAXIME SCHUHL. *Trois Essais de Montaigne: (I-39, II-1, III-2).* Paris: Vrin, 1951. (A highly illuminating explication of three crucial essays of Montaigne.)

LAUTREY, LOUIS (ed.). *Journal de Voyage.* Paris: Hachette, 1906.

MICHAUT, G. (ed.). *De l'institution des enfants.* Paris: Boccard, 1924. (A fine example of how scholarship can illuminate the subtleties of an essay.)

STROWSKI, FORTUNAT, *et al.* (eds.). *Essais.* 5 vols. Bordeaux: Pech, 1906–33. (A lucid edition, and the expositions are well founded.)

THIBAUDET, ALBERT (ed.). *Essais.* Paris: Gallimard, 1950. Pléiade Edition. (This edition was used in the present book because of its easy availability; it is not to be confused with a similar 1934 Gallimard edition, which has different pagination.)

VILLEY, PIERRE (ed.). *Essais.* 3 vols. Paris: Alcan, 1930–31. (Still the best French editiom.)

General

ENGLISH

ALLEN, J. W. *A History of Political Thought in the Sixteenth Century.* London: Methuen, 1960. (The best summary of the subject in English.)

Ayer, A. J. *Language, Truth and Logic.* New York: Dover, n.d.
Bainton, Roland H. *Here I Stand; A Life of Martin Luther.* New York: Abingdon-Cokesbury, 1950. (A classic of clarity, vivacity, and accuracy on this vast figure.)
——— *The Reformation of the Sixteenth Century.* Boston: Beacon, 1952.
——— *Hunted Heretic, The Life and Death of Michael Servetus, 1511–1553.* Boston: Beacon, 1960. (Servetus was one of the few men the Calvinists executed. This is a sincere attempt at a balanced study of the case on the part of a Protestant.)
Bishop, Morris. *Ronsard, Prince of Poets.* New York: Oxford University, 1940. (A general introduction; beautifully clear and interesting.)
Boas, George. *The Happy Beast in French Thought of the Seventeenth Century.* Baltimore: Johns Hopkins University, 1933. (A classic study of the origins of Montaigne's admiration for the cannibals.)
Boring, Edwin G. *A History of Experimental Psychology.* New York: Appleton-Century-Crofts, 1950. (A good study of Titchener and the Introspectionists, among others.)
Burckhardt, Jacob. *The Civilization of the Renaissance.* Oxford and London: Phaidon, 1945. (Still helpful for seeing the whole picture.)
Cambridge Modern History, The. A. W. Ward, G. W. Prothero, and S. Leathes (eds.). Vol. I. *The Renaissance.* New York: Macmillan, 1934.
——— Vol. II. *The Reformation.* New York: Macmillan, 1934.
——— Vol. III. *The Wars of Religion.* New York: Macmillan, 1934. (These volumes give the most detailed account of Montaigne's century to be found in so small a compass as three volumes.)
Cassirer, Ernst. *The Individual and the Cosmos in Renaissance Philosophy.* Mario Domandi (ed. and tr.). New York: Harper and Row (Torchbook), 1963. (A vital theme penetratingly studied.)
Castiglione, Baldesar. *The Book of the Courtier.* Charles S. Singleton (tr.). New York: Doubleday, 1959.
DeMornay, Charlotte Arbaleste. *A Huguenot Family in the XVI Century.* Lucy Crump (tr.). London: George Routledge, n.d. (These memoirs show at close range the state of mind and of body of many Huguenots at the height of the religio-civil wars.)
Descartes, René. *Philosophical Works of Descartes.* E. S. Haldane and G. R. T. Ross (trs.). 2 vols. New York: Dover, 1955.
Erasmus, Desiderius. *Ten Colloquies of Erasmus.* Craig R. Thompson (ed. and tr.). New York: Liberal Arts, 1957.
——— *The Enchiridion of Erasmus.* Raymond Himelick (ed. and tr.). Bloomington: Indiana University, 1963.
——— *The Praise of Folly.* H. H. Hudson (ed. and tr.). Princeton: Princeton University, 1941.

Erasmus-Luther Discourse on Free Will. ERNST F. WINTER (ed. and tr.). New York: Ungar, 1961. (A close look at a key problem of the age — a problem Montaigne pretty much ignored. Reading this, one learns a great deal about how different Montaigne was from these two thinkers.)

FROUDE, J. A. *Life and Letters of Erasmus.* London: Longmans, Green, 1894. (An intimate, illuminating biography.)

FRYE, NORTHROP. *The Well-Tempered Critic.* Bloomington: Indiana University, 1963.

GILMORE, MYRON P. *The World of Humanism 1453–1517.* New York: Harper and Row (Torchbook), 1952. (Not very penetrating or comprehensive, but handy for some reference.)

HALLIE, PHILIP P. "The Privacy of Experience," *The Journal of Philosophy,* June 22, 1961, pp. 337–346. (A common-sensical notion of privacy very close to Montaigne's is defined here.)

——— "Wittgenstein's Exclusion of Metaphysical Nonsense," *The Philosophical Quarterly,* Vol. 16, No. 63, Apr., 1966, pp. 97–112.

——— (ed.). *Scepticism, Man, and God.* Middletown, Conn.: Wesleyan University, 1964. (In this book, an annotated edition of the key work of the Greek Sceptics, I substantiate in some detail the claims about Greek Scepticism made in the present study on Montaigne.)

HAYDN, HIRAM. *The Counter-Renaissance.* New York: Scribner's Sons, 1950. (Paperback, New York: Grove, 1960.) (A perpetually illuminating study of the whole Renaissance. Excellent for seeing Montaigne's role in the thought of the time.)

HUIZINGA, JOHAN. *The Waning of the Middle Ages.* New York: Doubleday (Anchor Paperback), 1956. (A good preface to work on Montaigne's era.)

——— *Erasmus and the Age of Reformation.* New York: Harper, 1957. (A very comprehensive, useful summary of Erasmus' relationships to the religious problems of his age.)

IRWIN, S. T. (ed. and tr.). *Six Dialogues of Lucian.* London: Methuen, 1894.

JOWETT, B. (ed. and tr.). *The Dialogues of Plato.* 2 vols. New York: Random House, 1937.

KLEIST, HEINRICH VON. *The Marquise d'O and Other Stories.* Preface by THOMAS MANN. M. GREENBERG (ed. and tr.). New York: Criterion, 1960.

KRAILSHEIMER, A. J. *Rabelais and the Franciscans.* Oxford: Clarendon, 1963.

KRISTELLER, PAUL O. *Renaissance Thought: The Classic, Scholastic and Humanistic Strains.* New York: Harper (Torchbook), 1961. (The most concise, reliable treatment of Renaissance thought to be found in English.)

——— *Renaissance Thought II.* New York: Harper (Torchbook), 1965.

KRISTELLER, PAUL O., ERNST CASSIRER, and JOHN H. RANDALL (eds.). *The Renaissance Philosophy of Man*. Chicago: University of Chicago, 1948. (Useful for finding evidence of how deeply Montaigne differed from some Italian Renaissance philosophers and resembled others.)

NEWTON, A. P. (ed.). *The Great Age of Discovery*. London: University of London, 1932. (The explorations.)

OPPENHEIMER, J. ROBERT. *The Open Mind*. New York: Simon and Schuster, 1955.

PARRY, J. H. *Europe and a Wider World 1415–1715*. London: Hutchinson, 1949. (Excellent for the explorations.)

PIRENNE, HENRI. *A History of Europe*. Vol. 2. New York: Doubleday, 1956. (A modern classic on the period of the Reformation.)

PLUMB, J. H. *The Italian Renaissance, a Concise Survey of its History and Culture*. New York: Harper (Torchbook), 1961. (A clear and up-to-date book.)

POLANYI, MICHAEL. *Personal Knowledge: towards a Post-Critical Philosophy*. Chicago: University of Chicago, 1958. (In this monumental life-work Polanyi shows how in the most exact and exacting kind of knowledge it is always man we are dealing with. And he gives this claim a lucid, persuasive, detailed meaning.)

RABELAIS, FRANÇOIS. *Gargantua and Pantagruel*. DONALD DOUGLAS (ed.). New York: Modern Library, 1928.

ROEDER, RALPH. *Catherine de' Medici and the Lost Revolution*. New York: Viking, 1937. (A fresh point of view on Catherine. A biographical novel, but accurate on the whole.)

ROELKER, NANCY L. (ed. and tr.). *The Paris of Henry of Navarre as seen by Pierre de l'Estoile*. Cambridge: Harvard University, 1958. (An important book for its intimate insights into the religio-civil wars in Paris.)

RYLE, GILBERT. *The Concept of Mind*. London: Hutchinson, 1949. (A book which has considerably influenced the reading of Montaigne presented in the present essay.)

——— *Dilemmas*. Cambridge: Cambridge University, 1960. (A book whose tactics illustrate the careful use modern philosophers make of ordinary language.)

SABINE, GEORGE H. *A History of Political Theory*. New York: Henry Holt, 1946. (Still the best history of political thought available in English. Excellent on the Reformation.)

SILVER, ISIDORE. *Ronsard and the Hellenic Renaissance in France*. St. Louis: Washington University, 1961. (An up-to-date, compendious study.)

STICKELBERGER, EMANUEL. *Calvin, a Life*. DAVID G. GELZER (tr.). Richmond: John Knox, 1954. (An impassioned but well-supported defense of Calvin.)

THOMPSON, JAMES WESTFALL. *The Wars of Religion in France, 1559–1576*. Chicago: University of Chicago, 1909. (Still one of the best works in English on the subject.)
WITTGENSTEIN, LUDWIG. *Philosophical Investigations*. Oxford: Blackwell, 1953. (Wittgenstein's richest work.)
——— *Remarks on the Foundations of Mathematics*. New York: Macmillan, 1956.
——— *The Blue and Brown Books*. Oxford: Blackwell, 1958. (The best introduction to Wittgenstein's thought.)
YOUNG, G. F. *The Medici*. New York: Modern Library, 1930.
ZELLER, EDUARD. *Outlines of the History of Greek Philosophy*. L. R. PALMER (tr.). New York: The Humanities Press, 1955.
——— *The Stoics, Epicureans, and Sceptics*. O. J. REICHEL (tr.). London: Longmans, Green, 1870. (A detailed, still useful study of the "practical-wisdom" philosophers who so deeply influenced Montaigne.)

FRENCH

CHAMPION, P. *Ronsard et son temps*. Paris: Champion, 1925. (A very useful summary of Ronsard's relationships with his age.)
DESCARTES, RENÉ. *Œuvres Philosophiques*. C. ADAM and P. TANNERY (eds.). 12 vols. Paris: Cerf, 1897–1913.
JULLIAN, CAMILLE. "Bordeaux au temps de la mairie de Michel de Montaigne," *Revue historique de Bordeaux*, No. 26, Jan.–Feb., 1933, pp. 5–18.
MIREPOIX, DUC DE LÉVIS. *Les Guerres de Religion, 1559–1610*. Paris: Fayard, 1950. (A detailed, lucid study of the religio-civil wars, which often reads like a good novel.)
MONOD, A. "Montaigne après la Saint-Barthélemy," *Revue de Paris*, No. 2, 1910, pp. 95–125. (A revealing study of the relationship between Montaigne and the religio-civil conflict in France.)
PLATTARD, JEAN. *L'Œuvre de Rabelais*. Paris: Champion, 1910.
——— *François Rabelais*. Paris: Boivin, 1932. (A sensitive book.)
RABELAIS, FRANÇOIS. *Œuvres Complètes*. JEAN PLATTARD (ed.). 5 vols. Paris: Fernand Roches, 1929.
RENAUDET, AUGUSTIN. *Préréforme et Humanisme à Paris Pendant les Premières Guerres d'Italie*. Paris: Librairie D'Argences, 1953. (An extraordinarily perceptive study, the best on the subject.)
SABRIÉ, J. B. *De l'humanisme au rationalisme. Pierre Charron (1541–1603)*. Paris: Alcan, 1913. (An important study of Montaigne's only really philosophic disciple, Charron.)

Commentaries on Montaigne and His Writings

ENGLISH

AUERBACH, ERICH. "L'Humaine Condition," *Mimesis: The Representation of Reality in Western Literature.* WILLARD R. TRASK (tr.). Princeton: Princeton University, 1953. Pp. 285-311. (The best short essay on Montaigne's style.)

CROLL, MORRIS W. "Attic Prose: Lipsius, Montaigne, Bacon," *Schelling Anniversary Papers.* New York: Century, 1923. Pp. 117-150. (A very stimulating study of Montaigne's style as a mirror of his thought and way of life.)

DAWSON, J. C. "A Suggestion as to the Source of Montaigne's title: Essais," *Modern Language Notes,* No. 51, 1936, pp. 223-226. (An account of a possible origin for Montaigne's use of word "Essai"; commentary on a story or quotation from ancients — before the term reached its full richness in his work.)

Dow NEAL. *The Concept and Term "Nature" in Montaigne's Essays.* Philadelphia, 1940. (A modest dissertation tabulating the uses of the term "nature" in Montaigne's writings.)

EMERSON, RALPH W. "Montaigne; or, the Skeptic," *Representative Men.* Boston and New York: Houghton Mifflin, 1903. (A remarkably penetrating analysis of Montaigne's scepticism. One of the great brief studies of Montaigne.)

FRAME, DONALD M. "Did Montaigne Betray Sebond?" *Romanic Review,* No. 38, 1929, pp. 297-329. (A profoundly persuasive refutation of Sainte-Beuve's claims about Montaigne's atheistic tendencies.)

——— *Montaigne in France, 1812-1852.* New York: Columbia University, 1940. (A very important study of the attitudes of French writers toward Montaigne's personality and writings.)

——— *Montaigne's Discovery of Man: The Humanization of a Humanist.* New York: Columbia University, 1955. (One of the clearest and most illuminating books on Montaigne in English.)

——— *Montaigne: A Biography.* New York: Harcourt, Brace & World, 1965. (The best biography of Montaigne available in any language though short on intellectual influences. Indispensable for anyone at all interested in Montaigne.)

GIDE, ANDRÉ. "Presenting Montaigne," DOROTHY BUSSY (tr.), *The Living Thoughts of Montaigne.* New York and Toronto: Longmans, Green, 1939. Pp. 1-27. (A penetrating essay for revealing *both* Gide and Montaigne.)

GREENE, THOMAS M. "Montaigne and the Savage Infirmity," *Yale Review,* Winter, 1957, pp. 191-205.

Jones, Mansell P. *French Introspectives from Montaigne to André Gide.* Cambridge: Cambridge University, 1937. Pp. 22-41. (Indicated pages are very perceptive on Montaigne's use of the first person singular pronoun.)

Lüthy, Herbert. "Montaigne, or the Art of Being Truthful," *Encounter,* Nov. 1953, pp. 33-44.

Mauzey, Jesse V. *Montaigne's Philosophy of Human Nature.* Annandale-on-Hudson, New York: St. Stephen's College, 1933. (One of the commentators who believe that Montaigne's style is not simply a literary device but a philosophic method.)

Moore, W. G. "Montaigne's Notion of Experience," *The French Mind; Studies in Honor of Gustave Rudler.* Oxford: Clarendon, 1952. Pp. 34-52. (A sensitive study of Montaigne's efforts to keep philosophy or thought close to life by way of his notion of experience.)

Murry, John Middleton. "Montaigne: The Birth of the Individual," *Heroes of Thought.* New York: Messner, 1938. Pp. 49-62.

Pattison, Mark. "Life of Montaigne," *Essays by the late Mark Pattison.* Oxford: Clarendon, 1889. Vol. 2, pp. 323-349. (A suggestive warning not to emphasize Montaigne's public life.)

Popkin, Richard H. *The History of Scepticism from Erasmus to Descartes.* Assen, Netherlands: Van Gorcum & Comp., 1960. Pp. 44-87. (A lucid statement of Montaigne's role in the modern history of Scepticism.)

Poulet, Georges. "Montaigne," *Studies in Human Time,* Elliott Coleman (tr.). Baltimore: Johns Hopkins University, 1958. (Translation of an excellent French study noted in the following section of this Bibliography.)

Spencer, Theodore. "Montaigne in America," *Atlantic Monthly,* March, 1946, pp. 91-97.

Woolf, Virginia. "Montaigne," *The Common Reader.* New York: Harcourt, Brace, 1948. Pp. 87-100. (An always refreshing account of how Montaigne is trying to present his soul, his personality.)

Young, Charles L. *Emerson's Montaigne.* New York: Macmillan, 1941. (A fine study of how Montaigne affected Emerson.)

FRENCH AND GERMAN

Aymonier, Camille. "Montaigne à table," *Revue philomathique de Bordeaux et du Sud-Ouest,* No. 37, 1934, pp. 179-191. (A fascinating compendium of Montaigne's remarks on eating — an aspect of his self-portrait.)

Ballaguy, Paul. "La sincérité de Montaigne," *Mercure de France,* No. 245, Aug. 1, 1933, pp. 547-575. (Here is one of the few attacks on the autobiographical veracity of the *Essays*.)

BLINKENBERG, ANDREAS. "Quel sens Montaigne a-t-il voulu donner au mot Essais dans le titre de son œuvre?" *Mélanges, Mario Roques.* Paris: Didier, 1950. Pp. 3–14. (A careful study of Montaigne's use of the term "Essay.")

BONNEFON, PAUL. *Montaigne et ses amis.* 2 vols. Paris: Colin, 1898. (A classic study of Montaigne and La Boétie.)

―――― *Le progrès de la conscience dans la philosophie occidentale.* Paris: Alcan, 1927. Pp. 118–135. (A clear statement of Montaigne's governing intent in the *Essays.*)

BRUNSCHVICG, LÉON. *Descartes et Pascal, lecteurs de Montaigne.* Neuchâtel: Baconnière, 1945. (An important work, though weaker on Montaigne than on Descartes and Pascal.)

BRUWAENE, LÉON IVAN DEN. "Les idées philosophiques de Montaigne," *Revue neo-scholastique* (Louvain), No. 35, Aug., 1933, pp. 339–378; Nov., 1933, pp. 489–515. (A balanced study of Montaigne's key ideas, emphasizing the fact that he was less of a metaphysician than a psychologist.)

BUFFUM, IMBRIE. *L'influence du voyage de Montaigne sur les Essais.* Princeton: Princeton University, 1946. (Helpful supplement to Villey's great work on the evolution of the *Essays.*)

CHAMARD, HENRI. *Histoire de la Pléiade.* 4 vols. Paris: Didier, 1939–40. (A classic study of this Humanistic school.)

CHAMPION, EDMÉ. *Introduction aux Essais de Montaigne.* Paris: Colin, 1900. (A neglected but penetrating analysis of the *Essays.*)

―――― "Le scepticisme de Montaigne," *Revue Bleue*, 1921, pp. 189–192. (Brief, but stimulating.)

CITOLEUX, MARC. *Le vrai Montaigne, théologien et soldat.* Lethielleux, 1937. (Emphasizes Montaigne's Christian theology.)

COPPIN, JOSEPH. *Montaigne, traducteur de Raymond de Sebond.* Lille: Morel, 1925. (A classic study of Montaigne's translation of Sebond's work; it concludes that Montaigne did not try to refute Sebond, or betray him.)

DÉDÉYAN, CHARLES. "Deux aspects de Montaigne," *Bibliothèque d'humanisme et renaissance*, No. 6, 1945, pp. 302–327. (The distinction of public from private life in his thought is here examined.)

DRÉANO, MATHURIN. *La Pensée religieuse de Montaigne.* Beauchesne, 1936. (A book which quite thoroughly defends the thesis that Montaigne was a firm Catholic and distrustful of unbridled private judgment on religious matters.)

FRIEDRICH, HUGO. *Montaigne.* Bern: Francke, 1949. (A splendid summary of Montaigne's thought; one of the best. In German.)

GRAY, F. *Le style de Montaigne.* Paris: Nizet, 1958. (A workmanlike analysis of the details of Montaigne's imagery and syntax.)

GUITON, JEAN. "Où en est le débat sur la religion de Montaigne?" *Romanic Review*, No. 35, 1944, pp. 98–115. (An excellent summary of views on Montaigne's religious stance and a balanced evaluation of them.)

GUIZOT, MAURICE GUILLAUME. *Montaigne, études et fragments.* Paris: Hachette, 1899. (A remarkably ambivalent reading of Montaigne, seeing him as a sceptic and a non-Christian, weak of will but charming.)

JANSEN, FREDERIK J. B. *Sources vives de la pensée de Montaigne: étude sur les fondements psychologiques et biographiques des Essais.* Copenhagen: Levin and Munksgaard, 1935. (A beautifully argued book with conclusions rather similar to those of the present one.)

LANGE, MAURICE. "Le pragmatisme de Montaigne," *Revue du mois*, No. 19, Apr. 10, 1915, pp. 455–491. (A competent study of Montaigne as a Pragmatist before Pragmatism.)

LANSON, GUSTAVE. "L'art de Montaigne: l'art de se dire," *L'art de la prose.* Librairie des Annales, 1911. (A study of Montaigne's style as reflecting his imagination and logic.)

——— *Les Essais de Montaigne; étude et analyse.* Mellottée, 1930.

LÉVIS-MIREPOIX, ANTOINE, DUC DE. "Montaigne et le secret de Coutras," *La revue: littérature, histoire, arts et sciences des deux mondes*, Oct. 1, 1950, pp. 461–472. (Montaigne as a political force, with emphasis on Navarre's visit with Montaigne after Henry's victory at Coutras.)

MATTHIESSEN, F. O. "Florio's Montaigne," *Translation, an Elizabethan Art.* Cambridge: Harvard University, 1931. Pp. 103–168. (Shows the defects of the Florio translation and its virtues.)

MERLEAU-PONTY, MAURICE. "Lecture de Montaigne," *Les temps modernes*, No. 3, Dec., 1947, pp. 1044–1060. (A remarkable little study of Montaigne's self-awareness, written by a very distinguished philosopher.)

NICOLAÏ, ALEXANDRE. *Les Belles Amies de Montaigne.* Paris. Dumas, 1950. (Gossipy but illuminating.)

PLATTARD, JEAN. "L'Amérique dans l'œuvre de Montaigne," *Revue des cours et conférences,* Série 1, Dec. 15, 1933, pp. 12–21. (An informative study of Montaigne and the New World.)

——— *Montaigne et son temps.* Paris: Boivin, 1933. (A very insightful summary of Montaigne's relations with his century.)

PORTEAU, PAUL. *Montaigne et la vie pédagogique de son temps.* Geneva: Droz, 1935. (The origins of Montaigne's ideas on education and a good summary of these ideas.)

POULET, GEORGES. "Montaigne," *Etudes sur le temps humain.* Paris: Plon, 1950. Pp. 1–15. (A beautiful little study of Montaigne's notion that to be is to be changing, in body and in mind. Poulet sees action as basic to Montaigne's thought, not fixed metaphysical entities of any sort.)

IVe Centenaire de la naissance de Montaigne, 1533–1933. Bordeaux: Delmas, 1933. (Interesting essays by ANDRÉ LAMANDE on Montaigne as a Gascon, PAUL COURTEAULT on Montaigne as Mayor of Bordeaux, PAUL LAUMONIER on the thought of Montaigne, and various other writers on Montaigne's diseases, his thoughts on education, his activities as a jurist, and his relationship to Shakespeare.)

RIVELINE, MAURICE. *Montaigne et l'amitié.* Paris: Alcan, 1939. (A careful study of Montaigne's ideas on friendship, vital to any understanding of his personality and his personal philosophy.)

SACY, SYLVESTRE DE. "Montaigne essaie ses facultés naturelles," *Mercure de France,* No. 315, June 1, 1952, pp. 285–306. (Montaigne and his book are the same, his work consubstantial with his life.)

SAINTE-BEUVE, CHARLES A. *Port-Royal,* MAXIME LEROY (ed.). Vol. 1. Paris: Gallimard, 1953–55. (The great statement on Montaigne as an unbeliever.)

SAYCE, RICHARD A. "L'Ordre des Essais de Montaigne," *Bibliothèque d'Humanisme et Renaissance,* Vol. XVIII, 1956, pp. 7–22. (Concise and up to date.)

STROWSKI, FORTUNAT. *Montaigne.* Paris: Alcan, 1906. Revised, Paris: Alcan, 1931. (Early treatment of Montaigne as evolving, going from Stoicism to Scepticism, etc.)

TAVERA, F. *L'idée d'humanité dans Montaigne.* Paris: Champion, 1932. (A weak book, but an example of how Montaigne *can* be made out to be an atheist.)

THIBAUDET, ALBERT. "Le quadricentenaire d'un philosophe," *Revue de Paris,* No. 40, Feb. 15, 1933, pp. 755–776. (A concise treatment of some of Montaigne's contributions to modern philosophy.)

TOLDO, PIETRO. "L'homme sage de Montaigne," *Mélanges Gustave Lanson.* Paris: Hachette, 1922. Pp. 132–153. (An estimate of the *Essays* as autobiography; it concludes that Montaigne drew a flattering portrait of his own wisdom.)

VILLEY, PIERRE. *Les Sources et l'évolution des Essais de Montaigne.* 2 vols. Paris: Hachette, 1908. Revised ed., Paris: Hachette, 1933. 2 vols. (The classic analysis of the origins and changes in the *Essays.*)

——— *L'influence de Montaigne sur les idées pédagogiques de Locke et de Rousseau.* Paris: Hachette, 1911. (How Montaigne caused Locke and Rousseau to emphasize the growth of the individual and his adjustment to his environment in their educational philosophies.)

——— "Montaigne dans le mouvement philosophique," *Revue de Philosophie,* 1926, pp. 338–359. (Not up to Villey's best work, it is still clear and relevant to a depth understanding of the *Essays.*)

VILLEY, PIERRE. *Les Essais de Michel de Montaigne*. Paris: Société Française, 1932. (A splendid concise introduction to Montaigne.)
——— *Montaigne Devant le Postérité*. Paris: Boivin, 1935. (An illuminating summary, typical of Villey's best writings on Montaigne.)

Index

Action, 32, 46–47, 51, 55–57, 62–63, 64–68, 134
Affirmation, 24–26
Against the Physicists (Sextus Empiricus), 29
Alexander the Great, 102–103
Aloneness, 139–140
Amyot, Jacques, 12, 16, 71
Analysts, 89–90, 91, 93, 94
Animals, 31–32, 56–57, 83
Antiquity, classical, Humanists and, 9–11, 13, 71
Antithesis, 27–30, 166, 173
Aphorisms, 103
Apology (Plato), 48, 52
"Apology for Raymond Sebond," 5, 7, 8, 27, 30, 37–52, 55, 59, 60, 73, 88, 101, 110, 111, 131–133, 136; background of composition, 38–39; subject and structure, 39–40; quoted, 39, 40, 42, 44, 45, 46, 49, 50, 51, 55, 72, 75, 78, 79, 81, 84, 87, 96, 100, 107, 111, 132, 135, 163; Montaigne's objections to Sebond's arguments, 40–52
Aquinas, Saint Thomas, 38
Argument, Sceptic modes of, 30–31, 55, 172–173

Aristotle, 15, 79, 147
"Art of Discussion, Of the," *see* "Discussion, Of the Art of"
Assertive imagination, 77–85 *passim*, 93, 95, 128, 152
"Association, Three Kinds of," 139; quoted, 140
Aubigné, Agrippa d', 5
Austin, John L., 89
Avarice, 127
Axel (Villiers de L'Isle-Adam), xviii
Ayer, A. J., 89

Baïf, Jean Antoine de, *Epitaphe*, 6
Berkeley, George, 29
Biographia Literaria (Coleridge), quoted, 76
Bodin, Jean, 7, 8
"Books, Of," 108
Bordeaux, Montaigne as Mayor of, 4, 8, 120, 122, 126, 127–128, 148
Buchanan, George, 11

Caesar, Julius, 14, 124
Calvin, John, 3, 5
"Cannibals, Of," 30, 109; quoted, 17–18; *see also* Savages

Catherine de' Medicis, 7, 8, 20
Catholicism and Catholics, 3–7, 38–39, 41, 45, 51; Montaigne and, 5, 7, 8–9, 20–21, 33, 38, 41, 43, 107, 121–122; Catholic League, 6, 129; *see also* "Apology for Raymond Sebond"
Cato the Younger, 14
"Cato the Younger, Of," quoted, 76
Chateaubriand, François René de, *René*, 138
"Children, Of the Education of," 64, 98–99; quoted, 20, 65, 66, 79, 95, 99
"Children to Fathers, Of the Resemblance of," quoted, 129–130
Christianity and Christians, 40–41, 42
Cicero, Marcus Tullius, 9, 16
"Cicero, A Consideration upon," 105; quoted, 105–106, 148
Clarity of language, *see* Language — precision
Classics, Montaigne's interest in, 10–11, 13, 108, 111
Coleridge, Samuel T., *Biographia Literaria*, 76
Colloquy of Poissy, 51
Common sense, 23, 27, 32, 39, 59, 60, 61, 64, 67; custom and, 61–64
Communication, 135–136; and expression, 94–97; *Essays* as examples of, 97, 102; *see also* Language
Conscience, 16, 19, 117, 121; and public service, 123–125
"Consideration upon Cicero, A," *see* "Cicero, A Consideration upon"

Contradiction, 29
Copernicus, 45–46, 163, 164
"Cripples, Of," 82–83; quoted, 74, 82, 83
Custom, 20, 25–26, 29–30; and common sense, 61–64; *see also* Habit
"Custom, Of," 62, 117; quoted, 63, 65

Democritus, 52
"Democritus and Heraclitus, Of," quoted, 99–100
Dependence, 65–66
Descartes, René, xvi, xviii, xix–xx; comparison of Cartesian and Montaignian methods of philosophizing, xviii–xxi, 157–175; language doctrine compared with Montaignian, 159–167; *Principles*, 163; *Meditations*, 164, 168, 171, 174; doubt compared with Montaignian, 170–175; *see also Discourse on Method*
Discipline, 16
Discourse on Method (Descartes), xx, 58, 150, 159, 161, 166–167, 168, 169, 170, 171
"Discussion, Of the Art of," quoted, 15, 146–147
Divination, Montaigne on, 18
Docility, 33, 51–52
Dogmatism and Dogmatists, 25, 26, 27–31, 37, 72, 145
Doubt, 72; general function of in Scepticism, 23, 26–27, 37, 39, 147, 172–173, 174; Montaigne's philosophy of, 23, 31, 130, 147, 170–175 *passim* (*see esp.* 174–175); techniques of, 27–31;

Cartesian compared with Montaignian, 170–175
Du Bellay, Joachim, 12, 13, 71

Ease (laziness), Montaigne's love of, 118, 120, 123
Education, 64–68; "Of Pedantry," 64, 65–66, 67
"Education of Children, Of the," 64, 98–99; quoted, 20, 65, 66, 79, 95, 99
Epaminondas, 14
Epicureans, 15, 16
Epitaphe (de Baïf), 6
Erasmus, 14, 71, 81
Essays of Montaigne: Preface, "To the Reader," ix, xv, xvi–xvii, 15, 68, 96, 102, 112, 133, 152, 169; as self-portrait, ix, xvi, xix, xx, 20–21, 33, 43, 52, 54–55, 60–61, 64, 68, 96, 112–113, 117–118, 131–133, 144–145, 146–152, 169, 170; language of, xv–xvi, 13, 60, 96–113, 160; purposes of, xvi, 68, 96, 97–101, 102, 133, 150, 169; conditions in France during composition of, 3–9, 20, 38–39, 41–42, 43, 117, 125, 157, 163; as Humanist documents, 13, 15–16, 18–19, 20 (*see also* Montaigne as a Humanist); style of, 21, 101–113; Montaigne's concept of the essay form, 59, 97–101; epigrams in, 60, 103, 104, 105, 160; metaphors in, 77, 98, 101, 105, 107, 110, 111, 160, 166; order and unity in, 101–105; *Les Sources et l'evolution des Essais de Montaigne* (Villey), 22, 128; *see also* titles of individual essays under key word
Estienne, Henri, 12

"Experience, Of," 60, 146; quoted, xix, 74, 80, 138, 145, 150, 165–166
Explorations, by Europeans, 17–18, 37

Faith, 40–44, 50, 51–52
Fame, 73, 140–141, 145
"Fathers, Of the Resemblance of Children to," *see* "Children to Fathers, Of the Resemblance of"
"Feelings Reach Out Beyond Us, Our," 141
Ficino, Marsilio, 77
Fideism, 40, 44
"Fortune Is Often Met in the Path of Reason," *see* "Reason, Fortune Is Often Met in the Path of"
France, religious-civil wars in, 3–9, 20, 41–42, 43, 51, 157; Montaigne's attitude toward, 38–39, 117, 125, 163
Franciade, La (Ronsard), 12–13
Francis I, king of France, 5, 11, 86–87, 108
Francis II, king of France, 131
Freedom, 16; Montaigne's views of, 118–119, 123
"Friendship, Of," 135; quoted, 144
Frye, Northrop, *The Well-Tempered Critic*, 103

Galileo, 29, 157, 164
Gargantua (Rabelais), 13, 16
Gellius, Aulus, 9
"Glory, Of," quoted, 64, 73, 135, 143
God, 40, 41, 45, 48, 50, 51, 52, 57
Good and evil, 23
"Good and Evil Depends in Large Part on the Opinion We Have

of Them, That the Taste of,"
quoted, 23, 56, 61, 149
Good life, Montaigne's concept of,
16, 58; Sceptic view of, 26, 27;
see also Health
Goodness, 48
Grace, 40, 41, 43, 50
Gray, Thomas, 95
Guise family, 4–5, 6
Guyenne, college of, 11

Habit, 61–64, 136, 171; "Of Custom,"
62, 63, 65, 117
Health, national (peace), 8–9, 15,
19, 20–21, 39, 52, 60–61, 129;
natural (bodily), 16, 19–20, 32–33,
39, 54, 57, 58, 61, 62–63, 72,
129–130; Montaigne's views of,
19–22, 52, 54–55, 56, 60–61, 65,
66–67, 68, 126, 129
Henry III, king of France, 148
Henry IV, king of France, 157
"Heraclitus, Of Democritus and," *see*
"Democritus and Heraclitus, Of"
Hobbes, Thomas, xvi, 54, 164–165,
166
Honesty, *see* Lying
Horace, 17, 109
Huguenots, 5, 129
Humanism and Humanists, 9–17,
67; Montaigne as a Humanist,
9–10, 11–12, 13, 15, 16–20, 33,
92–93, 95, 96, 112–113, 151;
Italian, 10–11; French, 11, 12–18;
and language, 71–72, 95
Human nature, 15–16, 24, 25, 32
"Husbanding Your Will, Of," *see*
"Will, Of Husbanding Your"

Icaromenippus (Lucian), 87–88

"Idleness, Of," quoted, 96–97
Imagination, 56, 57, 58–68, 74, 126;
and language, 72–86; Poetic,
76–77, 78, 79; Assertive, 77–85
passim, 93, 95, 128, 152; metaphor
and, 77; reality and, 80–84
"Imagination, Of the Power of,"
quoted, 75, 85
Incertitude, *see* Doubt
Indicative Signs, 26, 29–30, 33, 43,
46, 74
Individualism, 64–68
Intelligence, 23, 65
Introspection, 136–139

Judgment, 55–57, 63, 66–68, 170;
suspension of, 30, 31, 55, 88, 170;
Montaigne's views of, 55, 56, 57,
59, 60–61, 62, 66, 68, 74–75, 85, 88,
99–100, 102, 104–110, 111, 112,
117, 130, 135, 137, 138, 151, 152,
172; *see also* Doubt

Knowledge, xvii, 43, 44, 46–47,
48–49, 55, 57, 65, 67–68, 132;
fount of (senses), 48–49

La Boétie, Etienne, 102, 135, 144
Language, 67, 71–113; ordinary
(common), xv–xvi, xix, xxii, 73,
79–80, 89–92, 95, 108, 123, 160,
161–162, 163, 165; of the *Essays*,
xv–xvi, 13, 60, 96–113, 160;
pedantic, 12–13, 66–67, 72;
Humanism and, 12–13, 71–72, 95;
simplicity of, 12, 80; Montaigne's
views on power and use of, 13, 72,
74, 76, 78, 79–80, 81–82, 84–86, 89,
91, 92, 93, 95–97, 160; gesture as,
54–55, 106; philosophy of, 71–113,
142; as a source of men's troubles,

71–93 (*see esp.* 73–75, 80, 84),
  89–93, 94; and imagination,
  72–86; metaphor and, 77; precision
  in, 79–82, 90, 92–93, 95, 160,
  161–162; rule or prescription in,
  80, 81–83, 161–162, 166; verbal
  disputes, 80, 83–84, 91–92, 162,
  165; artificial, 80, 81, 162, 165;
  modern philosophers and, 89–93,
  94–95; powers of, 94–113; of public
  service, 120, 123; Montaignian and
  Cartesian doctrines compared,
  159–167
La Noue, François de, 6–7
Laws, natural, 15, 19–20, 24, 32;
  see also Nature
Laws, public, 20, 24, 29–30, 32, 39,
  48, 62–63; *see also* Custom
Laziness, Montaigne's love of, 118,
  120, 123
L'Estoile, Pierre de, 120; quoted, 3
L'Hôpital, Michel de, 8
"Liars, Of," 86–87
"Lie, Of Giving the," 146; quoted,
  96
Life, *see* Good life
Living, Humanist style of, 13–17
Locke, John, 29
Loyola, Ignatius, 3
Lucian, 87–88
Lying, 86–87, 88

Man, doctrines of: Sceptic, 31–34;
  Sebond's, 38; Montaigne's, 51,
  59, 102–103, 149
Mann, Thomas, 76
Margaret of Valois, queen of
  Navarre, 38, 40
Martial, 17, 110
Materialism and Materialists, 29

Meditations (Descartes), 166, 168,
  171, 174
Method, x, xix, xx, 150–151;
  compared with style, 150;
  Cartesian, *see Discourse on Method*
Modes of Scepticism, 30–31, 32, 55
Mohammed II, 123
Monluc, Blaise de, 6
Montaigne, Michel Eyquem de:
  Mayor of Bordeaux, 4, 8, 120, 122,
  126, 127–128, 147; as a Catholic
  moderate, 5, 7, 8–9, 20–21, 33,
  38, 41, 43, 107, 121–122; private vs.
  public life, 11–12, 21, 117–133,
  142–145, 151–152; retirement,
  11–12, 96–97; early life and
  education, 11, 118, 126; attitude
  toward religious-civil wars in
  France, 38–39, 117, 125, 163 (*see
  also* "Apology for Raymond
  Sebond"); friendship with La
  Boétie, 102, 135, 144
Montaigne, Michel Eyquem de,
  personal philosophy of, ix, x, 31,
  68, 152–153; comparison with
  Cartesian philosophy, xviii–xxi,
  157–175; background, 3–34;
  Scepticism in, xvi, 22–23, 27, 28,
  30, 31, 33–34, 37, 128, 130, 132,
  138, 149–150, 170 (*see also*
  "Apology for Raymond Sebond");
  style (*façon*), 9–10, 13, 15, 21, 37,
  148, 150–151; Humanism, 9–10,
  11–12, 13, 15, 16–20, 33, 92–93, 95,
  96, 112–113, 151; antiquity and,
  10–11; language, 13, 72, 74, 76, 78,
  79–80, 81–82, 84–86, 89, 91, 92, 93,
  95–97, 160, 159–167 *passim*;
  health, 19–22, 52, 54–55, 56, 60–61,
  65, 66–67, 68, 126, 129; private
  life, 21, 119–120, 129–130, 141–142;

doubt, 23, 31, 130, 147, 170–175 *passim* (*see esp.* 174–175); sources of, 37–68; truth, 39–40, 45–50, 61, 62, 68, 138, 147–148, 152; as shown in "Apology for Raymond Sebond," 39, 40–52 *passim;* man, 51, 59, 102–103, 149; aversion to infliction of pain, 54–55; judgment, 55, 56, 57, 59, 60–61, 62, 66, 68, 74–75, 85, 88, 99–100, 102, 104–105, 108, 111, 112, 117, 130, 135, 137, 138, 151, 152, 172; imagination, 56, 57, 58–68, 74–86 *passim;* application to private and public life, 117–153; freedom, 118–119, 123; laziness, 118, 120, 123; public life, 119–120, 122–129, 131, 142–143, 148–149; the "Scar," 130–133, 152; privacy, 134–153 (*see esp.* 139–142); see also *Essays* and individual titles

Montaigne, Pierre Eyquem de (father), 11, 38, 39, 119, 126

"Names, Of," quoted, 74
Natural laws, *see* Laws, natural
Naturalness, *see* Simplicity
Nature, 19–20, 32, 54–55; variety of, 19
Nature (temperament), *see* Human nature
Navarre, Henry, king of, later Henry IV of France, 3–4, 7, 8; Montaigne as counsellor to, 21

"One Man's Profit Is Another Man's Harm," 53–54
Oppenheimer, J. Robert, *The Open Mind,* 151

"Our Feelings Reach Out Beyond Us," *see* "Feelings Reach Out Beyond Us, Our"
Outlines of Pyrrhonism (Sextus Empiricus), 23–24, 30–31, 49

Pain, 54–55
Pantagruel (Rabelais), 13
Paris, 3–4
Parliament of Paris, 5
Pasquier, Estienne, 12
Peace, *see* Health, national
"Pedantry, Of," 64; quoted, 65–66, 67
Petronius, 17
Phenomenalism, 29
Philosophical Investigations (Wittgenstein), 90, 93
Philosophy, modern, xviii–xix, xxi–xxii; and language, 89–93, 94–95
"Physiognomy, Of," quoted, 9, 76
Plato, 15; *Apology,* 48, 52; *Republic,* 77
Pleasure, 15–16, 26, 118; bodily, xv, 16
Pliny, 137
Plutarch, 15, 71, 108
Poetic imagination, 76–77, 78, 79
Poetry, Montaigne's love of, 98–99
Politiques, 7, 8, 15, 20, 33
Positivism and Positivists, 89–90
"Power of Imagination, Of the," *see* "Imagination, Of the Power of"
Practical Criterion (of Scepticism), 24–25, 26, 32, 37, 43, 45, 172
"Practice, Of," quoted, 137
Praise of Folly (Erasmus), 14
Prayer, 87–89
"Prayers, Of," quoted, 87, 89

"Presumption, Of," 133; quoted, 58,
  59, 61, 112, 118, 119, 125–126, 130,
  131, 132
Privacy, Montaigne's views of,
  134–153 (*see esp.* 139–142);
  absolute, 134–136; definitions of,
  134–135, 141; introspection,
  136–139; aloneness, 139–140; and
  personal publicity, 140–152
Private life, Montaigne's views on,
  21, 119–120, 129–130, 141–142
"Profit Is Another Man's Harm,
  One Man's," 53–54
Protestantism and Protestants, 3–6,
  26, 37, 41, 43, 78
Public life, Montaigne's views on,
  119–120, 122–129, 131, 142–143,
  148–149
Pyrrho and Pyrrhonism, 22, 23, 30,
  52, 53, 57, 79, 88; *Outlines of
  Pyrrhonism* (Sextus Empiricus),
  23–24, 30–31, 49

Rabelais, François, 16, 17, 71;
  Gargantua and *Pantagruel*, 13
Reason, 19, 23, 27, 28, 30, 31–32,
  40–41, 44–45, 47–48, 74, 84, 152
"Reason, Fortune Is Often Met in
  the Path of," quoted, 143
Recollective Signs, 27, 30, 32, 33, 46,
  52
Regrets, Les (Du Bellay), 12
Religion, 42, 44, 45; of Montaigne,
  42–43; *see also* "Apology for
  Raymond Sebond," Catholicism,
  Protestantism
Religion, wars of in France, 3–9, 20,
  41–42, 43, 51, 157; Montaigne's
  views on, 38–39, 117, 125, 163
René (Chateaubriand), 138

"Repentance, Of," 101; quoted, 140,
  144, 145, 147
Republic (Plato), 77
"Resemblance of Children to Fathers,
  Of the," quoted, 129–130
Revolutionibus, De (Copernicus),
  45–46
Rhetoric, *see* Language
Ronsard, Pierre de, 12–13
Ryle, Gilbert, x, 89

Saint Bartholomew's Day massacre,
  4, 6, 38, 120
Saint-Beuve, Charles A., 39, 59
Savages, 17; Montaigne's interest in,
  17–20, 129; "Of Cannibals," 17–18
"Scar" of Montaigne, 130–133;
  defined, 131, 152
Scepticism, 22–34; of Montaigne, xvi,
  22, 27, 28, 30, 31, 33–34, 128, 130,
  132, 138, 149–150, 170, 172,
  174–175; of Sextus Empiricus,
  22–23, 27, 30, 31, 32–33; doubt in,
  23, 26–27, 37, 39, 147, 172–173,
  174; Practical Criterion of, 24–25,
  26, 32, 37, 43, 45, 172; doctrine of
  man, 31–34
Sebond, Raymond: "Apology for
  Raymond Sebond," 5, 7, 8, 27, 30,
  37–52, 55, 59, 60, 73, 88, 101, 110,
  111, 131–133, 136; *Theologia
  Naturalis*, 38
Seneca, 31, 32, 50, 83, 85, 101
Sévigné, Mme. Marie de, 59
Sextus Empiricus, 23, 88; influence
  on Montaigne, 22, 23, 26, 27, 33–34,
  172, 174; *Outlines of Pyrrhonism*,
  23–24, 30–31, 49; quoted, 29, 30,
  33, 39, 149; *see also* Scepticism
Signs, Indicative, 26, 29–30, 33, 43,

46, 74; Recollective, 27, 30, 32, 33, 46, 52
Simplicity (naturalness), 21; of cannibals, 18–19, 129
Six Livres de la République (Bodin), 7
Skill, Montaigne's view of, 57
Socrates, xix, 14, 15, 47–48, 52, 63
Solipsism, 29
"Solitude, Of," 67, 130, 138; quoted, 57–58, 122, 137, 139
Sources et l'evolution des Essais de Montaigne, Les (Villey), 22, 128
Speech, *see* Language
Stoicism and Stoics, 15, 16, 31, 32, 49, 83
Style: Montaigne's *façon*, 9–10, 13, 15, 21, 37, 148, 150–151; of *Essays*, 21, 101–113; compared with method, 150
Suspension of judgment, *see* Judgment

Teaching: "Of Pedantry," 64, 65–66, 67
Theologia Naturalis (Sebond), *see* "Apology for Raymond Sebond"
Theophrastus, 46
Thrasymachus, 54
"Three Kinds of Association," 139; quoted, 140
Tradition, 25

Tropoi, 30–31, 32, 55
Truth, 19, 39–40, 45–50, 61, 62, 68, 77–78, 132, 133, 138, 147–148, 152, 170

"Useful and the Honorable, Of the," 117; quoted, 121, 123, 124

Vanity, 55, 57, 83
"Vanity, Of," 60, 104, 107, 109–110, 169; quoted, 37, 83–84, 101, 103, 104, 110, 120
Villey, Pierre, xvii; quoted on Montaigne, 22, 23, 128
Villiers de L'Isle-Adam, Philippe, *Axel,* xviii
"Virgil, On Some Verses of," 103, 104, 109; quoted, 73, 74–75, 76, 108, 110

"War Horses, Of," quoted, 143–144
Wars of religion in France, 3–9, 20, 38–39, 41–42, 43, 117, 125, 157, 163
Well-Tempered Critic, The (Frye), 103
"Will, Of Husbanding Your," quoted, 63, 110, 122, 126, 127, 148
Wisdom, *see* Knowledge
Wittgenstein, Ludwig, x, 89–91, 94